VINTAGE

THE PENGUIN BOOK OF MODERN TIBETAN ESSAYS

Tenzin Dickie is a writer and a translator. She is the editor of *Old Demons, New Deities: Twenty-One Short Stories from Tibet*, the English language anthology of modern Tibetan fiction.

Celebrating 35 Years of
Penguin Random House India

ADVANCE PRAISE FOR THE BOOK

'I have been waiting over the years for a collection of groundbreaking and current Tibetan essays, and this book delivers and then some. Vital and mind-blowing at the same time'—Gary Shteyngart

'This judiciously selected, masterfully edited and thematically varied collection reveals Tibetan life as it sparkles with stories, passions and insights'—Lama Jabb

The

PENGUIN BOOK OF MODERN TIBETAN ESSAYS

Edited by

TENZIN DICKIE

VINTAGE
An imprint of Penguin Random House

VINTAGE

USA | Canada | UK | Ireland | Australia
New Zealand | India | South Africa | China

Vintage is part of the Penguin Random House group of companies
whose addresses can be found at global.penguinrandomhouse.com

Published by Penguin Random House India Pvt. Ltd
4th Floor, Capital Tower 1, MG Road,
Gurugram 122 002, Haryana, India

 Penguin
Random House
India

First published in Vintage by Penguin Random House India in 2023

The views and opinions expressed in this book are the authors' own and the
facts are as reported by their which have been verified to the extent possible,
and the publishers are not in any way liable for the same.

The following essays are reprinted with permission from the author. 'Dram' by Gedun
Rabsal is from the Tibetan language memoir *Let's Go Into Exile*, published by *Tibet Times*.
'Traveling in Bardo' by Ann Tashi Slater was originally published in *Agni*. 'My Journey
to Lhasa' by Jamyang Norbu is from his forthcoming memoir *Echoes from Forgotten
Mountains*. 'Calcutta Evening' by Ann Tashi Slater is from her forthcoming memoir.
'An Amcho's Recitation' by Pema Bhum is from the Tibetan language memoir *Doring:
Remembering Dorje Tsering*, published by *Tibet Times*. 'My Kind of Exile' by Tenzin
Tsundue was originally published in *Outlook* India. A version of 'In the Embrace of
Letting Go' by Topden Tsering was published in Himal SouthAsian. The original of
'A Stranger in My Native Land: Kumbum' by Tenzing Sonam was previously published
in *Civil Lines*. 'Three Years in Lhasa' by Tsewang Pemba is from his forthcoming
memoir, reprinted with permission.

ISBN 9780143462323

Typeset in Adobe Caslon Pro by Manipal Technologies Limited, Manipal

www.penguin.co.in

For Marmay & her generation

Contents

Introduction

Literature in the *Bardo*

Tenzin Dickie

I remember the very first essay that I tried to write. I was in the sixth or seventh grade and my English teacher had told my class, 'Write an essay.' He said the word 'essay' in English. That was our assignment over the ten-day summer break.

My home was a Tibetan Buddhist nunnery in Dharamsala where my father was the principal. Living in a monastic compound surrounded by fields ringed by lesser Himalayan mountains in the distance, there was nothing for me to do but bother my older brother, disturb the nuns by skating outside their dorms and take long walks in the fields. Mostly, I was bored out of my mind. Still, I wasn't going anywhere near my assignment until the last day of summer break. Soon enough though, it was the last day of summer break. I had to write an essay.

But what was an essay? My teacher hadn't bothered to explain it properly. So, I went to my brother, like I still do when I'm at a loss. He said, 'It's a piece of writing. It can be about anything.' Anything. Well then. I started writing. One day, I wrote, I saw a fairy. I was not a mature middle schooler. I kept on writing. My brother leaned over, stifled a smile with all the wisdom of his fifteen years and said, 'One more thing about the essay. It has to be true.'

A piece of writing that has to be true. That's still as good a description of an essay as any.

Why does the essay have to be true? Why does it matter if the writing is true? Because the truth has power. We recognize the truth when we hear it. It speaks to us.

* * *

In the early Buddhist stories, there is something called 'an act of truth'. *Satyakriya*—a declaration of truth, something like ritual speech, which when spoken is like a wish that enacts itself, or a prayer which realizes itself. It's a declaration of truth. Similar to a 'speech act' in the philosophy of language and linguistics, it's a declaration, which by the act of speaking changes—performs, fulfils—an outcome.

This act of truth is illustrated in the Jataka stories, the genre of stories telling of the Buddha's previous lives. One story tells of a woman listening to a dharma teaching who gets so drawn in that she totally neglects her child. As a result of this neglect, the child gets bitten by a poisonous snake. The poison spreads rapidly throughout the boy's body—he's in imminent danger of dying. When the distraught parents ask a monk for help, the monk says that only an act of truth can save the child's life. The father starts. He says, 'By the truth that I have never seen a monk that I did not think was a scoundrel, may this boy live.' The poison leaves the boy's legs. Then the mother says, 'By the truth that I have never loved my husband, may this boy live.' The poison withdraws further up to the boy's waist—the lower part of his body is now free of poison. Finally, the monk says, 'By the truth that I have never believed a word of the dharma but found it utter nonsense, may this boy live.' The poison leaves the boy entirely. The truth works. The truth heals. The truth wreaks miracles.

This is a higher order of truth. It doesn't just describe reality, it creates reality.

Another story tells of a woman who was seduced by a king. Her young son wants to meet his father. But at court, the king refuses to acknowledge the child. So, the woman throws the child into the air and makes this declaration to the king, 'By the truth that you are the father of my child, may he remain in mid-air; but if not, let him fall to the ground and die.' The child remains in the air, and the king, compelled by the power of the truth he cannot deny, embraces the child as his.

The story of a child at court with its parentage in question reminds us, of course, of another king, another child. In the court of King Solomon, the question was: who is the mother? Who is the father, is a generally trickier question. In that story, King Solomon's justice draws out the truth. In this one, it's truth that draws out justice.

One lesson I can draw from the act of truth then, the Satyakriya, is that in order to have justice, we must have truth.

The monk in the first story and the boy in the second are said to be the historical Buddha in his previous lives. He's entirely implicated in the act of truth—he performs the act of truth and the act of truth is performed upon him, which is to say, he is both a catalyst for and catalysed by the Satyakriya.

How is this connected to writing?

An essay is an act of truth. The essayist is both catalyst for and catalysed by the essay. The essay—as an act of truth—changes not just the writer but also the reader. The essay, the personal essay, is a piece of deeply reflective writing and any true reflection—when we express it, when we see it, when we recognize it—changes us.

* * *

This brings us to the Tibetan essay. How did the Tibetan essay begin? Who was the first Tibetan essayist? It is worthwhile to try and trace this. Literature is communal culture, accretion as much as innovation. The future is history, as much as anything else.

By 1941, Gendun Chophel, often called Tibet's first modernist, had finished his long non-fiction tract, his masterpiece, *Grains of Gold: Tales of a Cosmopolitan Traveler*. But it's a historical tract, an academic tract. He wrote essays for the *Melong*, the *Tibet Mirror* newspaper, but these were academic or argumentative essays, laying out a case, for instance, about how and why the world was round and not flat. He did not write, what we would call, personal essays. Then, there is Dhondup Gyal, who many consider to be the first Tibetan essayist and who is certainly the watershed figure in the brief history of modern Tibetan literature. His poem 'The Waterfall of Youth' and his essay 'The Narrow Footpath' are both pioneering works. But again, 'The Narrow Footpath' is not a personal essay as such.

Both these men inspired a generation of readers and writers— they are the foundational figures of modern Tibetan literature. But regarding the birth of the literary essay, the personal essay, I think it is possible that that parentage may belong to neither Gendun Chopel nor Dhondup Gyal, but to Tsewang Yishey Pemba. A practising Western-trained doctor (the first one, naturally), Tsewang Pemba wrote what may be the very first modern personal essays by a Tibetan, in certain chapters in his autobiography, *Young Days in Tibet* (1957).

The key thing to note about Dr Tsewang Pemba? He wrote in English, not Tibetan. The other thing to note is that by the time Tsewang Pemba was writing his personal essays on Tibet, the country had been invaded and occupied by China. Like many of his compatriots, Tsewang Pemba was on the outside, in exile. And he was writing to tell his story to witness and to recover, which

is to say that one of the first modern Tibetan personal essays—
perhaps the very first modern Tibetan personal essay indeed—was
a literary exercise in recovering the lost land.

* * *

This is fitting because the essay has a long affinity with exile,
with distance and loss. The essay interrogates the interior
landscape—perhaps because the familiar exterior one has been
lost. Montaigne, who perfected the essay form in the sixteenth
century, and from whom we get the word 'essay' from the French
'essai'—for attempts—cut himself off from society and went into
a self-imposed exile at home for a decade, during which period he
wrote a book of essays.

* * *

The Tibetan word for the 'essay', whether personal and literary
or argumentative and intellectual, is *tsom*. Tsom is both noun and
verb. It can mean an essay and a composition. It can also mean to
compose, to create and, of course, it can mean to lie or to make up.
So, to write, to create, to compose, to lie—all of which is to say, to
tell the truth by lying. We know this is what art can do—tell the
truth by lying.

* * *

One of the very earliest pieces of writing from Tibet is the *Old
Tibetan Chronicle* from the eighth century. The *Chronicle* tells of
the old Tibetan empire, the Yarlung Pugyel dynasty and King
Songtsen Gampo—the Tibetan Arthur and Ashoka—who unified
the Tibetan plateau into Tibet. This is the story, from the *Old*

Tibetan Chronicle, of the marriage of Songtsen's younger sister, Princess Semarkar.

Princess Semarkar was sent to the neighbouring Shangshung kingdom not simply as a bride but to rule alongside the Shangshung king. Sometime after the wedding, Semarkar sent a message back to Songtsen in a song, a poem innocent in its verses, to the messenger. It was a coded message.

The political marriage had failed. The message to Songtsen said that Semarkar's husband, the Shangshung king, was not to be trusted. He had avoided consummating his marriage with her, presumably because he did not want a Pugyel heir to the Shangshung kingdom. Semarkar also sent her brother a sewn headpiece with thirty turquoises as a sign for him to go to war.

In 644, Songtsen Gampo led an invasion with his army, conquered Shangshung and established his Tibetan empire. Was he acting on intelligence provided by Semarkar? I like to think so.

I grew up hearing Songtsen's name and had no idea that he had a younger sister called Semarkar, or that she was key to his project of empire-building. I love this story because it tells us that one of the earliest pieces of Tibetan writing, one of the earliest and most important communiqués, was a coded message. And a woman wrote it.

* * *

Tibetans still write in code. Writings from Tibet still need to be deciphered and interpreted. Because there is so much they can't say, so little that can be said—truth-telling is not a safe pastime in authoritarian regimes—we need to pay close attention to subtext. Meanwhile, in exile, sometimes it can feel as if we say too much; we are always trying to shout, trying to underscore our exile, our oppression. If Tibetan writing from the inside can often feel like code, the writing from the outside can sometimes feel like caricature. They have to conceal, and we have to perform. This is the cross around our necks, for those of us writing in this time.

The best modern Tibetan writing, of course, threads the needle—conceals and performs in just the right way. The modern Tibetan essays collected here, through text and subtext, perform the act of truth.

To speak as Tibetans, and to write as Tibetans, is to continually recreate the Tibetan nation.

* * *

Gendun Chophel finished his masterwork *Grains of Gold: Tales of the Cosmopolitan Traveler* by 1941—in the Indian subcontinent, by the way—but it was only published in the 1990s. Interrupted by invasion and occupation, it lay hidden like a buried treasure for decades. (Its English translation by Thupten Jinpa and Donald S Lopez Jr was published in 2014.) Tsewang Pemba's *Young Days in Tibet* and his early novel *Idols on the Path* were published in England, in 1957 and 1966, respectively. His countrymen, in Tibet and exile, were unaware that these books even existed. Nor indeed could they have read them, even if they had been aware of them. The books were a casualty of exile. It was only fifty years later, when *White Crane, Lend Me Your Wings: A Tibetan Tale of Love and War* was published posthumously in 2017, that Tibetan readers and writers came to know of his work. Modern Tibetan literature, written in the in-between, in the *bardo*, is a literature of interrupted continuities, much like modern Tibetan people. As Tsering Wangmo Dhompa writes, 'The people of my childhood having lost everything were continually beginning.'

There's a genre of traditional Tibetan literature called the 'terma literature'. These are Buddhist texts that Tibetans understand to be buried or hidden a millennia ago and revealed hundreds of years later when conditions were more ripe for the Dharma to flourish. If this type of traditional Tibetan literature is concealed in time, a certain type of contemporary Tibetan literature today is concealed in place—texts that are meant to be read and comprehended, not hundreds of years later but thousands of kilometres away. Lhashamgyal's *The Man Who Can Never Go Home* resonates with Tibetan exiles in a way that the Chinese Communist Party (CCP) censors can't understand. It's also a reminder that it's not just Tibetans in exile who live in exile; and not just Lhashamgyal and Woeser in Beijing and the thousands of Tibetans in Chengdu and other Chinese cities, but also the millions of Tibetans who live in their ancestral homeland, exiled from the Tibetan nation. Exile is the essential Tibetan condition today—on and off the plateau.

* * *

In many ways, I have left my Tibetan refugee settlement in north India. In other ways, I can never leave it. Psychologists use the term 'ambiguous loss' to define a loss for which it is extremely difficult to find closure. This is often a traumatic loss, such as when a parent or a child goes missing in action. In such cases, those left behind have found that the way to finally find some form of closure is to arrive at a place of magical thinking, where the lost person is both gone forever and yet always with you.

For Tibetans, Tibet is our ambiguous loss, our open wound which refuses to close. This is why the twin strands of occupation and exile form the DNA of modern Tibetan literature. Our occupation grows long, as we turn from a single-source exile to a multi-strand diaspora. In our writing, we dig deep, deepening the wound but at the same time airing it out. Witnessing, voicing, reclaiming, imagining and creating. Here is why I think of modern

Tibetan literature, a de-territorialized literature that is obsessed with place and territory, as pre-postcolonial literature. We are writing, in the *bardo*, in the in-between transitory period between our old life and the new, towards the future.

I think of these essays as transcribing not just the Tibetan past, not just the Tibetan present, but the Tibetan future.

Nation of Two

Tsering Wangmo Dhompa

My mother and I were in Delhi in the winter of 1980, waiting for approval from the French embassy so she could begin a job at a Buddhist centre somewhere in France. It had taken her more than a year to convince various parties that she could do this work. This was in the early days when Buddhism was making tentative overtures of inner peace to the West, and the few existing centres were run by monks. She was considered for the job most likely because the then caretaker of the centre, Lama Namsey, was a monk from Dhompa, her nomadic village in the eastern Tibetan kingdom of Nangchen. Three individuals, including her, had made it to exile from her birthplace. Karyak, the other, lived in Mainpat, India, then later in Kathmandu.

'The three of us,' she would say when she spoke of her homeland.

They were a nation of three.

I did not ask when I was to follow her to France. My papers, or I should say, lack of them, were not under discussion. But by the age of eleven, I knew that my mother always put me first. She had pivoted from her worldview of 'everything is impermanent', to considering permanent legibility for me.

Delhi was pulsating with construction. Hotels, bridges, roads, water, and power facilities were being built in anticipation of making future foreign guests comfortable. Everything was going according to plan, the city's bureaucrats responded when interviewed on the status of the city's preparedness for the upcoming IX Asian Games.

'The best time of the year,' my mother said. The kaniar trees were in bloom past the corner where taxi drivers gathered in the afternoon, a short walk from our temporary one-room-*barsati* home in Sundar Nagar. It was from their conversations that my mother learned that colour televisions would be introduced in time for the Games. We had no country to root for and we did not own a television set, but still, my mother and I felt that for once, as refugees, we were in the right place and perhaps even at the right time.

The Games had almost been cancelled the year before, but Prime Minister Indira Gandhi had resumed power in January of that year. Now, Delhi was a tangle of metal, cement and confused ambitions. My mother and I were carefree in this upheaval; she had made her decision to start all over in a new country so I could one day become a citizen, even if it was of France, a country about which we knew nothing at that point. It was up to the French government officials to accept her. She had learned how to attend to hope. As a refugee, she knew how to wait.

'Let's watch all the films in the theatres,' she decided. Or maybe that is what I heard. She had memorized the names of the city's countless theatres. Regal, Sangam, Eros, Rivoli.

'Grand names. They sound English,' I agreed.

Movies allowed for longings other than what life's struggles tethered her to. Perhaps she wished for a life where characters did not have to flee to another country out of necessity. The celluloid family dramas situated in Indian settings reminded her of the irretrievable in her life. Our first outing was to see an older film, *Mughal-e-Azam*, a historical drama about the love between the Mughal Prince Salim (who became Emperor Jahangir) and Anarkali, a dancer in his court.

'No chance for this love story,' my mother predicted.

We did not know then about characters, setting and plot. My mother had been raised by nomadic chiefs and lamas in a Tibet that had faded when she crossed the borders into Nepal and then India. She fell back on karma to explain her life to me. Salim and Anarkali's love was the kind that gathered no allies. My mother was only satisfied when we watched the movie twice; it was as though she was unwilling to accept the outcome of that love, even though she had predicted it. Both times, I was unprepared for the screen changing from black-and-white to technicolour at the very moment when Madhubala twirled to 'Pyar Kiya to Darna Kya'. We alternated between translating the chorus as, 'There's no need to fear when you love,' and 'Why fear when you love?' depending on the kind of assurance we were seeking.

Each time Anarkali twirled, I think my mother sighed.

My mother's mother, my grandmother, Dechen, was the daughter of the secretary to the King of Nangchen. She had already given birth to a daughter whose father was the Chungho chieftain when my grandfather, also a chieftain of Nangchen, decided he wanted to take her as his wife. The ministers of Dhompa begged my grandfather to find a more suitable bride, the daughter of another chieftain perhaps. 'Or else,' they might have said, but my grandfather was in love with my grandmother, or so the story intimates. 'Or else,' my grandfather might have said to Dechen and the Chungho chief. Dechen was beautiful. And she was well-read, unusual for women of that region and of that time. I do not know what was in her heart.

That love did have life, according to my mother, who was her father's favourite. My aunt, the daughter of the Chungho chief, came to Dhompa with Dechen.

My mother hummed 'Pyar Kiya to Darna Kya' for days. I had not seen her with a lover, not then, not ever. As far back as I can remember, she was celibate, like the monks who surrounded us.

We did not go to France after all. In the winter of 1980, a man came, disrupting our film outings and bringing my mother news of her family. My mother heard of her family for the first time since 1959. She found out that her brother, her two sisters and their children were alive in Tibet. All elders, but for a cousin, had died in Chinese prisons or labour camps, the man told my mother. Her sagacious mother had jumped into the river when she was captured by the Chinese Communist Army, he said. It was rumoured she took a soldier with her. The man avoided the word 'suicide' when speaking of Dechen; he implied it was her karma. My mother cried all day after our guest left. Watching her, I wept. Her face had become rotund from grief. I worried her heart would break, that she might die from sorrow.

'We're moving to Kathmandu,' she said. This was the day after hearing about her family. 'Nepal is closer to our family in Tibet,' she explained.

She quit her temporary job in New Delhi—in a brief message by fax to her employers who were away on holiday—and took me to the sixteenth Karmapa, the head of the Kagyu order in Tibetan Buddhism, who was in the All India Medical Hospital in Delhi undergoing treatment for cancer. She explained to him why she could no longer work in his centre in France. She gave away what we could not pack in two suitcases, and after a week, we were changing trains and buses in the direction of Kathmandu.

It had taken my mother more than a year to decide on moving to France and it had involved the efforts of more people than my mother probably realized. She had resolved upon France after surrendering to the likelihood that nobody in her family in Tibet had survived the Cultural Revolution. She had acquiesced to a different set of hardships in exchange for the hope that the West would allow me a future that she could not furnish for me as a refugee in India. Mere proximity to family, however, replaced the pursuit of stability.

Family and people first was a mantra she had been teaching me, since I was a child. Her actions illustrated how one did that.

I don't remember the details of our crossing the border at Sonauli in India and Bhairahawa in Nepal. My mother must have shown her Indian government-issued Tibetan Refugee Identity Card. She might have offered *baksheesh*, a bribe—that was always the quicker and easier alternative. She would have had to offer money anyway, as she was a lone woman with a child, two suitcases and refugee documents. Once in Kathmandu, we moved into a room in the Sakya monastery in Boudhanath, or Boudha, provided by Tharig Rinpoche, the lama, who was a relative. And just like that, within twenty days of learning that some of her loved ones were not the subject of her prayers but alive in her homeland, we were in a different setting in exile.

* * *

Boudha offered to me a different understanding of the Tibet that my mother came from. It also made me see the imaginative and inventive ways in which Tibetan refugees were managing a life in exile—both in the ways they adjusted to disruptions related to the inner life of family and in the sleight of hand they improvised a livelihood. The Tibetans we knew in Boudha appeared to live in a state of their own, negotiating Nepali laws through a combination of calling favours, bribes and political chameleonics because most Tibetans didn't have any documents, but were unable to quash their feelings of injury when it came to the Tibetan exile government. Their relationship with the exile government was reflected in the way that they sometimes referred to it possessively as 'our government,' and on other days as 'the Tibetan government'. They seemed to weigh what they would have to lose if they were to reconcile with exile politics: an idea of who they were or what they hoped to be.

This, I now understand, is because the people I knew were from the nomadic eastern regions of Tibet, a large territory of kingdoms and diverse groups configured as Kham. It was as though they believed that as 'Khampas', people of eastern Tibet, they were always going to be misunderstood by 'the Tibetan government', which they accused of being Lhasa-centric. In their suspicion of centralized authority, they behaved as though they were still living as nomadic tribes. On one hand, they seemed to function without any caution because they didn't know the rules that did or did not apply to us as paperless people, and on the other, they lived in such fear that some of them never stepped beyond Boudha.

Unlike Tibetans living in India who were recognized as refugees, most of our community in Boudha were neither categorized as refugees nor recognized as Nepali citizens. We were living as both in-between and not-yet people, making up the rules as we encountered new situations. The elders had never needed to prove their identity in nomadic Tibet. The very idea of a nation-state was new to them as was the concept of formal citizenship.

Ironically, the only places where Tibetans were welcomed were at the casinos in Kathmandu. Prohibited to Nepali citizens, the casinos permitted Tibetans, those with an Indian government-issued Refugee Identification Card, to gamble. Once Tibetans stepped outside the casino doors, they would shrink back to the self that lived with the hazards of a present but invisible, socially-dead person status.

Tibetans claimed the Boudha stupa, *Jarong Khashor* in Tibetan, as part of Tibetan and Buddhist lore. A long time ago, a woman named Ma Jhadzima wanted to build a stupa. She approached the king of the region and requested land. The king granted her wish but on the condition that she can only build on land covered by the skin of a single ox. Jhadzima cut the skin of an ox into thin strips and used it to circle a boundary of the land. The king had to keep his word. That is why Tibetans call the stupa Jarong Khashor: Jarong means 'it can be done,' and Kha-shor translates as 'slipped out of the mouth'. Tibetans narrate different versions of this story but the central character, plot, and theme remain the same.

Jhadzima started the work on the stupa and her four sons completed it. The four sons were reincarnated as the crucial pillars to the establishment of Buddhism in Tibet: the seventh-century King Songtsen Gampo of Tibet, the famous minister of Tibet Padma Gungtsen, the abbot Shantarakshita, and the illustrious Guru Padmasambhava. As far as Tibetans were concerned, living in Boudha ensured their safety not only in the present life but also in the lives to come.

* * *

There is no guidebook to living in exile.

Tibetans in Boudha reinvented themselves regularly. One year, my mother's friend Pema ran a tiny general store; the following year, she transformed it into a restaurant. These decisions, made with an 'it can be done' attitude, were shaped by necessity, a change in circumstance or failure to get other things moving. Pema spent half her day standing at the entrance to her enterprise. She knew I was alone at home while my mother worked, so she would cajole me to step in to have a cup of tea, a bowl of *thukpa*, or a plate of chow mein. Monks from the monastery stored their soccer gear in her storeroom and she would often feed them when they returned from their games. Another family friend, who ran a general store, would leave it in the hands of passers-by to run errands. Every now and then, she would close her store at midday, saying she had made enough money for the day.

These businesses were probably never profitable, but they were hospitable to children and elders. Elders would rest on their way to the stupa, and they would be offered a soda or a cup of tea. I could visit these businesses whenever I was bored. Sometimes I would help serve a customer. Or elders would tell me to show a wandering tourist the way to a monastery. Even my mother, who knew absolutely nothing about running a business, contemplated opening a shop because, as was the case with many Tibetans without documents, working for an established Nepali outfit was not an option. Luckily, she abandoned the idea when she got an offer to work in a boutique hotel that was a joint venture between a rich American from Texas and a handful of ballsy Tibetan businessmen known to my mother. She became a housekeeping manager on the other side of Kathmandu without any training in running a hotel.

There were ten families, including my mother and I, living in a building designed as monk quarters. Three of the families, including ours, were related to Tharig Rinpoche. When my mother went to pay the rent for the year, Rinpoche would give the money back to her or keep a small amount as an offering, if my mother insisted. She was embarrassed by his generosity but acts like these helped us live with dignity.

To get to our house in Boudha, we had to walk through the monastery's main gate and around the schoolroom where monks memorized their prayers and alphabets all day. I played with the young monks and because they wore maroon and yellow robes, I stayed away from those colours. I did not want to be mistaken for a nun. The families in our building shared four toilets with the fifty or so monks. Mothers and daughters memorized the regimen maintained by monks: chanting prayers, memorizing prayers and writing prayers. Every time they got a little respite, the monks rushed to the bathroom.

My mother was adamant that I never carry a monk's baby, so I usually hung out with old monks. I wore loose shirts and long skirts; I dressed like the men who were *ngakpas* with long dreadlocks. When young monks sang songs from Bollywood films, 'Eh, Miss, dede kiss, Aya hain '86' (Hey Miss, gimme a kiss, it's '86), I sprinted home. When young school-going Tibetan and Nepali boys sang, 'I just called to say I love you,' I ran into the monastery and sat with the old monks till the beating of my heart slowed down.

There was a time when someone slipped a note to my friend, who was a year younger and an only child like me, that said, 'I like you'. Her parents were strict and so, she stayed indoors when she returned from day school. She and I scrutinized all the monks our age, but we could not figure out who could have written the note. We wanted our part in a love story but there was no ready plot in the movies that we saw in which a liaison with a monk ended with all parties celebrating.

We lived in one room. The stove was in one corner and within a few months, the wall around it turned splotchy with charcoal. Our two beds hugged the walls, serving as seats for visitors during the day. I had always shared a bedroom with my mother. She, on the other hand, as she explained to me, had been raised in a mansion in Tibet. Having visited nomadic Dhompa, her birthplace, following her death in 1994 and seeing the remains of the old house, I cannot say for certain that 'mansion' is an accurate description. Nevertheless, her father had been the chieftain of Dhompa in Nangchen, and as nomads, they had more than one home. Exile was the beginning of a diminished life as far as my mother was concerned.

My mother had arrived empty-handed at the borders of Lo Manthang in Nepal in 1960. Not a single other member of her family made it to exile. Her clothes hung to her frame and her shoes were filled with holes. She lived in tents for the first three to five years of her refugee life, first in Mustang, and then on road construction sites in the mountains of Manali in northern India where she worked as a labourer with her husband and his people. Every day she thought her body would break. Only her memories held intact. She frequently re-evaluated her losses in her attempt to teach me to honour her past as well as to learn Buddhist lessons on impermanence. Having lost her entire family, she taught me to love people.

'Fight for people, not for money or status,' she would say.

Exile was the only form of belonging I knew. While I could not and did not know how I fit into the world outside the Tibetan exile community, I had a clear sense of what was possible at home. Everything we owned was within view.

* * *

The first home I remember is the two-room house in Dharamshala in which one room served as the kitchen and the other was our everything room. When we had guests, I shared my mother's bed. We didn't have a private bathroom. We walked into the nearby forest at night or walked a block to the one bathroom that was shared by ten families. I don't remember clearly what we did for bathing; I think we heated water over our kerosene stove and took weekly baths in the kitchen. We brushed our teeth together, we shared the soap and face cream, we divided the shelves in the cupboard, and we each had an aluminium box for our winter clothes. We knew what the other owned. I stacked shoes neatly under the bed at night; I swept the floor in the morning. She stir-fried meals: chunks of bread with egg, rice with egg, rice with vegetables and slices of mutton. Once a week, she made her famous potato and beef curry. I knew when she forgot to say her prayers. I noticed when she ran out of clean socks. I knew the names of the people she wrote letters to, and there were some letters I wrote for her in English. She saved everything good for me. At the end of every month, she would offer me half of her salary.

Our single-room house in Boudha, like the room in Dharamshala, had a window that never knew the sun. Night or day, the light from the bulb hanging from the centre of our room was like our private sun. We never forgot we were in a monastery. Hence, we observed the decorum of ascetics: we woke to the early morning gong that roused the monks for prayers and we slept after the lull of night prayers at dusk. The chalky white walls of our living quarters contrasted with the traditional motifs ornamenting the building's awnings painted in deep reds and saffron colours. An American friend visiting Nepal compared our home to being in a railway station, or that is how my mother explained to me. It was the first time she was made to feel ashamed of the home that she had built for us.

'Maybe I should get a better place for us. Maybe it's not a good home for a young girl,' she apologized to me.

There were no rules in my mother's house, probably because we were always in each other's view. I could say that I was a dutiful daughter and I followed her well. Or that she observed me and arranged our lives to be harmonious. I think it had mostly to do with the fact that we were all we had. We guarded each other's happiness. We put the other first. We didn't have to make many decisions because we had few options. Our love, like our mobility, had a relationship with precarity. Unable to root ourselves wherever we were, we instead were grounded in each other—a nation of two.

All the rooms in our building in Boudha opened to a single room with walls painted in white that rubbed off on our clothes when we leaned against them. Some families had a small extension that served as a kitchen. Throughout the day, people popped in and out of our home. It was as though all the rooms in the building were connected. Nobody reprimanded me for disturbing them or for stopping by more than twice a day. Nobody complained that I asked them what they had cooked for lunch before deciding in whose home I would eat.

On sunny days, the women would bring out quilts and blankets for airing. The women, except for Dolma and my mother, would gather around the single tap in the courtyard to hand-wash clothes. My mother would be on the other side of Boudha, working in the hotel. Dolma would sit beside us while spinning wool while her husband, Tashi, a former monk, did the washing. We would soak clothes in water for an hour before squatting with *chubas* and with trousers gathered under our knees. I noticed that the women's ankles were three shades lighter than their hands. It was the only time I saw their calves. We also washed our utensils on the cement platform built around the tap. From the women, I learned to use ash as dish soap, to use soap meant for clothes as shampoo and to scrub pots stunningly clean with mud.

In between house chores, the women spun wool for local Tibetan-owned carpet factories. To earn more money, they wove carpets at home on small looms. The women spoke Nepali, while their husbands could barely negotiate their fare to reach the city's centre. I learned which women met at dusk to drink a shot of cheap local *rakshi* after they had served dinner to their families. I learned which family friend had discovered her husband had a girlfriend in Lhasa, and which one's husband caused the bump on her head. I learned that Dolma and Karma had been a couple for a long time before she fell in love with Tashi. They had settled the conundrum by living together, that is, Dolma decided to keep both men.

I also learned that my mother had been married to four brothers in Tibet.

My father had been the oldest, and the youngest had been too young so the remaining three were more like her brothers, the women explained. I concealed my shock at this discovery. I tried to discuss my mother's life as they did.

'Poor thing, she suffered a lot. He did not deserve her. I hear her husband was not good to her,' they said.

'She is so intelligent and beautiful,' they said.

My mother's marriage had been arranged to a neighbouring chieftain family when she was seventeen years old. She had not been a willing bride. She had separated from her husband as a new refugee around the time I was born. She took nothing from him. It was difficult for me to see my mother as a wife to four brothers.

In Boudha, I was reminded often that I had come to her life belatedly. I would never see her favourite brocade dress tucked under the sheepskin jacket in the chest in her room; I would not meet her father, her mother, her uncle, her brother or her childhood friends. I would viscerally know her past only through scars on her body: the tiny marks on her face that were remnants of the smallpox that had almost killed her when she was a child; the mangled distortion of her tailbone from the bedsores when she was bedridden while carrying twin babies in Tibet in 1959. In Boudha, a handful of elders who had visited Dhompa as children would tell me about my grandfather or grandmother. These elders referred to her as the daughter of the Dhompa chief. In calling her so, they kept her lineage alive. These stories kept me out and they drew me in. The elders called me the daughter of Tsering Choden Dhompatsang. Because of her, I was also a person with a past that preceded my birth. I was a member of the nation of three. This past gave me a sense of belonging in a present where I could not even obtain a document affirming my refugee status.

On cold days, we gathered in the warmest rooms. There was a *before* and an *after* to every narrative. No person amongst us had emerged unscathed from the break in time we referred to as 'when the Chinese came'. Who could have predicted that a mother would lose a four-year-old child attached to her horse in the darkness of night after three months on the road to exile? Or that a husband would take fancy to a sister-in-law and steal moments of pleasure while on a journey where death draped them like a rash? Or that an old, revered uncle would slide into his young nephew's wife's bed? Or that men who fought the Chinese during the day would weep quietly at night? Or that women who remembered everyone's names and held everyone together would also weep?

My mother's friend Tashi's husband left her and their two daughters behind in Lhasa in 1959 when he fled to India. I cannot remember if they had been separated while escaping or if she'd stayed back to wait for her parents. In any case, her husband had made it to India and searched for her in refugee camps for many years. He finally remarried but did not have any children. Then, after fifteen or so years, he got news from a trader in Lhasa that his first wife Tashi was alive. He left his second wife and invited Tashi to live with him in Kathmandu.

'Poor woman. Why should she have to sacrifice her life?' the women asked.

'But what would you have done?'

'Imagine living under the Chinese for twenty years and then finding out your husband is alive but with another woman,' the women said.

Most nights my mother and I would climb the stairs to our cousin's home and watch the news. This was our link with the world beyond Boudha. We wrote letters to friends and relatives in

India and Tibet and by the time we got their responses, it would be another season and new politicians would be running the country. So much would have happened on the television and yet our lives would be the same, suspended in waiting for external actors to step in and rewrite or rearrange the events of our lives towards action.

That I was in a different environment when we settled into life in Boudha was first evident in the language—not just the Nepali language which my mother and I had to learn, but also the Tibetan. My mother had switched almost immediately from the formal and more Lhasa-centric Tibetan (what government officials in Dharamshala called 'pure Tibetan'). I had become accustomed to hearing her speak the Nangchen dialect, which was stripped of all honorifics and niceties. The second was my understanding of family and politics. In Dharamsala, my mother had been the only single working mother in a building reserved for members of Parliament and their families. In our new home in Boudha, we were one of a spectrum of family systems that seemed to be cobbled together in response to unexpected life trajectories. For example, there was Dolma, Tashi and Karma, who lived together in one room. Then there was Tsering and her husband, both in their sixties when they adopted a baby they found outside their house in a plastic bag. No Nepalese relative came to claim her and so they held on to her. My mother's cousin, who lived on the floor above us, was raising a niece who had been smuggled out of Tibet in a jeep under big sacks of yak jerky, tea and dried cheese.

I had friends with two fathers, sometimes three fathers. I liked going to their homes—there was a constant hum. The children referred to the men as father and the fathers called the children 'gaga' (dearest), 'a-nyo' (child), or 'kho-re' (hey you)!

Boudha elders woke up at three or four in the morning to circumambulate around the stupa. They resumed the process at four in the evening. After prayers, they often gathered to have tea in small tea shops that proliferated over the years around the stupa. If I had a message to relay to an elder, I would wait in one spot around the stupa. Almost always, I would find the person. My mother only acquired a telephone when I was twenty years old. We didn't make much use of it; very few elders had telephones in their homes, and if they did have one installed, they rarely used them. Boudha was the safest place I knew.

Years later in college in Delhi, I met other Nepalese students, also from Kathmandu. One student, who lived in the centre of Kathmandu, said she had never been to Boudha.

'Is it safe there?' she asked.

It was only then that I realized Tibetans might have been viewed as dangerous. I was from a part of the city that good citizens avoided. Was it poverty that made us a threat? Was it because older Tibetans like my mother always wore their Tibetan *chuba*? Were our intentions unclear? Were we seen as ungrateful for refusing to fully assimilate, living as we did as though we were still in Tibet? I was too self-conscious and ashamed of being a refugee to ask her these questions. Instead, I intensified my deception, declaring I was from Tusal or Chabahil—areas adjacent to Boudha—to Nepalese friends who lived in Kathmandu's affluent neighbourhoods. This was also my strategy to deflect questions from immigration officers when I crossed the borders between India and Nepal. The question, '*Bhote ho?*' (Are you Tibetan?) paralyzed me. For how could I say 'yes' to the immigration officers while carrying documents that stated I was Nepali? At the same time, how could I say 'no,' without my heart breaking a little for the small deceptions that continuously eroded my sense of self and belonging?

Boudha sheltered us from such questions. I could ask Nepalis, '*Nepali ho?* [Are you Nepali?]' while being a Tibetan.

* * *

The people of my childhood, having lost everything, were continually beginning. My mother worked as a nurse in Shimla in the early 1960s, a nursery-school teacher in the early 1970s, a member of Parliament for the Tibetan Government in Exile through the 1970s and 80s and as a housekeeping manager of a hotel before her death. She was not trained for any of those positions. Now, after having lived half my life in the United States and having accrued enough time to be able to look back, I see exile, and what it means and does. I understand why my mother clung to history and her past. Memory was the only stability she could hold on to.

Karma is dead. So are Dolma, and the former monk.

I can call them back. I can turn to a moment, for example, when Karma entered our home presenting his grief.

'I am reduced to the figure of a father. I never get to sleep with Dolma anymore,' he says.

'I have feelings, too,' he says. My mother nods.

I heard him repeat the same sorrow month after month. There was no place for me to hide in our room. Whatever heartaches people shared with my mother, they shared with me. He had seemed eighty to me then, but perhaps he'd only been sixty-something. When he had arrived in India, he had taken Dolma, a young orphan, under his wing and when she had blossomed into a young woman, he had taken her to his bed. Nobody had asked then if she had wished for him, who had been like a father, to be her husband. Nobody had objected too much when she fell in love with a younger man and when she brought him home.

'I thought he was young and capable. I thought he would be of help to us,' Karma told my mother.

In the movies we watched, it was usually the husband who fell in love with a younger woman. The older wife remained devoted, waiting and praying that her husband would eventually acknowledge her love. And more often than not, he would return to the first wife. Love and virtue were the law. Love was the prize for those who waited. It was the reward for those who loved well.

Dolma and Tashi were always together. They would sit side by side in the garden when the sun was out, and they would walk to the stupa with their arms brushing. Tashi did all the washing, the cooking, and the cleaning.

'She has good karma,' the women would remark. 'Does she do anything at home?'

Karma would trail behind them, transformed from the first husband into the parent. I can understand now why he felt upset.

'You're the elder. They're taking care of you,' my mother would remind him.

'It isn't right,' he would respond. 'It isn't fair that I am alone in bed, night after night and they are in the bed across from me.'

My mother would nod her head in agreement.

'It is fate. Life is not always fair.'

This small admission of contradiction was not something she would offer to me, but having accepted some of Karma's burden, she would caution him to be careful as he climbed the stairs, one slow step at a time, to his room.

Our stories were often left incomplete, and because we were still living through the consequence of a cleft in time, we accepted the fragments. The conflict had already taken place and we were caught in a plot whose resolution was slow to unfold. And there was karma to contend with. While we waited, China grew stronger. Exile altered expectations and blunted convictions. It warped the lines of kinship.

What was right when life was wrong?

Unhealed

Bhuchung D. Sonam

'Did the Chinese beat you?' the little girl asked me. It was the first sentence I heard when I arrived in Dharamsala on a miserably cold December night in 1983. The bus shook and rattled up the winding mountain road. I was tired and my head felt swollen, but I said, 'Yes.' It sounded right.

1

I was born in a remote village to the north-west of the immense Tibetan Plateau. We had no running water, electricity or paved roads. The most advanced thing, to the wonderment of the villagers, was one family's sewing machine. In the daytime, grown-ups dug canals or worked in the fields. In the evening, at the blow of the whistle, they attended meetings at the commune hall, where cadres made them recite from Mao's *Little Red Book*. It was during these meetings that people were indoctrinated along the Party line to show absolute allegiance to the leadership of the Great Helmsman. At the end of each meeting, they strained their throats shouting: 'Long Live Chairman Mao!' Everyone learned to hold their tongues, to obey orders and instructions to the letter. No one had to think.

Occasionally, soldiers would arrive at our village on horseback, dressed in faded green uniforms and chain-smoking. They were treated with respect. Large meetings were staged in the village square, during which these important people made long speeches that were then translated for the villagers. The soldiers inspected the new canals, the commune's prayer-hall-turned-donkey-sheds and the barley fields where red flags fluttered. They were nice to kids, often giving us candies. They didn't scold us or chase us away for begging them to hand out more.

Nevertheless, years later, on that wet winter night in India, I told the little girl that the Chinese beat me. 'I know,' she said, 'they are terrible people.'

Layers of confusion enveloped me when I was sent into exile. To begin with, I didn't know that the Chinese were different from us. I couldn't understand why my great-uncle hated the blue canvas shoes, steel mugs and other items that my mother bought from the commune store; or why the Red Guards had destroyed the monastery in front of our house. I didn't know why I had to be smuggled out of Tibet.

I have had decades to find answers to these questions, and to dig into our history and the political dilemma we find ourselves in today. The years away from home have transformed me into a vastly different person from the small boy whom my parents—at my great-uncle's advice—sent away to become a monk at the Dalai Lama's monastery in Dharamsala.

My great-uncle was the abbot of the local monastery in Old Tibet, and his faith in religion was as unshakable as his resolution not to flee in the aftermath of the occupation. This belief was based on his understanding of Buddhism and trust that ultimately *ley-gyu-dey* or 'the law of karma' prevails. Even during the worst years of the Cultural Revolution, when he became the commune's shepherd, he continued to chant his daily mantras in the company of grazing sheep and goats, away from the prying eyes of the cadres. Until his death in 1988, he never betrayed his belief and steadfastly maintained his monastic vows.

My father, on the other hand, was a product of the great historical upheaval that had turned his familiar world upside down and forced him into a new socialist world, where the old value system had no practical application in life's daily struggle. His faith in religion was shallow and his understanding of the politics of occupation and suppression was even more limited. He smoked and drank. Worse still, he bought canned pork, fish and chicken (Tibetans generally don't eat these and they were strictly prohibited in our house) while my great-uncle was away in the hills with the flock. My father also befriended some of the men who, I learned many years later, were the first to volunteer when Red Guards ordered the destruction of the monastery that my great-uncle had presided over.

Once, when our rationed stock of barley was running low, my father wanted to sell the bronze Buddha image that our family had managed to hide during the destructive years of the Cultural Revolution. A heated argument broke out between my great-uncle and father. 'You cannot sell it,' great-uncle said, sitting cross-legged, kneading his rosary. This was in the early 1980s when there was a slight relaxing of the policy over religion in Tibet.

'We need money to buy food,' my father said, rolling up the sleeves of his *chupa* like a butcher about to slaughter a sheep.

'It's sinful. This will bring no good.' Great-uncle didn't raise his voice, but I noticed that his aged fingers were rolling hard on the beads.

Days later, the bronze Buddha was sold to a Tibetan merchant from Nepal for 200 yuan, a white nylon shirt and a digital wristwatch. The watch stopped working a week later. We were, however, able to buy more barley with the money so we didn't go hungry.

The incident had a deep impact on me. When reality knocks at the door, other things flee through the window.

My belief in religion has been shaped by circumstances in exile that neither my great-uncle nor my father had to negotiate. When I was young, I held the naïve belief that doing prostrations and chanting countless *manis* were the sole ways to accumulate merit, and that Buddhas, Bodhisattvas and deities would come to me in difficult times. Through my lonely and penniless years in school, I had never missed a single prayer session. My invocations, however, were met with silence. No deities jumped down from their gold-plated altars to assuage my pain. Doubt and scepticism soon took refuge in my impressionable teenage mind. I began to abhor the complex and often endless religious rites and rituals, which consumed huge amounts of our time, energy, and limited resources. The more I tried to understand the association between the rituals and fundamental Buddhist philosophy, the more confused I became.

The lasting influence of Buddhism on my life is its principle— that everything is interdependent and that every action will have an equal consequence in this or the next life. This guides me through the perils of exile, and I try to conduct my life based on these values. In this sense, perhaps I am closer to my great-uncle's understanding of Buddhism, and yet I certainly don't share his unshakable faith. Though I don't wave away Buddhist symbolism as easily as perhaps my father did during those terribly difficult times, my eyes always glance cynically at the rituals involved.

Tibet's spiritual leader, the Dalai Lama, often remarks that we have had enough elaborate religious ceremonies over the years since Buddhism was introduced in Tibet in the seventh century. He advises that the time has come for us to focus on its practical values. 'My religion is simple,' the Dalai Lama has famously said, 'my religion is compassion.' Even then, His Holiness still performs many rites and rituals. Furthermore, His remarks to simplify some of the extremely elaborate rituals have caused confusion and anxiety in the monastic community. Monks have been unable to decide which ceremonial rituals to discontinue and which aspects to retain.

Despite Buddhism's newfound popularity, only a handful of parents in my generation want their children to join monasteries as opposed to the traditional practice of putting at least one child from each family in robes. We may still visit monasteries or light butter lamps on special holy days, but we do these with a pinch of salt, a dose of doubt. A friend complains that his very religious friend makes offerings of soft drinks and wine by opening them and placing them on his altar. 'Such a waste,' he says. 'We can't drink them afterwards.'

Born and raised in exile, today's youth are equipped with the linguistic skills and technical know-how to absorb the shock of harsh reality far more maturely than the generation that came into exile in the late 1950s and early 1960s. This gives them the confidence to venture into other communities and migrate to places that the older generation never dreamt of. The interactions with diverse groups of people and exposure to other spiritual practices make our beliefs less conservative. We ask more questions and rely less on faith.

However, the common dream etched in the collective consciousness is to go back to a free Tibet. Connected by the invisible thread of our common history, culture and language, each of us has created a mini-Tibet within. As Salman Rushdie writes in his essay 'Imaginary Homelands', we know this is 'one version of all the hundreds of millions of possible versions'. For the moment, this mini-Tibet in our heart is the home we inhabit in our dreams even as we transport ourselves into newer environments and more unfamiliar circumstances.

2

My mother did not cry on the day I left Tibet. She took out a fist-sized lump of crystal sugar and said, 'Keep chewing on it and you won't get tired.' For years in exile, I held on to her voice, her face, and the taste of that rock sugar.

Distance blurs memory and kills intimacy. In the boys' hostel at the refugee school in Dharamsala, I would stare at the ceiling each night and wish for my mother's voice and her warm pats on my back. The darkness never responded. The wet pillow laughed at me, and the bedbugs continued their bloody assaults. On hot summer nights, a stink emanated from the cheap canvas shoes of eighty-five boys in the fanless C-shaped dormitory. The monsoon brought mildew in every nook and cranny. But the worst season was winter. After the year's final examinations were over in early December, everyone left for long holidays with their parents or relatives. The vacant classrooms stared at those of us who had nowhere to go. To fill our empty days, we would be given odd jobs such as whitewashing the walls, re-arranging the desks in the classrooms or fruitless tasks such as planting trees on cold days. The activities were organized perhaps to keep us occupied and sane. These rituals were repeated each winter, year after year. Meanwhile, my mother's voice grew more distant. I forgot the taste of her rock sugar. I thought less about her at night. The image of her face in my mind gradually thawed and disintegrated like ice cream splattered on a pavement.

When I left school and joined an Indian university, my mother was no longer number one in my imagination. Every now and then, she cleaved to my thoughts but then disappeared as soon as other pressing issues crowded in my student-mind. To begin with, I had to stretch my monthly Rs 500 scholarship by spending not more than Rs 16 a day. This meant that three meals a day were out of the question. Films, snacks, soft drinks or a cup of tea during recess were luxuries. I settled for lunch and dinner at the hostel mess. No breakfast. Occasionally, when a friend sent some money, I would spend it on audiocassettes and books. Piled on top of this acute student poverty were endless classes with mind-numbing professors talking about economic theories, development models and regression analyses.

There is a Tibetan saying that goes: it is better to keep an appropriate distance from fire and loved ones. The word 'appropriate' is crucial. If the distance is too far, the warmth does not reach you and the fire remains just an image as in a photograph.

It has been over three decades since I saw my mother. She lives in her world, her thoughts and ideas shaped by circumstances that are beyond my imagination. I live in exile, my thoughts and values shaped and influenced by a different set of circumstances. Books and friends have played important roles in my life. During my days in college, I found solace in literature. The fate of Robinson Crusoe on his godforsaken island in *Robinson Crusoe*, Edmond Dantes in the dreaded Château d'If prison in *The Count of Monte Cristo* and the terrible hardships endured by Hasari Pal, the rickshaw-puller in the *City of Joy*, somehow assuaged my hunger and loneliness. These fictional characters gave me the strength to face each scorching Indian day with renewed resilience.

My mother does not automatically pop into my mind these days. Unrequited love and affection go stale. I have to force myself to think and refresh my memory to be able to hear her voice—'Keep chewing on it and you won't get tired.' A photograph I received along with a letter from Tibet about seven years ago shows an old woman, her face wrinkled like a drying radish, her hands folded in front of her, nails black with dirt and her mouth slightly skewed towards the left as if to scorn decades of socialist indoctrination.

Memory plays tricks. Worst still, it crashes when reality bursts through the door. My friend Tenzin used to soak his handkerchief with tears when talking on the phone with his mother. Two years ago, his mother escaped from her village in southern Tibet. Along with a small group, she crossed the Himalayan mountains in the winter, braving snowstorms and avoiding the Chinese military check-posts. Their joyous reunion after sixteen years was over within months of her arrival in India. Today, Tenzin lives with his wife and kids, while his mother is alone in another rented room, ten kilometres apart. 'We look at life so differently and we never agree on anything,' he says.

And so, we adjust to our lives like a fish that changes its colour to survive. Exile is a reverse logic feeding on confusion and disappointment and hardening our memory-burdened hearts. Exile is love lost, found and rearranged. Above all, exile is a compromise.

Every once in a while, when I phone my mother, we swim in tears at both ends of the line. Our occasional calls are made worse by our inability to understand each other properly. My mother speaks in a dialect particular to the area around my birthplace, I have long exchanged it for the dialect spoken by the majority of Tibetans in exile. The loss of my native dialect was as inevitable as getting used to fits of monsoon rain beating down on my rented room. In the process, however, I gained two other languages— English and Hindi.

English—which the foremost twentieth-century Tibetan scholar, Gendun Choephel, during his self-imposed exile termed as 'this not-so-useful foreign language'—has become an integral part of who I am and how I define myself. Though I talk in Tibetan most of the time, I read and write primarily in English. I sometimes even think in this acquired tongue, giving a new colour to my spectrum of identity. I have not mastered this language. Perhaps I never will. But the fact that my identity as a writer comes mainly through writing in this alien tongue is a powerful indication that acquired things can replace indigenous characteristics. Those of us who are ejected into strange environments by occupation and social upheavals do not have the luxury to choose what we desire or fend off undesirable factors. Survival trumps everything else.

3

My life in exile revolves around one central untruth; that I was born in India and not in a tiny village in Tibet. All legal papers have to be obtained with this lie in mind and every form with a 'Place of Birth' section has to be filled with falsehood. If I fail to write 'Dharamsala, India' in this small white space, and if I fail to obtain any legal paper through illegal means, my life will fall apart.

This is how telling lies becomes a part of us. If a policeman refuses to thump his official stamp on the application form to renew our Registration Certificate (RC), or an immigration officer asks too many questions, we back up our lies with more fabrications. We sit on a layer of precariously piled lies. When this pack of lies eventually crumbles, neither argument nor tears work. The only other option is an under-the-table operation. We cannot afford to differentiate between rights and wrongs under such circumstances. Truth hardly ever triumphs.

In our heavily accented Hindi, some of us try to prove that we have rights and try to put our scattered facts together, often making matters worse. The irate officer then waves us aside or sends us to the end of the queue. Our assumptions about having rights are often wrong. The man behind the desk knows this. We are a bunch of 'stateless' people surviving in host countries on humanitarian grounds. At best, we are 'honourable guests'. When dinner is over, we have to leave.

And so, we continue with our lies. Another friend Kelsang is a young university-educated Tibetan, born and raised in India. When he sought political asylum in the US, he became 'Dakpa', an illiterate nomad from a small town in Western Tibet. On the day of the interview, he discarded his Levi's jeans and Nike shoes and instead donned dirty corduroy pants bulging at the knees and sported a pair of worn-out leather shoes. To complete the image makeover, he wore a *dzi* sandwiched between two corals around his neck. His asylum application was okayed. Later his Green Card came out too with a new name. We now call him 'Drokpa Dakpa' or the Nomad Dakpa.

'I would certainly not have survived in our terrible time without lying,' wrote Nadezhda Mandelstam in *Hope Against Hope*, her searing account of Russia under Stalin. 'I have lied all my life: to my students, colleagues, and even good friends I didn't quite trust. This was a normal lying of the times, something in the nature of a polite convention. I am not ashamed of this kind of lying ...'

Unlike Mandelstam, most of us live in exile in relative freedom. We do not have dictators breathing down our necks or bayonets poking at our bellies. Nevertheless, when survival bangs at the door, everything goes asunder, making it hard for us to live with dignity and truth. It trumps everything else. We must survive at any cost because our survival is a resistance to being forgotten, a resistance against occupation and a resistance against some of our own faulty memories that do not match reality.

What shines across our lives in exile—wrapped in confusion, lies and endless daily struggles—is the individual resilience and collective fortitude that manifest in victories such as the establishment of our cultural institutions, schools, and monasteries and above all, a legitimate democratic government in exile.

Our new generation, mostly born and raised outside Tibet, has modern education and yet is deeply rooted in our history, culture and language, firmly dedicated to our struggle for freedom and at the same time pursuing individual goals. This is not to state that exile is a blessing in disguise. It never is. Exile is pain and dislocation and sorrow. But these have moulded us into a hard-edged breed, capable of challenging new realities with hard facts, much less dependent on faith alone. This new generation is, as the contemporary Tibetan artist Tshering Sherpa writes, 'the promise of the future amongst the black clouds' of separation, loss and fading memories.

'Did the Chinese beat you?' the little girl asked. I said, 'Yes.' It sounded right.

It still sounds right.

Fragments of Gontse: Remembering My Friend Gonpo Tsering

Pema Bhum

Translated by Tenzin Dickie

1

By the fall of 2011, it was clear to him, and to all of us that Gonpo Tsering didn't have long to live. Still, when I heard the shocking news of his death the other day, I was so stunned that for a while my mind went blank, and I couldn't pull up any memory of him at all. However, various memories of him, both blurry and clear, soon began to surface and crowd my mind. I have put them down here.

I must be among those who knew Gontse the longest. In the 1970s, when I was a teacher at Malho (Henan) Mongol Autonomous County Middle School, he was a student there. I don't have a clear memory of him at school. What does come to my eyes is an image of a boy in a fur-lined coat, hair falling to his eyebrows and covering half his ears. I recall somewhat more clearly that he was not fond of maths class.

In his second year at the middle school, Gonpo Tsering's maths teacher was Tsering Dondrub from Rebkong. I was the maths teacher for the grade above his. Whenever Tsering Dondrub and I got together, we talked about the students in our classes who hated maths. Gonpo Tsering's name came up often.

In the 1980s, Gonpo Tsering studied at Tsongon (Qinghai) Teachers' College. At that time, I was at Northwest Nationalities College. One day, I was in Ziling (Xining) and somehow ended up in Gonpo Tsering's dorm room. He was there that day, lying atop a bunk bed, reading a book. I still remember that image. He was now studying physics. I even wondered how does someone who hated maths now study physics. Later, Gontse told me that he had studied just enough physics to clear his exam. He spent most of his time studying Tibetan literature.

In the fall of 1987, the Lhasa Uprising occurred. During this time, mimeographs of His Holiness the Dalai Lama's 'Five Point Peace Plan', delivered in front of the US Congress, were posted all over the classrooms and residential buildings of the Tibetan teachers and students at Northwest Nationalities College. We also got them in the mail. I received a copy from a factory in the Chinese town of Shenyang. The mail included a strongly worded appeal to rise up against the Chinese. I have no idea who wrote it. I can't remember the letter's contents now, but it was written clearly and fluently, and the appeal was strong and true. The students of Rebkong Middle School went out into the streets to protest. Apparently, this same letter had been distributed among the students before the protest. On the morning of the protest, the letter had even been pasted to the door of the school.

Did the concerned authorities suspect me of authoring the anonymous appeal? The public security bureau in Lanzhou called me in for secret meetings—to question me about these anonymous letters. At least they said they were from the public security bureau but in reality, I think they were from Public Security. They called me to a hotel room on the Northwest Nationalities University campus. When I went in, a hotel staffer told me that someone from my hometown was staying in that room and that he was asking for me.

After many meetings, this man finally believed that I had nothing to do with these anonymous letters. But he said he wanted to be friends with me. Clearly, they wanted to keep up some sort of connection. I guess they wanted to keep tabs on me. One day, the same officer told me that a high-ranking official from Beijing wanted to meet with me. I could not agree to this. Later when I was in India, during a long conversation with Gonpo Tsering about all kinds of things, I learned that he was the author of that letter. He had a partner, whose name I no longer remember.

One night during the uprising in Lhasa, Gonpo said, he and his friend were discussing Tibet and drinking. They wrote that missive in a fit of angry inspiration and mimeographed it. The next day, they took a leave of absence from school to travel elsewhere to mail and distribute the letters.

2

Towards the end of 1988, not long after I had arrived in India, Gonpo Tsering, Chapdak Lhamo Kyab, Gonpo Tsering's nephew, Lama Jabb (the Tibetan Studies scholar who now teaches at Oxford), and a few others arrived. They had a great story. On their way to India, they ran out of money in Lhasa. So, they started a game on the streets of Lhasa, throwing steel rings over the necks of bottles. Gonpo and his friends made a tonne of money but then proceeded to lose it all.

One thing we noticed when we arrived in India was the lack of Tibetan journals and newspapers in Dharamsala. One day, a group of us discussed this on the hill behind the Dharamsala Reception Center. Many *Amdowas*, who were also new arrivals, were there, including Gonpo Tsering, Lhamo Kyab, Palden Gyal from

Radio Free Asia, and the former member of Parliament Dungkar Tsering. Though we talked about the need for more Tibetan-language newspapers and journals, we did not say anything about starting these ourselves. We were new arrivals, we didn't know anyone, and we didn't know the place at all. We had no confidence that there was anything we could do; we didn't know what we could achieve.

Most importantly, we had no idea where we would get funds or who would write in these journals or newspapers. But, as we kept having these discussions, I slowly began to get the sense that maybe literary work could indeed pave the way forward and sustain us. It was Lhamo Kyab and Gonpo Tsering whose encouragement really inspired this confidence in me. To tell the truth, before then I had not read Lhamo Kyab or Gonpo Tsering's writings, and though I wondered at their confidence, I also began to have faith. The two of them were straight and true, and not the kind to pretend to what they didn't know or couldn't do. Other friends also insisted that we wouldn't lack for contributions.

I took our ideas to Secretary Lhamo Tsering (who was the former deputy of Gyalo Thondup, the older brother of His Holiness the Fourteenth Dalai Lama), who was very pleased with them. He told me to write up a proposal for the Kashag, the governing council. And so, this venture was sketched out into a real functioning organization. It was a highly detailed proposal, to the extent that I remember we even laid out what kind of curtains we wanted for the office windows. However, this proposal did not receive support from the Kashag. But later, Taktser Rinpoche (another brother of the Dalai Lama) supported and funded us personally, and this is how we started the journal, *Jangshon: Young Shoots*.

Prior to the journal's launch, I was worried about whether we would be able to fill it up, but I soon realized that I need not have worried at all. Although we didn't have as many pieces as the journals in Tibet, filling up a few issues per year posed no challenge. Some of the pieces, such as those by Gonpo Tsering, would have been among the best pieces even in the journals in Tibet. I was surprised at myself for not having read Gonpo Tsering's work before since I had always paid attention to literature. People can't see the truth and so they eagerly follow only the famous and the celebrated. As I began reading Gonpo Tsering's writings, I realized that his words weren't just empty words—they conveyed much meaning. Whatever he wrote, he wrote from knowledge and experience and not from confusion. He wrote with feeling and precision so that the writing was always clear and meaningful, and never opaque.

There were no boasts or quarrels in his writing. He just wrote clear, flawless prose with seamless structure and without a word out of place. If you knew him well, you saw that the virtues of his writing were very like the virtues of his character. He was an honest man, clear and transparent as a glass marble, and these virtues had sunk into his writing as well.

3

Not long after Gonpo Tsering arrived in India, he went to Shimla or thereabouts to teach. But he couldn't stay there long. At the time, most of us had no Registration Certificate, the document which allowed us to stay in India. In Bir and Dharamsala, the Indian security office was used to many Tibetans not having their documents and they didn't care much. But if you went to places where there weren't many new arrivals from Tibet, then the security office took notice, and you became a person of interest to Indian security personnel. They found out Gonpo had no Registration Certificate and were about to seize him when he fled just in time and came back to Dharamsala.

Then one day when Gonpo, I and a few others were eating our lunch in the staff mess at Gangkyi administrative compound, we received word that the Indian security office was searching for him. Cutting short our meal, Gonpo and I ran to my place and hid there. As it was no longer safe for Gonpo to be in Dharamsala, the Tibetan Education Ministry sent him to Bir to teach. Bir had many Tibetans with no Registration Certificates, certainly many more compared to the number in Dharamsala. In Bir, he would be just one more paperless Tibetan.

In 1992, the Amnye Machen Institute was established as a research centre. I was among the founding board members. A few of us had previously founded *Mangtso* (Democracy) newspaper and *Young Shoots* literary journal, which we now folded into *Amnye Machen*. As my duties and responsibilities had expanded and I could no longer manage the work for *Mangtso* and *Young Shoots* alone, we invited Gonpo Tsering back from Bir to be the Tibetan editor that we needed. Although Lhasang Tsering and Jamyang Norbu were still the chief editors of *Mangtso* newspaper, I was responsible for the Tibetan language content. Led by the two of them, after we finalized the contents of the journal, I wrote up the copy.

Computers were just starting to make an appearance in Dharamsala. But I wasn't used to them, and I wrote faster by hand. What I wrote by hand, Gonpo Tsering typed into the computer.

At the time, *Mangtso* was the only major newspaper published by a non-governmental organization. It had a clear point of view and covered various current topics in simple language. Gonpo had a big influence on the newspaper in this regard. He didn't just input my handwritten content into the computer, he also edited and revised the grammar and spelling, and spent much time simplifying and clarifying my writing. Sometimes we disagreed and even argued over a particular phrase's construction. I usually lost our arguments. He could cite all the grammar rules and never got tired of arguing the finer points of Tibetan grammar. There was no way I could compete with him on grammar and spelling.

Gonpo was amazed at how quickly I could write the pieces. He said that I composed faster than he could input on the computer. To be honest it wasn't simply that I was a fast writer. He wasn't all that used to a computer. As he typed, he sat with a grim expression, his face so close to the computer that it touched the screen at times.

Our newspaper design and layout person was a man named Peter from Switzerland. Peter joked that the computer was Gonpo's girlfriend. Whenever he saw Gonpo, he stuck his neck out, held up his arms and with fingers sticking out in front of his chest, pretended to be Gonpo pecking away at the computer. The first time Gonpo saw this, he laughed so hard that he cried. Whenever someone joked about him, Gonpo's eyes, half hidden under those bushy eyebrows, brightened with a smile, and he just ran with it and laughed.

In 1994, after I left for the US, Gonpo's duties at *Mangtso* increased and I think he took over the editor's role for Tibetan pieces. From the very beginning of *Mangtso*, Gonpo played a significant role. He cared very much about the newspaper. When *Amnye Machen* stopped publication in 1996, Gonpo wrote a piece about his sorrow and disappointment in the *Nyenchen Thangla* newspaper.

4

Palden Gyal did most of the work on *Young Shoots* before it was absorbed into *Amnye Machen*. After it became part of *Amnye Machen*, Gonpo was the real editor of *Young Shoots*, though I was the editor in name. It was he who did most of the work of reaching out to the authors, selecting the pieces, typing the selected pieces into the computer, and then editing them. I really just gave him the final permission to publish.

Between *Young Shoots* and *Mangtso*, the latter was a lot more work; it was also extremely stressful. Even so, as far as the responsibility for producing the final copy was concerned—setting the issue, seeking, and gathering the news, writing the news and the op-eds, and doing the translations—the work was distributed among quite a few people. However, the final copy had to be input into the computer in Tibetan and then edited, and that responsibility was Gonpo Tsering's alone, so really, the pressure of finalizing the newspaper copy all fell to him. Still, no matter how intense the pressure got, it was not in Gonpo's nature to get flustered, or to fall short of his responsibilities or to do things sloppily. Instead, he gave up a great deal of his personal time for the job. He usually worked late into the evening. Very often, we gave up our Saturdays and Sundays to work on the newspaper. All of us did that, but especially Gonpo. He never bragged or boasted about anything he had done. After the proofs were ready, Gonpo and Peter had to work on them together. In the beginning, they had a lot of trouble understanding each other as one of them spoke no Tibetan and the other only spoke a little bit of English. But as time went by, they managed to find a way to communicate and Peter even started to understand Gonpo's nomadic English. When Peter was designing the layout and the text didn't fit or there was leftover space on the page or when the text had to be moved, he went looking for Gonpo. Sometimes, instead of calling Gonpo's name, he would simply stick his neck out, with his elbows behind his back and fingers sticking out from his chest, and walk from room to room, staring at people's faces.

Since there was nothing feigned or contrived about Gonpo's behaviour, sometimes it led to funny incidents. Once, on a Sunday,

I went to his place. He rented a room in an Indian family's house. I knocked on the door. He called out an answer but didn't open the door. I went in and the room was empty. When I scanned the room, I saw two calves sticking out from under the bed. Now I was worried. I said, 'Hey, Gonpo.' Gonpo's voice came from under the bed, 'Wait a minute, I just saw a cigarette butt under the bed.' Having run out of cigarettes and craving one, he was searching for a cigarette butt that he had already smoked and thrown away.

With this scene fresh in my mind, I started a short story but couldn't finish it. It was the story of Gonpo and his lover and the unfolding of that relationship. I made up a scar on Gonpo's ankle, from a dog bite sustained on an outing one night to search for a lover. Gonpo read the story and said he had had some problems because he never did know how to stop any dog from barking.

Gonpo threw himself wholeheartedly into whatever he did. If he was making a joke, he made it wholeheartedly. After reciting the Phowa funeral prayers for Gonpo, we looked at a picture of Gonpo in a red scarf and told stories of Gonpo that made us laugh. On the night depicted in the photo, Gonpo had sent us into gales of laughter. A foreigner had given each of us a gift and Gonpo's gift was the red scarf he wore on his head. He was a little drunk. His girlfriend, Pema Khangsar, was next to him and his friends insisted that he must sing a song. He was ready to sing but could not think of a song. He said, 'Shit, what should I sing? What?' and kept looking at the ceiling. I had an idea. I had once been to Gonpo's hometown, a nomadic village in Amdo. At the start of summer, the nomads laid out the fleece to dry, to turn them into felt. Surrounded by about ten lambskins strewn around each fleecer, they sang a Mongolian song as they worked. It went like this, '*Zone nege, Zone dolong, Zone hoyo*'. As they twisted the fleece, they sang the song, keeping count of it and setting aside a pebble as they did so. As this scene came to my mind, I softly sang '*Zone nege.*' No sooner had this tune slipped my mouth than Gonpo picked it up and, running with the tune, sang out, '*Zone dolong, Zone hoyo.*'

Swiping a dishcloth from the table, he began to twist it, working it as if it were a nomad's felt and as he twisted the cloth, his voice rose higher with the song. The tail of the red scarf fluttered back and forth on his chest. His face completely serious, he stared at the 'felt' in his hands. Looking at him, all our friends burst out laughing. Some of us were wiping tears from our eyes. Others overturned their drinks. Gonpo kept on twisting his felt and singing, '*Zone nege, Zone dolong, Zone hoyo*'.

5

Those days when we worked for *Amnye Machen* were a happy time for all of us. Our work earned us some abuse in the community. We made enemies. There was even a time when those of us who ran *Amnye Machen* had to carry weapons in our backpacks for safety. However, it was work that we were all passionate about, work that we felt was necessary in the service of the enlightenment of Tibetan society. And for Gonpo and me personally, the work and the pay meant that our lifestyle improved. Previously, our lives were truly poor.

For instance, Gonpo came up from Bir one night to stay at my place. I had only enough blankets to keep myself warm. That night, I had to give him one of my blankets. It rained at night and then thundered, waking me up. I realized that I was cold. I looked at Gonpo who was sleeping on the floor. He was all curled up under his blanket. Was he sleeping? I didn't call out to him. The next morning, I wrote a poem about the night, which I later found in one of my notebooks.

Night of Wind and Rain

World devoured by fog
From sky to earth
From earth to sky
It's all empty
All dark

The heart is cold
Under a thin, frayed blanket
A poet with no money, no god and no fate
With knees to his chest
Heels to his butt

Through cracks in the door
The cold wind howls
Hands clutch the blanket
The rain drips against the window
Head under the covers
Forehead kissing his knees
Sour breath mingling with
The smell of passing wind

As poor as we were, Gonpo didn't mind it at all. When he had money, he ate and drank. When he had none, he made no complaints. He was content with what he had. He didn't ask for more. When he had money to drink, he drank till he got sloshed. The next day he would say, 'What did I do yesterday?' When he made a joke, and we added to it, he smiled widely with his eyes under those bushy eyebrows and then went off into peals of laughter. But he only drank with his friends and at parties and shows. He did not drink otherwise. As we new arrivals were all very poor, many felt that the other Tibetans looked down on us. But Gonpo never thought that—Gonpo, who when he laughed, did so in ringing peals of laughter. I remember a night when he just could not stop laughing.

I had just had my dinner. Gonpo and Palden Gyal came by. Gonpo's eyes were smiling, and Palden Gyal had a small smile on his lips. I asked if they wanted dinner. Gonpo just laughed and laughed. I thought they had been drinking and I asked if they wanted some tea. Gonpo leaned back on the folded blankets and broke off into peals of laughter again. I didn't know what to do, or what to say. 'You should go to bed,' I told them. Gonpo pressed his face into my blankets and kept chortling into it. Palden Gyal, with a big smile on his face, said, 'Let's go' and the two of them left. Gonpo kept laughing even as he left. Later I found out that Gonpo had plucked some marijuana leaves, rolled a joint and smoked it. Apparently, when some people get high, they can't stop laughing. I never saw Gonpo smoke marijuana again, it was just that once. I think he was just experimenting that one time.

6

If I were to look back on my time in Dharamsala, one memory spills into another, and that memory spills into yet another in an endless swirl of memories, but I'll tell of two more memories and leave it at that. These are two memories of fear and dread. In 1992, after my essay 'The Heartbeat of a New Generation' raised a big brouhaha, my friends actually began to worry about my safety. My friends and colleagues at *Amnye Machen* made sure that at least one of them accompanied me home at the end of each workday. Gonpo Tsering, Sonam Tsering, Bongyal, Yangbum Gyal and others spent the night at my place, sleeping over as my guard. None of us really thought that my life was under threat, Gonpo

Tsering, in particular. He was himself so free from malice and deceit that he had a hard time believing in the malice and deceit of others. At the same time, we didn't want to take any chances with my safety. There was a rumour of a price tag of Rs 1,00,000 on my head.

One night, Gonpo Tsering and I were preparing dinner at my place. He went outside saying that he was going to the toilet. As soon as he stepped outside, I heard a noise, some footsteps and a ruckus. I thought for sure that an attacker had come for me. It was quiet when I stepped out, but I couldn't see Gonpo anywhere. By the gate, there were some stone steps, and he was laying there, fallen on the steps. I ran down, pulled him up and asked him what had happened. He didn't know. As he stood up, I realized that he was bleeding from the back of his head. Luckily, an empty taxi was coming down the road. I stopped it and took Gonpo to Delek Hospital. After a couple of hours, he woke up from his sleep and asked where he was. I said, 'You are in Dharamsala.' 'What do I do in Dharamsala,' he said. 'You work for *Amnye Machen*,' I said. 'I know now,' he said. A little while later, he asked the same questions again. At times, he didn't seem to know that he was in India. The next morning when I went back to the hospital, he was fully awake and his memory had returned. But he still had no idea how he had fallen down the stairs the night before. I asked, when he was going down the steps, did he trip and fall? He said he didn't think so. The toilets were in the back and there was no need for him to go near the stone steps. He had no memory of anyone pushing him either. But after that, he became much more concerned about my safety. In fact, he said he was going to move into my place.

The second memory is a happy one at first. On a spring day in 1994, a bunch of us including Gonpo had gathered at Jamyang Norbu's house. We stayed until late in the evening. It was warm but not hot. We sat out on the grass in his garden at the back of the house, talking and laughing, singing, and playing music. His mother was quite old, but she also sat out on the grass with us. Jamyang Norbu's mother had been a pen pal of Gendun Chophel. She said that when she heard us speaking the central Tibetan dialect in an Amdo accent, it reminded her of Gendun Chophel when he came to Tethong House during her childhood. Afterwards, we laughed and sang as we walked back home down to Gangkyi.

The next morning, as I was finishing my tea, Sonam Tsering and Bongyal stopped by and wanted to know where I had gone yesterday. They said there had been a fight between some Indian youths and some Tibetan youths near Lower TCV School and one of the Indians had died. The local Indians had started beating up any Tibetans they came across. A couple of Tibetans were even now laid up in the hospital. We were very lucky not to run into any Indians the night before as we were returning from Jamyang Norbu's. In a little while, we started to hear an Indian crowd protesting on the road. We were still figuring out exactly what was happening when suddenly there was a rain of stones and rocks flung on my roof and thrown at my windows. The three of us ran into the kitchen, which had no windows. I thought the Indians might come into the apartment. I was frightened. After some time, we could hear no more breaking windows. The crowd had shifted further down the road. The Indians weren't going to burst in—that set my mind at rest.

When we came out of the kitchen, not a pane of glass was left in its frame. The houses that were off the road had been left alone by the Indians. We gathered in one of those apartments and waited anxiously. We didn't know if the Indians would return. We waited there till the afternoon, the mob didn't come back. The Tibetans started to come out of hiding, some of us needed to go out. I went to check in at Gonpo's place. He and his girlfriend Pema Khangsar were fine as nothing had happened there. Most of the Tibetan government offices in Gangkyi had been looted and destroyed.

We heard a rumour that thousands of Indians were on their way from Chandigarh to protest against the Tibetans. Everyone in Gangkyi was very scared. All my windows were broken. If the Indian mob returned, my building, which was right on the road, would be one of the first to be looted. I couldn't stay there. I had to seek shelter with Gonpo and Pema Khangsar. Gendun Rabsal was Gonpo's neighbour at that time. The three of us spent a few terrible days together. As soon as that episode ended, Gonpo and I wrote about it in *Mangtso* newspaper. And that is my final memory of me and Gonpo in India together.

7

When I returned from the United States to Dharamsala to attend the Writers' Conference, the *Amnye Machen* staff was very busy organizing it. Another issue of *Mangtso* newspaper was due to come out. I stood in for Gonpo and co-edited the issue with Lhasang Tsering.

It had been a few years since our Dharamsala friends' group had scattered all over. Because of this Writers' Conference, a few of us old friends, including Palden Gyal, Dorje Tseten and Rabsal were all able to get together again in Dharamsala. But as the conference kept everyone busy, we didn't really get a chance to hang out like we wanted. One night, Palden Gyal, Dorje Tseten and I went to visit Gonpo's newborn, Kalden La, at his place and we got to relax a bit.

We also did a poetry reading during one of the conference nights. Rakra Rinpoche exclaimed that this was an opportunity for him to read poetry with fellow poets from the homeland of Gendun Chophel. He had even written a poem for the occasion, which he read. Chabdak Lhamo Kyab and Lunyon also read their poems that night. I have no memory of whether Gonpo Tsering read that night. That conference was the first and last conference of Tibetan writers and editors in exile. While it was a hectic time, it was a great opportunity for these writers and editors, who are spoken of but never seen, to gather and mingle amongst themselves.

Eight years after this conference, there was another opportunity for us old friends, including Gontse, to get together. This was at the Gendun Chophel Conference held in 2003 at Latse Library in New York City. In the fall of that year, Latse organized a major conference, the Gendun Chophel Centennial Conference, to mark the 100th anniversary of Gendun Chophel's birth. Gonpo Tsering came from Canada for the conference. While we were getting ready for the conference, he even sent me an audiotape of him interviewing his father about Gendun Chophel. His father had been a monk at Labrang Monastery in his childhood. Later he became a nomad, but he continued his studies. He knew a great deal about Gendun Chophel and had read almost everything written by him. One night during this conference we got together at my house and drank, talked, and debated as we used to. As we talked and talked, everyone had more and more to say and listened less and less, and one could hardly get a word in edgewise into the debate. Among us it was Gonpo who was the quietest; he was not vocal about dominating the conversation. According to Rabsal's memory of that night, Gonpo opened his mouth to say something many times but before he could get any words out, one of us would jump in and run off with the conversation. I think our gathering then was a precious thing to Gonpo. When we went to visit Gonpo after he got sick, he showed us the framed photo of us that he had kept and gave us all a copy each. All the leaders of *Amnye Machen*, except for Lhasang Tsering, had gathered for the conference, and in the photo you could see, from the right, Gonpo Tsering, Jamyang Norbu, me and Sonam Dhargye. Tashi Tsering was missing from the picture, but he had been at the conference.

8

After that even though we didn't meet much, we spoke on the phone constantly. Khangsar Dorje's observation was quite true: every time you talked to Gonpo Tsering, it was a very long call. Mostly, he talked and I listened. I had to switch my phone from hand to hand and ear to ear. I always made sure that I had plenty of time when I called him. Otherwise Gonpo wouldn't get to say all he had to. He spoke about Tibetan culture, Tibetan politics, and the news from Tibet. We often got into debates and disagreements over several issues. For example, I was very opposed to the changes that the Chinese government had made to the Tibetan language during the Cultural Revolution. Gonpo supported those changes. He thought the changes were good and that we should implement these changes now to make Tibetan easier to learn. Otherwise, he said, the kids thought that Tibetan was just impossible to learn. Adhering to the rules of this new 'reformed' Tibetan, Gonpo said he would no longer use the grammatical particles '*gyi*' and '*kyi*' in favour of just one simple genitive case and for a while, he stopped using them in his writings on *Khabdha*. I don't remember when he started to go on Tibet tours, but after he did, our main topic of conversation was Tibet. After visiting Tibet, he had some uncomfortable realizations. For instance, he was shocked that the lower-level chiefs and the upper-level chiefs back home were all so corrupt. Not only did they not hide it, but they even bragged about it when they were out drinking.

On one of his visits back home in Tibet, he saw a stream clogged with lots of bottles and plastics, and he waded into the water to pick up the trash and clear the stream. He also told me about his uncle's horse, which routinely won races and had such a reputation that people from far away came with offers to buy it. In the years before Gonpo became ill with cancer, he used to read a lot of books on Tibetan literature and culture in Tibetan, English, and Chinese. He was very interested in the Western fascination with Tibet and how that had come about. He knew a great deal about the Westerners who had travelled to Tibet in the old days. As I requested him, he wrote an essay for Latse Journal's sixth issue called *Acharya George Bogle*. He wanted to write again for the journal, but later he became too sick. Even after he fell ill, he was still very involved in his literary activities. Once he was doing some research on the place historically known as 'Garlok'. He had been looking into old Chinese and English language sources and he told me what he had found. I was very surprised at his Chinese. I had assumed that his Chinese was average, just good enough to read the newspaper and regular books, but I was wrong. As we were talking, he cited many old Chinese sources from the old documents that he had been reading. He talked about the mentions of Garlok in the old Chinese texts.

Another time he was reading *The Black Treasury of Milarepa* and he spoke about all the differences between this Milarepa narrative and the narrative written by Heruka. I had bought *The Black Treasury of Milarepa* for Latse Library but I had never read it. And because I had not read it, I didn't have anything to say about it, so I just listened. It was like that with Garlok. Anyone who has read any of the religious histories of Tibet has seen the name of Garlok, but as for me, I had never thought about where Garlok was actually located. Gonpo had not only thought about it, but he had researched the old documents in various languages, to determine its location. One day in the spring of 2011, Gonpo gave me a call and said he was planning a trip to Tibet. Then, I didn't hear from him again until the end of summer, and after that, I heard nothing from him. Then one day Palden Gyal called me. The radio station had sent him to Canada, and he had met up with Gonpo. Palden Gyal told me Gonpo had stomach cancer and only a few months left. Two days after that call from Palden Gyal, Gonpo himself called me and said, 'I am at the mouth of Lord Yama.'

About a month after that, with Palden Gyal driving, we went to visit Gonpo. I can still see my first sight of him that day. He straightened up from the box of books next to him. His hair was short, his forehead had grown higher and larger, and his thick eyebrows were even thicker and darker. His cheeks and his nostrils were sharper. But more than all that, what struck me the most was how the clothes that he was wearing seemed to be half empty—just hanging off him. I still see him as he looked again on the second day, when we were saying goodbye to him. Gonpo stood on the porch, looking at us through an opening in the railing. A ray of light fell on one side of his face while the other side lay obscured in shade. What the shaft of light illuminated—his eyebrow, his nostril, his cheek—looked to me sharper and starker than ever. My eyes misted over with tears as I got into the car. Gonpo waved at us through the railing. His figure blurred in my eyes.

Palden Gyal started the car. For quite a long time, we drove in silence. A few days later when I called Gonpo, his wife Pema picked up. 'Good news,' she said, 'Gonpo didn't throw up his food. Here, you speak with him.' Gonpo said he had stopped throwing up after eating food. It looked like maybe his body would be able to stand the chemotherapy after all. He began the chemotherapy and he turned from someone who had two-three months left to someone who had a year or more. During that time, I didn't call him much because I didn't want to tire him. The few times I called, I listened to him talk for a long time. He had started reading books again. He even went online. I think it was around this time that he wrote the essay, 'This is What Garlok Was, for Those Who Don't Know'. Towards the end of the 2012 summer, my wife and I went to visit him. At that time, he even said he was going to see if he could write the essay that he had promised for *Latse Journal*.

About three weeks before he died, I had called him. That was my last phone call with Gonpo. His body had been failing under the chemotherapy for some time. He now weighed only seventy-something pounds. He didn't have much energy to talk. After we had chatted for six or seven minutes, he said, 'Aro, I should go. I am going to rest and sleep.'

Three weeks after that, he rested forever.

Love Letters

Topden Tsering

In January of 1991, the Upper Tibetan Children's Village (TCV) School in Dharamsala was covered in fresh snow. A dazzling whiteness blanketed the school's sprawling campus which bore a deserted look on account of the annual two-month-long vacation. The few students and staff who had stayed behind had been forced indoors by the biting cold. Outside, occasional footprints in the soft powder served as the only reminder of the activities from earlier in the day: students fetching food from the main kitchen, adults running essential errands and kids playing, throwing snowballs at one another.

From where I stood—the balcony of the boys' hostel dining area nested in a wooded hillside at a soaring height from the school grounds—these imprints and echoes of exertions past looked like crawling columns of ants.

I was in the 12th Grade (12 Arts, to be precise) and had been hunkered down in the hostel since the school closed for vacation a month ago after our final examination. We were some forty boys, half from my grade (including 12 Science) and the other half from 10th Grade (10A, 10B, 10C), holed up in this medieval castle-like structure to prepare for the All India Secondary School Examinations, also called board exams, which were two months away.

For me and my friends, Dhondup Wangyal aka Shawa and Norbu Wangchuk, these were wonderful times. Not because we were particularly pumped about the life-changing moment that awaited us—bidding goodbye to school and saying hello to college (that is, if we made it to college), or not because we appreciated the momentous transition into adulthood that lay ahead. These matters were of little consequence to us. We had no mind for ambitions or seriousness. We simply existed in an excitable limbo, for which the current setting—when the hostel was half empty, when the food was a little bit better and the servings more generous, when the authoritarian supervision was minimal, when there were no classes and we were left on our own for self-study, when we did not have to wear our uniforms—was just perfect. We rolled without any plans. And half the time, we were bored out of our minds.

I made my way down the labyrinthine corridors, towards my room. As I reached for the door, I could hear familiar voices inside. Shawa, Norbu Wangchuk and a few other friends were standing or sitting around the study tables. As always, my roommate, a serious boy from Class 12 (Science), who was a bit of a genius in mathematics, was away to escape the shenanigans of my less study-minded friends. He had taken refuge in another classmate's room, poring over complex Algebra problems.

Seeing me, Shawa got up, full of excitement, from the bottom bunk of the bunk bed—my roommate's bed—and said, 'There you are. Guess what? You will write a love letter for me.' Others in the room cheered and nodded their heads, grinning widely.

At first, I suspected a prank; something of the sort that had involved four boys stripping me to my bare bottom, picking me up from each arm and leg, and dumping me onto frosty snow. Or the kind that had involved Norbu Wangchuk and me rolling crushed cow dung into cigarettes and offering them to Shawa and another boy, who had puffed away until they started retching and throwing up. Or when on our return past midnight and through the dark, thick forest, from watching movies back-to-back at a video parlour in Mcleod Gunj—the nearest town—we had made Norbu Wangchuk believe a ghost had slapped him on his back, sending him sprinting (and with him the rest of us, to keep up the trickery) the remaining half mile to the hostel.

Searching their faces carefully, I asked why me. 'Because you are the only one who can write a love letter without a great many grammar mistakes,' Norbu Wangchuk said. 'Because you scored the highest marks in English,' Shawa added. I didn't have to ask who the letter was for because the answer was obvious. The whole year, Shawa had been in love with Tsamchoe Dolma, a tall, thin, and beautiful girl from Class 10A who sported hair like Lady Diana. He had never spoken to her. Yet, he had never passed up on any opportunity to steal glances at her whenever she walked past him, alone or with her friends. He had never loved anyone before like he loved her, and he claimed he would never love anyone like that again.

* * *

Shawa (Tibetan for deer) had always had good taste in clothes and shoes. Unlike most of us, he wore "original" brand sneakers—Nike, Adidas—and imported denims. He liked loose sweatshirts and bright-coloured ski jackets, and he put an effort into matching ensembles and coordinating colours; he liked to show up sharp. Way below average in his studies, he had made it thus far by just making the minimum percentage (33 per cent) required to pass his final exams. He didn't have a favourite subject; he had least favourite subjects: all of them. He was, however, good at sports, especially track and field, for which his tall and lanky frame seemed custom-built. As such, his appearances on occasions such as the sports day—in tracksuits or jersey and shorts, sprinting, jumping and leaping, his straight hair falling over his eyes—triggered adulations and gossip reserved only for the popular kids.

Shawa's love for Tsamchoe had grown a hundredfold in the last month or so since the school closed and the students reconnoitred in classrooms along the same hall, for the fifteen-day advanced preparation before the two-month-long internment, the boys in the boys' hostel and the girls in theirs, until the board exams. During classes, he waited for the bell to ring for breaks so he could stand in the hallway and watch her from a distance, hoping she'd look in his direction and smile at him. Norbu Wangchuk and I, as well as a few of our friends, did the same. We shared his longing and desperation for the very same thing—a look and a smile in 'our' direction from her. As such, we took our positions beside him during recesses and kept our eyes peeled at doors and corners around buildings so we could alert Shawa as soon as we spotted her. We had thought up a secret language, some elaborate codes, but whenever we saw her, inescapably the same undignified words—half ruffian, half urgent—tumbled out of our mouths: '*les ke, les ke* [here she comes, man, here she comes].'

With the boys, Shawa was a hit because he was upbeat and fun, ready with jokes, and always concocting some mischief to keep them entertained. His parents lived in Delhi, and he had generous pocket money which he splurged equally upon himself and his friends. The boys liked him mostly for his nonchalant ways, an 'I could care less' attitude that was a welcome antidote to our somewhat oppressive reality enforced by a staff and a band of prefects, all too happy to administer punishments for the slightest insubordination, fortified by a system that fed on fear over flexibility. His foolhardiness was infectious—it made us feel free.

He was popular among girls too, despite him not having much experience talking to them. Until Tsamchoe happened, he had avoided having anything to do with them. This reticence might have been construed as some sort of mystery which, when combined with his good looks, his impressive height, his dominance in the track field, and his unique style, gave him an aura of charm. But this charm, it seemed, was lost on Tsamchoe and her friends. It appeared they focused instead on the many descriptions of disrepute that surrounded him and our group: the boys who smoked, snuck out at night to catch movies at video parlours in the nearby town, crossed school boundaries for their juvenile escapades, fared terribly in academics and whose names were always called out during the morning assemblies for punishments.

By now, as if to mirror Tsamchoe's unconventional hairdo, Shawa had begun to copy Sanjay Dutt's hairstyle: spiky at the top, close-cropped on the sides, and longish at the back. True to the Bollywood macho man's avatar, Shawa had traded his bright white sneakers for distressed ankle-high work boots, the more worn out the better. Instead of fluffy coats, he had taken to wearing leather jackets. Against the perennially overcast, desolate and oftentimes snowy landscape, his new look was fitting. Love had worn him down, and for love, he was fighting back.

* * *

I was happy I could help Shawa, who I considered my best friend (there were many others too who considered him their best friend). Grabbing a notebook and a pen, I sat myself down at one of the tables, and on a blank page I wrote: 'My Dearest Tsamchoe Dolma.' Some six or seven pairs of eyes were trained on me, following the slightest movement of my pen. I do not remember what I wrote next. It might have had to do with how she had set up a permanent home in his heart; how his every waking moment was spent thinking about her, and his every sleeping hour dreaming about her; how happy it made him whenever he could see her, how miserable he would become on the days he could not see her; there was nothing in the world he treasured more than her; that if only she could be his girlfriend he would do whatever it took to keep her happy; and that there was no length he wouldn't go to if it only so much as meant making her smile.

Upon finishing the letter, Norbu Wangchuk took the paper from my hand, stood up on a chair and read it aloud. After every sentence, the room broke out in a loud celebration, the boys banging their fists on the table and pumping them in the air. Shawa looked pleased, hopeful. Then he asked Norbu Wangchuk why he didn't write a similar letter to Kalsang Wangmo, the girl from our class he liked. Norbu Wangchuk didn't protest; he seemed flattered by the consideration. Soon, the names of other boys in the room were mentioned, as well as the names of the girls they liked. I was surprised that even the boys who had appeared most uninterested in the opposite sex had secret crushes of their own—I was impressed by their duplicity. At one point, one or two of these boys dashed out of the door, as if carrying some big news for the world to hear, before returning with two or three more boys, who looked equally gripped with fervour, as though they'd been newly enrolled in a cult.

After the ruckus died down, it became clear I was writing nine more love letters. And this included one for me. After much prodding by others and deliberations among themselves, it was decided that the occasion called for a similar letter for the girl I liked. Her name was Tenzin Choekyi; a close friend of Tsamchoe.

The two were seen together all the time, as though they were joined at hips, like Siamese Twins.

So, I copied the contents of the first letter, over and over, with minor variations here and there, the most important being the names of the girls; occasionally I mixed up some girl's first name with another's last name, which made the corresponding suitor or suitors promptly offer corrections, looking slightly hurt. The last letter I wrote was from me. It was also the least authentic letter, a copy of eight copies before: the words were mine but since I had already used them for others, they were not really mine. At best I was a forger of my own work.

Each time I finished a letter, Norbu Wangchuk read it aloud, to resounding whoops and the Tibetan war cry, 'Kyi hi hi!' And even though the letters were identical, the group lavished praises upon my penmanship. 'What poetry!' they said. 'What big words!' they exclaimed.

It was five minutes or so before the warden would start his nightly rounds, poking his head in the rooms to see we were retiring to beds and ensuring all the lights were promptly switched off. Therefore, the important question was raised: 'Who would deliver the letters and how?' After a heated discussion, it was decided that Norbu Wangchuk was the best person to do that. Unlike Shawa, who was shy and avoided talking to girls, Norbu Wangchuk enjoyed talking to them and was often seen in their company, mostly talking girl stuff, for which whence he got the confidence, let alone the authority, no one knew. Also, he was one of the few boys who had been inside the girl's hostel and knew his way around it. According to the plan, Norbu Wangchuk would sneak into the girl's hostel, and deliver the ten letters, separately, to their addressees. A satchel bag was produced for him to carry the mail, and he practised taking the letters out from the stack, singly, without moving the two or three others attached to them.

He looked like a cowboy practising a fast draw of his gun from its holster.

* * *

A few days passed. Then, one evening, trailed by Norbu Wangchuk and a couple of other boys, Shawa burst into my room. Tsamchoe Dolma had written back. She had agreed to be his girlfriend and accepted his request for a date. She had proposed a time and location: 5 p.m. by the Dal Lake. Shawa was overcome with joy. But quickly his happiness turned into terror. 'What should I talk about? What if she doesn't like me?' he thought.

Understandably, we were all overjoyed for him. Norbu Wangchuk, myself, and the others who had packed my room the other day, just like now, when I had written ten letters, each salutation uniformly beginning with 'My Dearest' before the girl's name: Tsamchoe Dolma, Kalsang Wangmo, Tenzin Choekyi, Passang Lhamo, Nyima Bhuti, Yangchen Dolkar, and so on. More than that, we were curious. What had happened to our letters?

But there was a more urgent matter at hand: Shawa's date was in a couple of hours. Gripped by fear, Shawa had begun to wonder if he should back out and be a no-show. All the five or six boys present in the room objected to this notion. What about all the trust we had put in him? All the rooting we had done for him? All those hours we had stood as his sentry, like *chowkidars*? All the supplications we had offered for the success of his love, even during short prayers before each meal in the dining hall? 'If you back out now,' said one of them, 'we will consider it a betrayal of our friendship.' Finally, Shawa relented and started taking mental notes on how to initiate a conversation with Tsamchoe, while one boy, lathering hair gel on his fingers, gave touch-ups to his Sanjay Dutt hairdo. For wingman, Shawa picked me to go with him.

Now I was terrified. Choekyi was surely going to be there with Tsamchoe. I hadn't gotten a response to my letter yet, which could mean any number of things, including rejection. What was I to say to her? I tried to excuse myself, but the boys stared me down and shut me up. Someone even mentioned honour. It was a boy from the room next door, a Hindi film aficionado, who quoted movie titles and dialogue at will. He said, '*Praan jaye par vachan na jaye* [never renege on a promise even if it puts your life in harm's way].'

* * *

The Dal Lake, its water muddy all year round, lay outside the school's boundary. Next to it, by the side of a road, sat a small tea shop. The road led away, on a gradual incline, through the woods before meandering all the way to the top where stood a couple of small villages, holding close-up views of the mighty Dhauladhar ranges. A narrow trail circled the lake. To the left of this walkway, the terrain climbed upward with its slope thickened by forest. A couple could take two steps off the path and be shielded from the world's prying eyes: these swathes were the TCV students' favourite canoodling spot.

Shawa and I reached the tea-stall first. Throughout our walk from the hostel, we were both silent, each preoccupied with his own dread. We didn't have to wait long before Tsamchoe showed up. She had brought along Choekyi as her wing woman. The four of us nervously exchanged greetings. Then, Choekyi suggested Tsamchoe and Shawa be on their way, pointing to the trail and its many crevices. With his hands in his pockets, Shawa obliged, rarely looking up from the ground. Choekyi and I watched them disappear around the corner before we ordered tea and sat down on a bench. Looking back, I don't remember what we talked about or if we talked at all. All I remember is wondering whether, whenever I said something, she looked quizzical or cross.

The date didn't last long. Shawa and Tsamchoe were back in less than twenty minutes. Unceremoniously and hurriedly, our two groups went our separate ways: Shawa and I towards the boys' hostel, Tsamchoe and Choekyi towards the girls' hostel. Back in my room, where eight boys, including Norbu Wangchuk, were waiting for us to return and give a full report on the date. Shawa told his story.

'*Kunchok sum*, Tsamchoe was even more beautiful up close,' he said, evoking the three jewels of Tibetan Buddhism (Buddha, Dharma and Sangha). 'She was dressed so fashionably, too. Hearing her voice, spoken directly to me, I became nervous right away. But I tried to look confident. I put my hands in my pockets and walked slowly beside her, all the while trying to find a good spot for us to sit. We found a big boulder and next to it a grassy patch. I asked her to take a seat on the grass. I kept standing, leaning against the rock.'

'I was surprised by her frankness. She told me she was glad I had sent her the letter. She said her friends thought I was trouble, just like my friends, and had tried to persuade her to reject my proposal. They had pointed to the ten identical letters, all written in the same hand, composed with the same words of love and affection. But she said she told them she didn't mind it. Then she started asking me about my hobbies.'

'At that point, I saw her shoes. They were brand new Reebok sneakers, sparkling white. Then I looked down at my shoes, and suddenly saw how old and damaged they looked, like the shoes of a *mistry* (cement worker). I was so embarrassed I could barely hear what she was saying. To make it worse, I saw the double stitches had come undone around the toe of my left boot. A long white thread was almost standing upright. Alarmed, I pushed my left foot behind my right foot. I remained like that for a couple of minutes, struggling to stand still. Then I saw my right shoe which looked ugly too, screaming destitution. Now, instead of listening to her, I was switching between my two feet to stay balanced on one foot. I decided I couldn't continue any longer. Finally, I said I had to go because I had to help the hostel cook with dishwashing—I had kitchen duty today.

* * *

The room fell silent. Then, one by one, everyone broke into laughter. While Shawa was sharing his story, I had picked on what Tsamchoe had said, regarding knowing about all the ten letters. I was bothered by it. Midway through the romp, I put my hand up for quiet and, turning to Norbu Wangchuk, asked him: 'Tell us again how you delivered the letters.' The day after his mailman mission, he had told us he had delivered the letters to all the girls. The news made us—all of us—both so excited and anxious that no one thought to ask for details.

Norbu Wangchuk started off by explaining how difficult it would have been to catch the girls separately in their rooms. 'This would have required roaming around in the girls' hostel for a long time,' he said. 'This would have meant me getting caught by the warden before I could deliver one letter, and being thrown out, ending my operation.' So, he said he had no choice but to sneak into the dining hall during evening study, when all the girls were gathered under one roof, and deliver the letters, moving from one dining table to the other.

It was no surprise that, except for Shawa, no one had heard anything back. The girls we had written to had chosen to express their rejections with uniform silence. 'Of course, they wouldn't write back. They'd think this was a terrible joke,' I said. At this,

Norbu Wangchuk made a face, his expression belying a secret. Then he pulled out a note from his pocket. It was for me, from Tenzin Choekyi. I didn't want to read it in front of everyone, but I had no choice.

Opening it, my eyes rested on two sentences, in beautiful handwriting. 'I am sorry. I cannot reciprocate your love.' We all suspected from the word 'sorry' that it was a rejection letter. But we were not sure. Nobody knew the meaning of the word 'reciprocate'. Not even me. Surrounded by nine pairs of eyes, I had to look it up in the dictionary.

Norbu Wangchuk said in consolation, 'At least now you know one more bombastic word.'

The Embassy of Tibet

Tenzin Dickie

The Office of Tibet in New York is not an embassy.

The office does not issue visas to the land of Tibet, although every once in a while, during my two-and-a-half years at the office, I had to reluctantly tell some hopeful-but-mistaken soul inquiring into visa procedures for Tibet that the first step was, unfortunately, contacting the Chinese Consulate. It's funny, how embarrassed I felt when I said this, as if the continuing occupation of my country was a job that I had personally bungled. Over the years, I have felt many different emotions over the fate of my country—disbelief, despair, pride, loss, hopelessness, resignation, resentment—but it was only during these calls that I ever felt embarrassment. A perverse embarrassment, a furry feeling in the mouth of some intimate personal failure that was yet tinged with a grateful pleasure at this unsuspecting American's generous belief in the dignity and self-possession of our Tibetan office.

The office was housed then in a nondescript three-storey townhouse in the Manhattan neighbourhood of Murray Hill, also called Curry Hill for its fleet of Indian restaurants. The coat of whitewash, hanging on by its (chipped) fingernails, looked as if it would appreciate a relief of duty. It was a nice, quiet residential street with trees that cast leaf-shaped shadows on the sidewalk in summer. Although there was a small gold-plated plaque on the door saying 'Office of Tibet'—many Tibetans preferring not to deal with articles which are non-existent in the Tibetan language—I don't think the neighbours even knew that they lived next door to the Dalai Lama's office. In my two and a half years working there, I saw the guy living to our left exactly once, when he asked to bring in a large sofa through to our back door because his front hallway was too small for it to pass through. He certainly didn't seem like he knew that his sofa was passing through the Dalai Lama's office. To our right was a house that underwent noisy renovations for a full year. I never saw the owner, but I saw the silhouettes of her two kids once or twice. They gutted the house and remade all four floors from the basement up. The airy first floor became an enormous living room with windows and skylights everywhere and a patio leading down to a stone garden in the back with a Buddha statue and lush new foliage. I never saw anyone in the garden ever.

We had renovations too, on a much smaller and less professional scale. They were imperative. Pre-renovation, the first floor lay fallow, the kitchen buried beneath ten years of junk furniture, the backroom empty and useless, the front used only once a week by the board members of the Tibetan Association of New York and New Jersey. On the second floor, the five of us who made up the office staff were cramped in a single room. Across the hall, the head of the office, the Representative of His Holiness the Dalai Lama to the Americas, at least had his own office. Between us was the second-floor bathroom, where we kept our tea supply and electric kettle. 'So, you are making your tea in the toilet,' my brother said when I described my working conditions. I was about to object to his phrasing when he pointed out, 'Better to make tea in the toilet than to shit in the kitchen.' Post renovation, I happily fixed myself six or seven cups of Earl Grey or Lipton in a day, wallowing in the luxury of a designated kitchen area with a proper marble countertop.

The renovation was a labour of love and ingenuity carried out on a shoestring budget—overseen by my colleague, the Latin American liaison officer Tsewang Phuntso—involving the kind expertise of a Korean architect friend, the wage labour of a Czech handyman, and the generous help and services of a Tibetan monk, a friend of the office and a fixture in the community, who daylighted as a construction labourer. They redid the entire first floor, tearing down the walls and putting up built-in shelves to create a beautiful open-plan office that was cool and cozy, spacious and sunlit, painted a bright Valencia red that sounds awful in print but was gorgeous on the walls. Tsewang la even produced a lovely red carpet that lit up the whole office with its brilliantly rich colour but some of our other colleagues felt uncomfortable walking over the eight auspicious symbols that decorated the carpet and soon, to my deep regret, it was rolled up to make way for a less pleasing and less auspicious specimen.

We had large and comfortable new desks, custom-made by a Tibetan carpenter based in New Jersey. He also built us a terrific outdoor table for the patio that would have been a centrepiece in any Manhattan showroom. The table was square and comfortably seated twelve people. We ate our lunches communally with the staff of the Tibet Fund, a non-governmental organization on the third floor and our landlord. As long as the weather was warm, we ate out on the deck. That summer, the wood swelled and in the winter when it contracted, there remained a thin crack running through the table.

* * *

So, how did I end up working for the Office of Tibet in New York, the unofficial agency of His Holiness the Dalai Lama and the Central Tibetan Administration to the Americas? The short answer is that I was a recent graduate looking for a job. The longer answer is that I was taking a slow stock of my interests and abilities, considering a Master of Fine Arts (MFA) in a few years and making a list of publishing houses big and small. The only job I had tried out for so far was that of a US Foreign Service Officer (the requirements of foreign travel and language acquisition making the job something like a paid vacation in my fevered imagination). But to my surprise and embarrassment, I failed the test. The knowledge portion of the test covered, among other things, management theory, psychology, finance and economics; subjects I hardly knew anything about and had to read up on. So, I was quite prepared to fail that portion but in the event, I passed the knowledge portion and failed the writing. Writing was supposed to be one of the few things I could do competently. Well then, I was calculating that I would like reading slush-pile novels (and eating sour grapes) better than writing reports anyway when the Office of Tibet announced a vacancy.

My father forwarded me the vacancy announcement from the Office of Tibet, my father being the kind of person who subscribed to the Office of Tibet listserv. Working for the Tibetan government? I hadn't even considered the possibility because I lived in the US and the Central Tibetan Administration was based in India. The Office of Tibet usually had its staff posted from India, but this time they were hiring someone in the US. It was clear they wanted a Tibetan American—someone bilingual in Tibetan and English, with an American education and a Tibetan Green Book. Special assistant to the representative of His Holiness the Dalai Lama to the Americas. I thought that had a nice ring to it. The job description sounded challenging and interesting. The application process was fairly simple. My resume was pretty good, and I had a recommendation from Dr Lobsang Sangay, the research scholar at

Harvard Law School, who two years later would win the election for Tibetan Prime Minister and become my boss's boss.

There were four of us whom the Office called for an in-person interview. The interviewing panel comprised a three-person board that included the charismatic and larger-than-life Professor Robert Thurman, famous for being the most famous Buddhist in the United States, and the possessor of an unblinking glass eye that in no way diminished the symbolism and discomfort of sitting across from three people who were deciding my fate for the next few years of my life. My nerves were wrecked but I acquitted myself honourably. In retrospect, I needn't have been so nervous. Of the other three candidates that they had called in for an interview, one was a schoolmate of mine and I thought both my English and my Tibetan were better than hers. Another man, quite impressive on paper—he had worked at the Supreme Justice Commission in Dharamsala, India—in actuality, turned out to be the kind of person who was so proud of his Indian law degree that he had taken his certificate down from his living room wall and brought it to the interview, *still in its large, ornate frame.* The third man was quite forgettable. I have forgotten him.

I got the job. My father approved because he was civic-minded and public-spirited in general, and my mother approved because she thought working for His Holiness's office would increase my personal merit and good fortune. I was terribly pleased but slightly apprehensive. There seemed to be a strong organizational component to the job, and I was the kind of person who had distinguished my tenure as president of the Students for a Free Tibet club in high school and college by having meetings to plan the next meeting.

* * *

There was a triangulation of paperwork that needed to be sent back and forth, from me in Boston to the Office in New York to the Kashag Secretariat in Dharamsala, India. So it was months later, in March, that I finally moved to New York to begin working. There was a minor hiccup when my mother consulted the handbook of The Tibetan Medical and Astrological Institute, which had made life difficult for me before. She looked up from the book, frowning. Apparently, the day I was supposed to report for my first day of work was not a good date for new beginnings. 'Take the day off,' she said. 'Ask to come in the next day.' I said I couldn't possibly take the day off on my very first day of work. What would my new boss and colleagues think? 'Surely they'll understand when you explain why,' she said. 'Talk to the Representative,' she insisted. 'He'll think you are preserving your culture.' 'Why don't you talk to the Representative?' I said, forgetting that one did not make facetious suggestions to my mother. She did call him, only to have him suggest that surely the meritorious nature of the work itself ensured its good beginning. My mother conceded the point.

On my first day, I broke into my computer at work, a feat which, considering my computer illiteracy, seemed like its own kind of good beginning. I didn't want to be late, so I arrived at the office around 8.30 a.m. I thought I would get a coffee around the corner. To my surprise, the office was open. The Representative welcomed me, showed me to my desk and then went back to his work. I could wait for the person who was to give me my orientation or I could start guessing passwords. I started typing words into the computer. To my infinite surprise and self-satisfaction, I got the password right on the third try. It was '*BhodGyalo*'—Victory to Tibet.

Dram

Gedun Rabsal

Translated by Dhondup T. Rekjong and Catherine Tsuji

Around dusk we began to move again, walking along the road until we were finally in the middle of the forest. We seemed to be getting closer to the Nepalese border—to the town called Dram (Tatopani).

Datak began talking. 'From now on, let's split up into two groups. If one group gets captured by the Chinese, the other might still have a chance to escape to India. That group could ask His Holiness to do prayers for us.'

'Yes, we've made it this far already. As the saying goes, if we die, we die together; if we survive, we survive together,' I said, agreeing with Datak.

'How about this, Tenzin and I will go first, Datak and you follow us, and then Aku Tsachuk Kawa can come last,' said Gelek. We all agreed.

Although Tenzin and Gelek left first as planned, they walked slowly and couldn't cover much ground before Datak and I caught up to them.

'Why didn't you two go ahead?' I asked.

'There are fifteen to twenty lights below, one after another. Maybe it's the bandits,' Tenzin said.

'So what if they are bandits? We have no choice but to go on,' Datak said, summoning extra courage.

'In that case, we both will go on first and you two follow us,' I said.

We set off. Datak even picked up some stones to use if we came across any bandits. I began to pray to my Dharma protectors and followed Datak, making up my mind to have absolutely no fear of death. Although we could still see the lights, there was no sign of bandits anywhere. Maybe some people were cutting wood in the forest or maybe there were fire ghosts. Who knew?

However, the faster Datak and I walked, the closer the others followed along. For whatever reason, our plan didn't go well that night. So, we decided to just walk together. It was now nearly dawn, and we had arrived at the foothill of a mountain where a village appeared in sight.

'Is this Dram?' I asked.

'It can't be. Dram's supposed to be a big city,' Datak said.

'I don't see a big city from up here.'

Datak couldn't believe it. 'There are many shops in Dram. There can't be any shops in such a remote place like this.'

'You guys wait here. I will go to ask that kid,' I said, seeing a kid reading a book on the side of the road. I went down to the highway. The student was startled by my sudden appearance from out of the forest.

'Where is Zhangmu?' I asked in Chinese.

'This is Zhangmu,' the student answered with a curious look on his face.

'Thank you.'

The student continued reading his book. Sneaking past him, I used another path to go back to the forest.

'It *is* Dram. What should we do?' I asked, panting.

The others looked surprised that we had arrived in Dram.

'Wait a bit. We need to talk it over some more,' Datak said.

I took a good look at all of us and thought that Datak looked presentable enough—he was even wearing newish clothes. So, we decided that Datak would go find the shopkeeper named Jampel from Amdo Ngawa. If Jampel couldn't be found, then Datak would look for another shopkeeper. Datak felt up to the task. He cleaned his face, dusted off his clothes, and off he went.

We hid in the same spot. Datak returned after almost an hour. He had found Jampel, who had told him that we should go deeper into the forest and find a better hiding spot there. He'd come out later in the night, around 11 p.m. The shopkeeper had also sent a lot of food. We were a little nervous but very relieved and had no problem hiding out there.

Around 11 p.m., we came out one after another, and followed Datak. We kept a ten-foot distance between each other so that we wouldn't look suspicious to any officials or spies. We arrived safely at Jampel's store. He was waiting for us. A plate of steamed buns and a large bowl of boiled pork ribs were ready for us to eat. We devoured them like wolves preying on sheep. The boiled pork ribs soon disappeared and only a few steamed buns remained on the plate. We hadn't had such a delicious meal in a long time.

Jampel had already arranged a guide for us. He had also exchanged all our Chinese renminbi for Nepalese rupees and prepared enough *tsampa* for us for the road. 'The guide will take you all to the Boudha Stupa in Kathmandu. Give him this piece of paper when you safely arrive there. I will give him the rest of the money when he returns. I only gave him two thousand rupees in advance. So, you guys don't need to worry,' Jampel advised us. He told us that the total fee was five thousand Nepalese rupees.

'Yes, yes,' we all agreed.

Jampel wasn't quite done yet. 'When you meet His Holiness, have him pray for us. Be sure to study and work hard under the precious guidance of His Holiness.'

He might have had more to add but we had to leave because it was now past midnight.

'Sure, Aku Jampel. Thank you very much. We won't forget your help.'

We said goodbye to Jampel and took off.

A Day in Exile

Dhondup T. Rekjong

The year 1999 was a significant year in my life. That summer, I left my parents, relatives, and childhood friends—all those beings I knew and loved—and fled to India to join a Tibetan school. I, a young boy from a small village in Amdo, Rebkong, escaped to India.

From Xining in Amdo to Lhasa was a three-day bus ride. From Tingri, near the Nepalese border, twenty-five other Tibetans and I travelled on foot for almost eighteen days, passing beneath Mount Everest and through many villages. At Jiri, we found local buses that would take us to the International Refugee Centre in Kathmandu. After a week in Kathmandu, the Tibetan reception centre sent us to New Delhi. We finally made it to Dharamsala twenty-eight days after our departure from Tibet.

Dharamsala is in the upper reaches of the Kangra Valley, surrounded by dense coniferous forest. Its name means 'Place of Dharma' and His Holiness the Dalai Lama and the Tibetan government in exile took up residency here in 1960, following the events of 1959 and the atrocities in Amdo and Kham earlier that decade. Because of the Dalai Lama, this little hill station has become a major tourist attraction for people around the globe. Tibetans call it Little Tibet.

I attended the Tibetan Children's Village school in Suja, a village in the Mandi district of northern India. This small village sits at the base of Mount Billing, which is famous for paragliding. Part of the larger Tibetan school system in exile, the school's purpose was to preserve the Tibetan language and culture in a foreign land. The students came from different regions of Tibet. However, most teachers were born in India and had never visited their homeland. Under such complex and challenging conditions, we try to preserve Tibetan culture. But exile is not an ideal place for preservation.

My first class was called Opportunity Class, or O/C. It met near the girls' hostel—Gyaza Kangtsen. Gyaza was the Chinese wife of the seventh-century Tibetan king Songtsen Gampo. The king had five wives—she was one of them. In exile, Tibetan schools use historical names for hostels, school halls, senior homes, government offices, cafes, restaurants, and pretty much everything else. A visitor can learn Tibetan history just by studying these names.

Our class was on the second floor. From one side of the room, we could see some Indian houses, their holy cows, and rice paddies. I was astonished at how small the Indian houses appeared, they seemed much smaller than the barns in my village. From the other side of the room, we could see the classroom buildings, arranged in a semi-circle behind the basketball court. Inside, there was a blackboard, a photo of the Dalai Lama on the wall, and a simple altar below his photo. There were no chairs and tables. A torn carpet was laid out on the floor and the students scattered to find their spots like sheep on grassland.

We were from various parts of Tibet and as I sat down, I could hear Chinese, while others spoke in their regional dialects. We students didn't have a common language yet. I sat near other Amdo students since the Utsang and Khampa dialects were foreign to me. Some students had joined the school early in the year and some a month ago. I had arrived only the day before, in the middle of the school year.

The classroom was filled with the sound of various dialects when our teacher, Chime, entered. When she introduced herself in the Utsang dialect, all the students mimicked her smile. It quickly became obvious that more than half of us had no idea what she was saying. She wrote English letters on the blackboard and read them aloud. Every time she uttered a letter, we read after her. The more we increased our voices, the higher her voice got. Her glasses fell down the bridge of her nose and as she grew more excited, spittle flew towards us through her teeth. She then paused to see whether we understood the English letters.

When a student beside me said, '*Ah?* (What?)' in Amdo, she was quick to correct him, 'It is not *ah*. It is *lah.*'

'*Ya Ya* (Okay),' the Amdo student responded.

'It is not ya ya. Say *la so*,' she corrected him.

The student then said, '*La so.*'

Hearing that, other students burst into laughter. I laughed with them, though without a specific reason. It was obvious Miss Chime disliked the student's responses. I was quite baffled.

After the class, an Amdo student—Gongko, who had arrived three months earlier—explained to me that students were expected to speak in the Utsang dialect. Gongko was the class monitor; he seemed to understand the other students quite well. When the teacher was absent, he tried to show off his English skills by teaching us words such as teacher, classroom, book, and pen. I envied him. When the teacher asks, one should respond with 'la' instead of 'ah,' he explained. When the teacher asks for affirmation, one should respond with 'la so', not 'ya ya'. Both 'la' and 'la so' are honorific terms, typical of a central

Tibetan dialect. I made a mental note to replace my Amdo expressions with these others.

At the assembly that morning, the students and teachers sang the national anthem of Tibet. Listening to it, I felt deep pride and courage. It was followed by reciting the *Manjushri Mantra*—the Mantra of wisdom. Suddenly, I felt like we were in a monastery. I used to hear prayer recitations at monasteries and religious festivals, but never in the Chinese schools that I attended.

The school headmaster's name was Choegyal Tashi. His short height and flattop were prominent and his face was humourless. He was born in India—his grey Nehru jacket was a good sign of that. He made several announcements, but I couldn't understand any of them. I could only recognize his repetition of the Tibetan expression '*lab na dha* (such as)'. He used '*lab na dha*' a lot.

Over lunch, I asked my Amdo roommate, Phakmo, a senior student, about the headmaster's announcements. Phakmo had been at the school for almost three years. He was a very quiet person, he only spoke when he was asked a question. I didn't know whether his quietness was a mark of his loneliness or his personality.

He explained that the headmaster loves to use synonyms because he was a graduate of the Central University of Tibetan Studies. This university has produced many Tibetan language teachers in exile. Students joke that everyone who went to that university loves to parade his or her Tibetan language skills. For the headmaster, the morning assembly was a great platform to display his skilful use of the Tibetan language.

My roommate taught me how to learn the Utsang dialect quickly. He said I should drop the prefix and suffix from the root word when reading Tibetan. In the Utsang dialect—unlike the Amdo dialect—the prefix and suffix are totally unstressed. As I neither spoke nor understood the dialect, I was relieved to learn this technique.

That evening, a debate was held in the Tibetan language at the school auditorium. The debate was among the four houses—*Nyatri*, *Triral*, *Songtsen* and *Trisong*, each named after one of the great kings of Tibet. The title of the debate was 'Morality is more Important than Education'. A large white banner hung on the stage, announcing the theme. The calligraphy of the Tibetan words seemed to advocate the topic. The debate contenders were sitting on either side of the stage with the moderator between them. Three judges were stationed in the audience. The contenders took turns presenting their arguments.

I wasn't fully able to grasp their points. However, one contender was from Amdo. I felt the melody and clarity in his voice every time he raised it to make a point. His Amdo accent became thicker when he tried to make an argument. Other students threw their heads back and laughed each time they heard his accent. That got the judges to laugh along with them. I mimicked them and laughed even harder. The debater from Amdo managed to entertain everyone but failed to receive any trophy when the results were announced.

When I returned to my room, I asked Phakmo about the laughter. He told me that hardly any teachers at the school could understand either Amdo or Khampa dialects. That is why the students love to use certain Amdo or Khampa expressions to tease others or joke about things. They also sometimes used them to trivialize an otherwise serious dialogue.

From the window beside my bed, I could hear frogs calling in the rice fields. A magnificent moon hung in the clear summer night sky. The moon seemed to laugh at me. The stars reminded me of my family, relatives and land—everything I had left behind. I imagined my family having conversations in the Amdo dialect under the same moonlight—they might even be talking about me—while I debated whether to keep my dialect or replace it with the Utsang dialect. If I didn't replace it, I wouldn't understand my teacher's lessons, I wouldn't understand the headmaster's announcements and I might become the target of mockery. But then, if I lost my Amdo dialect, I might lose my regional culture, customs, and even my expressions.

Losing one's dialect in exile is not just a loss to an individual rather, it is a cultural loss to the nation at large. My worries that night speak about the nature of the Tibetan freedom movement, which has been struggling for its survival in the face of China's colonialism.

Over the past sixty years, China has developed numerous policies designed to extract natural resources and control Tibetans, including a monolingual education system, nomad relocation, and land redistribution. None of these policies has been entirely successful in fostering Tibetan loyalty to Beijing, but they have had many harmful effects on the Tibetan language, religion, and culture. My experience of being in exile was the direct consequence of China's colonization of Tibet.

Exile is a political project that requires rebuilding everything from scratch. That is why unity has been the primary goal of the Tibetan government in exile in every field, including education. In prioritizing that goal, sometimes diversity was lost, unfortunately. But while exile is a matter of being out of place, it is also a flexible space to create new meanings.

As for me, I learned the Utsang dialect. My friend's technique of dropping the prefix and suffix from the root word worked. For more than a year, I struggled to find myself in the new system. It wasn't easy. Eventually, I became our house debater. But I made sure to hold on to my Amdo dialect, too.

Oral Traditions

Mila Samdub

Momola is boiling lamb. She dips a ladle into the simmering broth, carries it over to the sink, and blows on it through pursed lips. A film of opalescent grease slides into the sink. The soup under it remains undisturbed. Momola saves a couple of spoonfuls of the grease to return to the pot; a little fat enhances the flavour, she says. Boiled lamb is our family's traditional picnic food. It should be a fatty cut of the meat, bone-in, from the ribs or shoulder of the sheep, seasoned only with salt, ginger, garlic, and *erma*—the Tibetan name for Sichuan pepper—the little kernels of fire that numb your tongue on contact. Over the next few hours, the house is filled with the smell of lamb. We are going for a picnic in the local state park in eastern Tennessee.

At a picnic table next to the parking lot, my grandmother slices pieces of the joint and distributes them to us. My two younger cousins are given tender, boneless slices. I get the fattiest bits, with a warning about my health. My aunt gets the lean meat. For herself, my grandmother saves the boniest pieces, on which flesh clings desperately to bone. She manoeuvres her false teeth with considerable dexterity to get every morsel. When I was younger, my grandmother would commend me on the way I ate, with reckless abandon—dunking my meat into chilli and soy sauce, sucking the marrow out of bones, smacking my lips in contentment. The lamb is cool, dry, and delicious; the spiciness of the chilli is refreshing in the southern summer. With the meat, we have cold noodles and laphing, a slippery, translucent jelly made from mung-bean starch. Both dishes are topped with onion, garlic, and tomato sauce. Afterwards, overfed and unsteady, we descend through the forest to the waterfall.

Our family picnics, in Dharamshala, Delhi, and Tennessee, have always revolved around these three foods: boiled lamb, cold noodles, and laphing. My grandmother has always presided over their preparation. But like most of the food she cooks, our picnic trinity is not eaten in the part of Tibet she is from. This food, and especially the cold egg noodles, is from my grandfather's homeland in Kumbum located thousands of miles away from Lhasa. Momola only learned to cook like this after coming to India, from Majen Dambala, my grandparents' cook in Darjeeling. Yet in the days following the picnic, Momola remarks many times that this was such excellent lamb, fatty and flavourful, just like in Tibet.

* * *

Kumbum is near Siling, on the far eastern edge of the Tibetan plateau. I remember arriving there, in the living room of relatives I had never met before, stunned from the travel and the altitude, and being handed slice upon slice of boiled lamb. I remember the griminess of the hands that wielded the knife and handed me the meat. I remember finding familiar the taste and the texture of the lamb. Surrounded by these friendly strangers, who spoke a language I didn't understand, I felt oddly at home.

This was a region I had heard little about. Sometime in the early 1960s, when he was already living in India, my grandfather stopped using his native tongue, Siling kye—the language of Siling (Xining)—which is customarily categorized as a dialect of Chinese. His diary, which since his student days in Nanjing he had kept in Chinese, he started writing in Tibetan. With decisions like these, our family began to shed part of its distinct history and traditions. The new Tibetan community in exile was dominated by central Tibetans, and as the government in exile became functional, the culture that emerged was a distinctly central Tibetan one. Since my grandfather's home was close to China—was, in fact, like much of eastern Tibet, politically a part of China—his traditions, like his language, would have been deemed irremediably sinicized. His transformation was an act of the will, an attempt to become, in advance, a citizen of the new Tibetan nation he would commit his life to. Nevertheless, this was a gradual transformation. My father recalls having to prostrate in front of his parents every Tibetan New Year during his childhood, a practice which he believes might be related to Chinese traditions of ancestor worship. By the time I was born, such traditions were no longer practised in our family.

* * *

When I visited my grandfather's home in Kumbum in 2010, two years after the uprisings of 2008 and just as Tibetans were beginning to self-immolate in protest all over the plateau, I went as a near-complete foreigner. My plan had been to visit central Tibet and meet for the first time my relatives from my grandmother's side. But in an attempt to hide the violent crackdown from the rest of the world, the Chinese government had closed the region to outsiders. I decided to go instead to my grandfather's family home in Kumbum, in the Chinese province of Qinghai, for which no special permissions were required. This was a charged moment to be visiting Tibet, and I expected to witness, if not explicitly then at least in the pauses between words, as it were, the Chinese repression and Tibetan resistance.

One morning, my cousin Lobsang Sangye, a monk at Kumbum monastery, took me to a grassy knoll covered with identical grey gravestones on which Chinese characters were carved. The sky was windy, the grass rippled, and the stones were still. Lobsang pointed at one and told me that it was the spot where my grandfather was buried. There was my grandfather's name, and on either side of it, the names of his parents. Lobsang pointed at an empty spot in the grass next to it: this was where my father would be buried. I didn't know what to make of this. Growing up, I had heard so much about the Tibetan tradition of feeding corpses to vultures so that even in death one can generate good karma. And in India, the dead are cremated, as my grandfather had been. Lobsang told me to take pictures to show my family in India. I did as I was asked, wondering, as I took the photographs, three careful rectangles with monoliths framed centrally, what everyone back home would make of this.

I didn't know it then, but I was repeating a scene from a documentary film that my parents had made two decades ago about my father's first and only visit to Kumbum. My father too had been taken to this hill by a drunken relative, now dead, who sobbed and shouted at the camera. In the film, the hillside is not a site of commemoration so much as one of loss. My father was disillusioned by his visit to this homeland he had inherited. This was no longer the contested borderland of my grandfather's youth when it was ruled not from Lhasa or Beijing but by a Hui warlord in Siling. More tragically, the independent nation-state my grandfather had dedicated his life to seemed now more distant than ever. But Kumbum was also different from central Tibet, and what seems natural in one place might be ill-suited to the other. As I was finding out on my trip, like so many borderlands, Kumbum seems deeply incompatible with the project of the nation-state. Yet Kumbum was still his homeland, and after my grandfather died, a part of his ashes was sent back and interred on that hill.

The mixture of cultures and traditions I encountered in Kumbum—the language, incomprehensible to mainland Chinese and central Tibetans alike, the strange gravestones, the food—is a result of a historical diversity that is unimaginable in central Tibet. Here, ethnic Tibetans are one minority among many, and this has been the case since before my grandfather's time. Even now, when it is clearly a land under colonial Chinese rule, I don't know that a state ruled from Lhasa would be any solution here. Kumbum is a place all of its own, with ties in many directions. It doesn't admit the territorial fantasies either of Chinese colonizers or Tibetan nationalists.

So, it was that when I visited my relatives, I felt I had stumbled upon a parallel world, in whose cosmology my grandfather, my father, and even I had our assigned places, but which I had previously been unaware of. In India, we have all but forgotten these relatives and their way of life but in the house of my father's half-sister in Kumbum, I found, among the photos cello taped to the cabinet in the living room, baby photos of myself and my sister. I experienced many such moments of uncanny recognition in my grandfather's homeland; it was the food that made me most aware of my kinship to this place and my relatives who lived there. The hand-pulled noodles, the pan-fried bread, the stir-fries, the boiled lamb—these I knew from my grandmother's kitchen. Besides the visceral connections of blood—a gait that reminds me of my father's, a familiar nose on a young man—it was food that imbued this visit with the sense that it was to a place to which I belonged.

* * *

A book, a film, or a photograph: these stay more or less the same with the passing of time. Even though the circumstances of their reception change—language shifts, words fall out of use, ideologies shatter—some constancy remains. In contrast, food, especially the way my grandmother does it without written recipes, is alive and constantly changing. Like the tale of King Gesar of Ling, the Tibetan epic which is still performed and passed on orally exists in differing forms, subject to countless permutations, in Tibet and Mongolia, in Bhutan, in the Russian republic of Buryatia and beyond; like this and other epics, food is an oral tradition. No author binds it ahistorically to a time and place. The story of the boiled lamb grows each time it is cooked and eaten. Flavours intensify, ingredients are substituted, and this animal is gristlier than the last. As I eat boiled lamb, I recall the boiled lambs I have eaten—by a gushing stream in Dharamshala, at Nehru Park in Delhi, at home in Kumbum and in a forest in Tennessee. The flavour of the meat and the context in which it was eaten meld into one. And it is the flavour and texture of the boiled lamb that unites these disparate times and places in my past so that all the picnics come together as an extended memory of the senses. I know the next time I taste boiled lamb, the previous memories will float out on a breeze of ovine pungency, and the new encounter will join the others, to be recalled later, at another picnic, maybe even someday in Kumbum.

But that is not all. The boiled lamb is not just a source of warmth and comfort. If we choose, we can taste unexpected and uneasy kinships in it—with pastoralists and predatory animals, with warlords, landowning monasteries and transnational corporate entities, with shifts in climate both slow and sudden, with plate tectonics that lifted up a vast plateau in the centre of Asia, with the rearing and slaughter of millions of sheep, with caravan routes long forgotten, with colonization and exile and the labour of mothers and grandmothers through the ages. Out beyond the comfort of individual memory and the certainty of national history extends a vast web of relations, openings into other ways of being, with which we can puzzle out our affinities, ignoring or heeding them as we must.

* * *

We are on the way to Tso Ngonpo, the great blue lake. My cousin, who is a truck driver, has borrowed his friend's car to make a day trip. I am in the passenger seat. His mother—my father's half-sister— wife and two children are piled into the back. We pass by rolling hills covered in mustard fields and grim towns that have been torn down and built anew. This is a landscape I've driven through in another life: the yellow mustard flowers and the rapid development remind me of many journeys through Punjab; and I know the turquoise skies from some primordial memory. We stop for lunch in a small town, a collection of concrete blocks and tiled government buildings clustered around a crossroads. Like most restaurants in these parts, it is run by a family from the Hui ethnic group, who are famed for their cooking. The dishes bear a family resemblance to the ones I've been eating in Kumbum, and ones I know from home. We order bowls of hand-pulled noodles and a succulent hunk of lamb. The lamb is roasted rather than boiled, and it is spiced with cumin. The meat falls apart like the flesh of a tropical fruit. The skin has been cooked till blistered and crispy. The little restaurant is pungent with the smell of animals that have roamed the high plateau.

* * *

My visit to Kumbum ends abruptly. I have been spending time in Zorgye Labrang, the section of the monastery that my family is connected to, writing furiously to record the flavours and experiences of the past few days. One morning, Lobsang Sangye calls me on the phone. Something is the matter, he doesn't say what. He has booked me a ticket on a bus leaving that very afternoon. A series of self-immolations has been taking place in monasteries throughout eastern Tibet, and though nobody in Kumbum has taken their own life yet, the monastery is full of plainclothes security agents. Before I know it, I am in a taxi to Siling, then in a bus barrelling down the winding highway that descends to the upper reaches of the Yellow River. I can only hope that my visit, which has shaken my world, hasn't put my relatives in danger.

* * *

My grandfather never completed his transformation. Although he stopped speaking his language and wore the staid suit-fabric *chubas* favoured by the exile establishment, he never gave up the food of his homeland. Most exile Tibetans, who arrived impoverished in a foreign land, had little choice but to take to rice and dal. Living and working in proximity to the Dalai Lama's family in Darjeeling, my grandparents were relatively privileged and had fewer material constraints on their diet. In that situation, I imagine it was hard to bend his appetite to a political project. Some things did change over time. The whole pig's heads my family used to prepare on festive occasions haven't been served in decades. But my grandfather kept eating noodles every day till the end of his life.

Even if taste lives beyond conscious intent, it is still shaped by the values of the world around us. I suspect part of the reason we still cook and eat the food of my grandfather's homeland is because we think our food, with its obvious Chinese influence, is better. While most exile Tibetans might shun Chinese influences most of the time, I think it's a common view that Chinese food is more refined. Historically in Lhasa, the banquets of the central Tibetan aristocracy consisted of multiple elaborate courses of Chinese-style dishes. The Dalai Lama, who like my grandfather is from near Kumbum, often says, only half-jokingly, that from India, Tibetans got Buddhism and from China, they got good food.

Maybe this is why my grandmother sometimes dismisses the food she grew up eating in central Tibet as peasant food, which is not to say she doesn't like it or feels that it is not her own. It continues to occupy the privileged place that things from childhood carve out for themselves. In Tennessee for breakfast, with toast and a boiled egg, Momola eats two slices of mozzarella cheese, microwaved for a minute and with the water wrung out. It makes a *chak-chak-chak* sound, like meat, she tells me. One morning, I am given a slice, squeezed out and folded over on itself, and she asks, in expectant confirmation, isn't it just like meat? I'm not sure, but something about its stringiness and rich, animal-protein flavour makes it a fitting comparison. It reminds her, she says, of the fresh cheeses the nomads made when she was young. She remembers out loud, over breakfast one morning, her childhood and the late summer festival of Ongkor, when there were horse races and archery competitions and the meat was boiled in large quantities and, if you had nomad friends, they brought you fresh cheese as a gift. Sometimes, she says, she likes this village food better and, eyes twinkling, smiles a wry smile, as if she knows this is a silly thing to say.

Some Things Are Felt through the Body

Lekey Leidecker

I have always been what can be described as 'sensitive'. This is shorthand for, literally, some days I can't get out of bed because the Amazon is burning, or I have to recover each time I remember that Selena is no longer alive. Another way of describing it is my diagnosis of anxiety and depression.

There is a disconnect in these instances, between what I know and what I feel. While I recognize the complex structures and causes behind these feelings, I still struggle painfully not to see them as failures or weaknesses. I shame myself thinking of how many people do not have the luxury to shut down like I do, which only worsens things. Until now, I have only devised ways to survive these periods, and every time I return to this state, I struggle anew.

My inherited faith prescribes plenty of solutions for what I experience, plenty of explanations for its occurrence. When I have dared to share my struggles, the well-meaning and serotonin-privileged, in a special kind of irony, suggest meditation or yoga.

So far, excluding a brief run of antidepressants, the feelings always return—an undeniable fact, an unstoppable force. Here, I attempt to derive logic, to find a thread that connects a new way to understand what happens to me.

* * *

This essay began when I learned the name Ahmaud Arbery, the twenty-five-year-old Black man killed by three white men in Georgia while jogging, about his life and those who love him, and the horrific circumstances of his murder. I felt sickening, devastating, exhausting grief and rage, and a twinge of horrible recognition as the murderers were shielded by the very institutions that are supposed to uphold justice. I felt it spread through individual cells, communities, planes of spirit and ancestors. I knew, too, that this rage never really left. For far too long, the story has been the same.

As the summer of 2020 boiled into a global uprising, distractions kept me functional, until they didn't. For days, I was moody, irritable and quick to anger or dissolve into tears. I could not focus on anything. I stopped and started two yoga videos in a row. I left the grocery store with none of the items on my shopping list. I sat still, seized by mounting anxiety, rising dread, rushed to distraction, and the cycle repeated itself. My mind darted around my brain, desperately avoiding something.

It remains alarming that it requires years of unlearning for non-Black people to acknowledge the wrongness that pervades our world. It remains alarming how unwilling we are to change, with each instance of mass rebellion against these systems of murder, of absolute violence and immense, oceanic pain.

There exists some rage that cannot be fixed by breathing. Some things are felt through the body.

At some point in this writing process, sometime in the interminable summer of rebellion and uprising and liberation, I recognized that I could not bring my world back into order. The bad feelings were not internal failures, they were indicators. I cannot cut the threat down any further. I confront it at its true size.

* * *

When anxiety begins, I cycle through a brutal, exhausting mental list: potential antidotes, reasons to not be anxious, and reasons I am a let-down to myself and the world. If I am lucky, the solution is simple: I am over-caffeinated and have forgotten to eat, a biological force-quit. Maybe I've been on a search engine or feed too long, and I shut them off and go outside. If I am unlucky, I fall into a depleted, empty state and remain there for days.

Anxiety is a disproportionate reaction to a perceived threat, so if I guide my body to perform actions that slow the spiral, my perception shifts, and the threat fades. What if you have assessed the threat correctly? I had not devised this protocol, and my body was sounding the alarm.

* * *

The problem is trying to fix an experience of the body with a solution of the mind.

I am a writer. I wholeheartedly believe in the power of words to make and change worlds. But I also have a literal, whole heart that pumps life through my literal body. Our bodies hold what we ask of them, but they are not infinite. They are the most finite. Bodies crumble, contradict themselves, get sick, age, and die. Things like epigenetic trauma and myofascial release therapy show us that bodies hold and can pass on trauma.

I miss Tibet through my body. I do everything I can to feel close, but the loss feels immense as the sky, wide as the grasslands.

There is nothing like being on the land. So, nothing I have done is like being on the land. There are things I may never get to feel. There are things I may always feel. I cannot think my way out of this. Some things are felt through the body.

No matter how much I love reading writer Robin Wall Kimmerer's world-altering words on planting corn, I have not yet planted corn. To reap the benefits, I must actually eat *tsampa*, not just rhapsodize about its many virtues, its centrality to Tibetan ancestral lineage and living tradition and survivance.

This is embodiment: there is an unbreachable distance between the intellectually known and the physically, materially felt.

Land is a body. I am a body. My body is land.

We attempt to discipline, control and marshal the body because we don't like what it tells us. We do not want what it offers, terrified of the poison or medicine. We try to outrun the terror or the pain to which it alerts us, and in these attempts at control, we miss the joy or the possibility of love.

* * *

Any measure of success I have attained has been through betrayals of my body.

Foregoing sleep, exercise, food, and other fundamental needs, I have moved mountains and performed miracles. Once, during a particularly stressful period, I developed an ulcer. Consuming coffee threw my body into incapacitating nausea. Deprived of its usual fuel, my body, ever faithful, pushed through on pure adrenaline.

Afterwards, ensconced safely at home, I sobbed so violently that my terrified family members could not understand me. I fell into a deep sleep listening to the Heart Sutra. My body, having served so well in the heat of battle, had finally come to collect the many debts I owed. Some things are felt through the body.

I cannot help but think of these feelings as results of the struggle against deep colonial structures of violence. Maybe practising the truth of having a body will allow me to slowly disentangle the structures of ableism, colonialism, patriarchy, and white supremacy that my wise body rejects, even as my mind tries again and again to force her into acceptance.

* * *

I wonder if I write because of the feelings of my body. I have learned—or learned how to make it so—that grief can be generative. Sometimes it comes out of the body and creates things. And so, I am grateful to the grief, for what it has spurred me to create. I am trying to let the grief move, hear it say: 'I am alive, and it hurts.'

Here are three elements: pain, joy, and the body. The first two deepening the other; the third, the conduit, the vessel, the barometer of it all.

What I have gleaned from my inherited, patchwork understanding of Buddhism—to grossly oversimplify—is that pleasure and suffering, joy, and pain, are two sides of the same coin. One hollows out space for the other, an immutable bond. The path out of this cycle, we are taught, is to recognize their connection, and to sever our attachment to both.

Perhaps this is the link I so often miss. We are taught that as we attune to our own experience of suffering, it enhances our ability to empathize with others and recognize our inextricable connection with them. We should allow this to increase our desire to end the suffering of all beings. Isn't this, the heart that breaks with grief at the horror of the present, the beginning of the desire for a better world?

Feeling things through the body, especially when unaccustomed to doing so, is near unbearable. Perhaps I am learning to be a body in the struggle. Perhaps I am learning, for the first time in this life, to have a body. I am learning how not to think, but to pray and use my body to access the sacred; to locate the sacred of my own body.

Perhaps my body is the intermediary for my existence on this earth, the vessel through which I receive the message. Perhaps I need to stop thinking, even listening, and start feeling.

Travelling in *Bardo*

Ann Tashi Slater

O nobly-born, although one liketh it not . . . one feeleth compelled
involuntarily to go on; . . . noises and snow and rain and terrifying
hail-storms and whirlwinds of icy blasts occurring . . .
— *The Tibetan Book of the Dead*

On September 13th, 2010, I lay in a Tokyo hospital, my joints
aching and my skin burning hot. Only a faint glow of daylight
penetrated my curtained cubicle. The routine of temperature-
taking, breakfast, and doctors' rounds hadn't started yet, so
the room was silent except for the beeping of monitors and an
occasional rattling snore from the elderly woman in the next bed.

Sunk in that dimness, and staring up at the white ceiling, I
remembered my grandmother's account of a morning in 1912
when her father, my Tibetan great-grandfather, was coming down
into India by pony. He lived in Darjeeling but, deeply involved
in the affairs of British India and Tibet, had been carrying out a
diplomatic mission in Lhasa. On the way home, he was caught in
an avalanche and buried along with several of the men in his party,
their ponies, and their mules. But somehow my great-grandfather
was able to work his arm loose. He thrust it through the snow
and waved his rosary back and forth, muttering to himself, 'Save

me, Guru Rinpoche! Save me!' Someone spotted him, and he was saved.

I imagined that winter day: the turquoise Himalayan sky, the sun glittering on the ice-encrusted pines; the groaning of the pack animals, their musky smell; the laboured breathing of the trapped men as panic rose in their throats. I saw my great-grandfather struggling in his twilit underworld to pull his rosary free and reach for the air; heard him call to his beloved Guru Rinpoche, the eighth-century Indian sage who brought Buddhism to Tibet.

I'd been admitted to the hospital a week earlier, suffering from a severe headache and nausea, an unremitting fever of 103 Fahrenheit, and violent chills. My husband, David, and I, American professors at Japanese universities and residents of Tokyo for over twenty years, had been on summer holiday with our children in Indonesia, and my doctors thought I might have contracted dengue fever or malaria. None of my symptoms had abated and every day new ones were appearing: a jaundiced tinge to my skin, tiny red petechiae dots on my hands from subdermal bleeding, a pebbly rash on my knees, and photophobia. The pain in my joints was so excruciating that I now understood why dengue, if that's what I had, was known as 'breakbone fever'. The only way I felt slightly less miserable was by lying motionless with a gauzy hand towel over my eyes, hour after hour. All I could eat were giant purple *kyoho* grapes—their burst of coolness a fleeting relief in my fevered state—so I'd been put on an intravenous therapy (IV). When Dr Ando, the internal-medicine specialist, stopped in later that morning and saw my untouched tray of mackerel, rice, and miso soup, he asked if I couldn't try to eat just a little. A slight, sombre man of about fifty, he stretched out his arms in a pleading gesture and smiled. 'You may have whatever you want,' he said, 'Even ice cream.'

* * *

My Tibetan grandmother was psychic. On Christmas Day, 1936, as my great-grandfather prepared to travel to a town near Darjeeling to campaign for an assembly seat, she went to him and whispered, 'Father, I didn't have a very good dream. I don't think you should go.'

'I can't help it, darling,' he said, picking up his valise. 'All the preparations are made, everyone is waiting for me. I have to go. I can't let the people down.'

'If you do, Father, you will never come back.' She'd seen his body being brought up to the sky, with a few drops of rain, but also sunshine. Everyone was saying, '*Look! Look!*' and pointing as his body rose to heaven.

'I pre-saw all of that,' my grandmother told me fifty years later over tea in her sitting room in Darjeeling. I was perched on the leathery elephant's-foot stool that had fascinated me as a small girl, next to the ancient gramophone my grandparents played when they threw parties, and everyone danced the Tibetan Charleston. Outside, the snowy peaks of 28,000-foot Mount Kanchenjunga glistened in the sun, towering over the Raj-era bungalows and tea gardens of the fabled former British hill station. 'But he wouldn't listen. On the platform, he spoke for five or six hours, and the same night, his heart failed. In his sleep, he expired. When the servants went to knock with the tea and toast, he was dead.'

If my grandmother were still alive, I wondered that day in the hospital, what would she prophesize for me? I'd had strange feelings before getting sick. Had I inherited her powers? David, the children, and I had been in Indonesia during Ramadan, and every morning I lay sleepless, listening to the muezzin sing the call to prayer in the still, blue dawn. Regret over matters large and small flooded through me. Hurtful things I'd said or done, lost opportunities, actual and imagined slights—it all flowed past in an endless loop. As if mirroring my inner state, the surroundings were surreal: women in white burkas, their faces veiled, gliding along the roadside; a band of silvery langurs leaping from a tree.

In mid-August, we flew back to Tokyo, and a few days later our children started the new school year. But my unease continued, especially one evening towards the end of the month. Our neighbourhood—an old area of the city where wooden tile-roofed houses and temples sat among high-rise apartment buildings and international supermarkets—was quiet, as if resting after the sweltering heat of the day. We'd opened the windows, and a twilight breeze brought in the odour of damp earth from the garden, along with laughter from a neighbour's TV, the occasional cooling *ting* of a glass wind chime, and the plaintive song of the *gyoza* dumpling vendor as he wound through the streets in his little truck. An evening like so many others, but glancing up from the newspaper, I was transfixed. David sat at the dining table in a tattered Cape Cod T-shirt and khaki shorts, working on his computer. Fourteen-year-old Sophia was sprawled on one of the Tibetan carpets doing geometry problems and eating *mikan* tangerines, her earphones in and her head nodding to the beat. Twelve-year-old Henry, his cowlick standing straight up as always, sat cross-legged on the sofa, mainlining gummy bears and writing out Japanese *kanji* characters. Our Westie, Mac, slumbered under the table next to his bone, paws twitching as he dreamed his doggie dreams.

Before long it would all fade away. Sophia would leave for college. Henry would go soon afterwards. Not much later, Mac would be dead! I saw David and myself retiring from our universities and growing old and someone else living in the house we'd built. All the things that hadn't happened yet but inevitably would.

The passing years are like dust, the Buddha said. *Regard this phantom world as a star at dawn . . . a flash of lightning in a summer cloud, a flickering lamp . . . and a dream.* Even though I'd been raised without religion in 1970s California (my mother, after marrying an atheist American, had cast aside the rituals and prayers of her Darjeeling girlhood), I felt a deep connection to Buddhism. At first, this tie was only a familial inheritance, but as I grew up, it became a secular affinity, a way to better know myself and the world. I understood—or thought I understood—the fundamental principle of impermanence especially well, having written a novel based on the Tibetan Buddhist belief in an after-death journey to rebirth. This journey was one of the 'between states', or *bardos*, we are said to experience, including periods during life when ordinary reality is suspended, as during sleep or illness. I was aware nothing lasts forever, but until now, I realized, I'd never really *felt* impermanence.

* * *

On the day I was admitted to the hospital, Dr Ando stopped by. Turning the bedside chair around, he straddled it, resting his arms on the back. He gazed at me with an expression both intrigued and perplexed, as if he were wondering how this very sick American woman had come to be under his care. Rubbing his jaw, he asked, 'Have you . . . been in Japan for quite a long time?' When I told him I'd lived in Tokyo for almost a quarter of a century, he looked surprised. When I told him I was a mother of two, writer, and literature professor, he looked astonished. I shared his amazement: in my diminished state, the person I'd described seemed like someone else. I'd taken leave of my full, rich life and was viewing it from afar, just as a spirit hovers in the after-death *bardo*, gazing back at the existence to which she can never return.

I told myself these feelings were only a symptom of whatever illness I had, some kind of temporary hallucination disorder. I was at the Japanese Red Cross Medical Center, a state-of-the-art hospital that attracted the best doctors in the country, and there was no doubt they would cure me.

'Dr Ando said there was a guy in much worse condition than you who was here with dengue,' David said as he helped me get settled that first night in my surprisingly attractive room. The hospital had recently been renovated and, with its cream-coloured walls, muted lighting, and panoramic views of the city, seemed more like a hotel than a place of suffering. The effect was intensified by the willowy, soft-voiced nurses and the Japanese custom of patients wearing their own nightclothes rather than hospital gowns.

'The guy lasted eight days,' David said, plumping my pillow and arranging my slippers next to the bed.

'And then he died?' I asked, appalled. Why hadn't they been able to save him? And how could my husband act so offhand?

David laughed and hugged me. 'No, he was discharged.'

The first week passed in a blur of pain and confusion as my symptoms worsened and Dr Ando and his junior, Dr Kondo, a cheerful, earnest young man who wore scuffed white Crocs, tried to figure out what was wrong. New words entered my Japanese vocabulary: *samuke* (chill), *darui* (extreme lassitude), *enshou* (inflammation), and *tenteki* (IV). I had head computed tomography (CT) scans and full-body CT scans, regular magnetic resonance imaging (MRI) tests and contrast-enhanced MRIs, X-rays and echocardiograms, agglutination and nephelometry tests, serum glutamic-oxaloacetic transaminase (SGOT) and serum glutamic pyruvic transaminase (SGPT) liver function tests; tests for lupus, Sjogren's syndrome, and rheumatoid arthritis, including antinuclear antibody (ANA), erythrocyte sedimentation rate (ESR), and CCP (cyclic citrullinated peptide antibody). The C-reactive protein (CRP) test, an indicator of inflammation in the body, showed that my level was sixteen instead of less than one, and my complete blood count (CBC) showed thrombocytopenia, an insufficient number of platelets in my blood. If my platelet count got too low, I'd need a transfusion to prevent spontaneous internal bleeding. Too weak to walk, I was taken for the tests in a wheelchair, and though Tokyo was experiencing a record heat wave, I needed an electric blanket to ward off my intensifying chills.

Every night I prayed for heavy, narcotic slumber, but whenever I managed to drift off, it was into a world of nightmares. I dreamed that my credit cards and identity document (ID) had been stolen and wild dogs were attacking me. Driving on a dark winding road in torrential rain, I lost control of the car and plunged off the edge. I was trapped inside a shack in the hottest desert in the world, dust blowing through gaps between the floorboards, everything shrivelled, brown, desiccated. Once, I shot up in bed and called to David, who was dozing in the chair next to me, but he didn't wake. *This is the after-death bardo*, I thought. I was in the stage of the journey where not yet realizing we are dead, we call out to our loved ones, but they cannot hear us.

* * *

On September 15th, my tenth day in the hospital, a woman I'd known since our daughters were first-grade classmates came to visit. We adored books and fashion and parties, and always had fun together. Her horrified expression when she saw me pale and listless in my sweat-soaked nightgown sent waves of dread through me. We struggled to reassure each other by acting as if all was—almost—normal, chatting about our book club and whether our girls would make the basketball team. Gradually, the talk of everyday things soothed my nausea and the terrible headache. It even began to seem that my affliction might vanish as mysteriously as it had appeared. Spontaneous remission sometimes happened—why not for me?

A clattering in the hall interrupted our conversation. Moments later, two nurses charged in with a wheelchair. One of the blood cultures had yielded a positive result and the doctors thought there was a nest of bacteria in my heart.

'Everything will be fine,' my friend said in tears, running by my side as they rushed me out for another echocardiogram. I noticed how lovely her feet looked: the rose-pink polish on her toenails, her strappy lavender sandals.

Two hours later, I was lying in bed with the hand towel over my eyes when Dr Kondo hurried in. No matter how bad my condition, he always remained calm and upbeat, striving to find what he called 'happy points', like my temperature dropping by a few tenths of a degree. But now something was very wrong: his face was flushed, and the armpits of his blue scrubs were dark with perspiration.

'Final diagnosis!' he announced breathlessly, flinging his arms wide like an umpire. 'Endocarditis.'

He spoke fast, yet unbearably slowly: endocarditis was a life-threatening infection of the heart lining. Bacteria got into the bloodstream, attached to the endocardium—often in a heart valve—and formed a mass, or vegetation. The vegetation in my mitral valve had proliferated to 20.3 mm—so large it would have begun forming four to six weeks earlier, which explained my strange feelings in Indonesia. 'It is lucky,' Dr Kondo said, 'that you have not experienced a heart attack.'

'How does this happen?' I heard myself ask.

How *could* this happen? I'd been running and doing yoga for years. I didn't smoke, drank in moderation, and ate well.

'Sometimes such an illness arises due to a dental procedure!' Dr Kondo said, his voice still animated from the excitement of the diagnosis. 'The bacteria may enter through the gum. Also, when you are old or have some defect in the heart, this disease is somewhat possible.'

I hadn't had dental work, I was young, and my heart, he said, was strong and healthy.

'In your case,' he told me, 'it just happened that some germs got into your body.'

I'd need to stay for four more weeks to receive intravenous ceftriaxone and ciprofloxacin, antibiotics that might or might not work.

That might or might not work. I contracted into a knot of fear and bewilderment.

They'd called David and he was on his way. I lay frozen, listening for my husband's step outside the door. A siren shrieked from somewhere in the city. The rhythmic swish and pulse of a ventilator sounded from one of the other curtained cubicles. Whispers floated on the dim air: unmoved by the no-cell-phone rule, the elderly woman in the next bed was chatting on her mobile. I stared at the travel clock on my night table, tracking the second hand's oblivious, circular march. Near the clock, the delicate freesias sent by a friend (cut, not potted, because the Japanese believe plants with roots suggest a permanent hospital stay) glowed spectrally white and funereal.

Everything would be fine as soon as David arrived. We'd been inseparable since we met on a rainy March evening in 1985, two English teachers at a Tokyo beer party, and together we always knew what to do. A child of divorce, I'd planned never to marry, to live by the sea with a dog and write. David—witty, irreverent, brilliant, with the bookish good looks I found so attractive—had changed my mind. As soon as he got to the hospital we'd talk, because that was what we did, whether going over the day's events while we made dinner, critiquing each other's work (a keen editor, he'd read drafts of my novel more times than anyone should ever have to do anything), sharing funny things the kids had said, brainstorming ways to help our ageing parents, ruminating on the future. Ideas, crises, musings—we talked it all through.

But when David strode in, still holding his wallet and the receipt for the ten-minute taxi ride, he sat mutely on the edge of the bedside chair. His shoulders were slumped, and he smelled of fried onions from the dinner he'd been cooking for the kids when Dr Kondo called. I waited for him to say, *Everything will be okay*, as he had on the way to the hospital the summer we'd rented a cottage on Cape Cod and I'd had a miscarriage. He'd been right: though we lost the baby, I'd gotten pregnant with Henry just a few months later. But for the first time, he was silent.

When we spoke at last, it was to seek control in logistics. He would contact my university to tell them I couldn't start teaching at the end of the month, call the organizer of a Tokyo writing conference to say I wouldn't be presenting, and cancel the appointments in my datebook. Each step felt like a cutting of another of my ties to the world, an ever-deeper entombment in *bardo*.

Soon David left to finish making dinner. Friends had been offering to help, but we felt it was important for the children that David be home as much as possible and keep to the family routines. After he went, I hobbled with the IV stand to the hallway computer to google endocarditis. The smooth, cool feel of the keys under my fingertips calmed me, as always. Now I'd be able to see the whole picture. I would put my thoughts in order and formulate a plan. But as the information flashed onto the screen, my mind grew charged and staticky, my breathing ragged: *Complications include congestive heart failure, severe organ damage, intracranial haemorrhage, stroke, neurological failure. Difficult to cure. Significant mortality.*

* * *

Tibetan birth horoscopes indicate the year you will die. I'd never asked about my horoscope, partly because I didn't want to know when my end would come, but mostly because I felt sure it wouldn't be before my time.

Yet after the diagnosis, I realized with chilling clarity that in the Tibetan way of looking at things, there was no such thing as 'before your time'. When my grandmother died on a winter night in Darjeeling, the moon setting over Mount Kanchenjunga and dogs barking in the mist-shrouded valleys, she wasn't sick. Her body had just wound down. 'It was her time,' explained one of the monks who came to do the prayers from *The Tibetan Book of the Dead*—she'd reached the end of her allotted lifespan. Calculating age from the womb, as the Tibetans do, she had made it to one hundred.

When my grandmother suddenly couldn't get warm in the drafty, wooden house where she'd lived for over sixty years, the family moved her across town to Tinkerbelle's Cottage. This was a homey bungalow on the grounds of the Windamere, the Raj-era hotel my grandfather had taken over after India became independent in 1947 and the two Britons he had owned the hotel with returned to England. At Tinkerbelle's, my grandmother felt more comfortable but stayed mostly in bed, not talking or eating much. Sometimes, she sat on the veranda and gazed out over the houses and shops of the storybook town where she and my grandfather had ridden through the streets on horseback the day of their wedding in 1930, where her five children had been born, and where her husband had been cremated. This continued for three weeks, until at 1:16 a.m. on November 30th, 2004, her heart stopped and, peacefully, she exhaled for the last time.

If this was the end for me, I wanted to embrace it with the same equanimity, and yet I refused to accept that I might be fated to die in my forties. There had been moments when I could have died but didn't: at nine, I was chased through the woods by a knife-wielding man; at seventeen, I missed an oncoming car by inches as I flew around a curve, driving to my boyfriend's house one sunny California morning. Surely getting sick with endocarditis was just another one of these moments.

* * *

From the day I'd been hospitalized, David had been in contact with everybody who might know something, anything, about my condition. Each morning he hurried to the hospital with a legal pad full of notes to discuss with my doctors, trying frantically to understand what was wrong and what could be done. By an improbable stroke of luck, it turned out his family physician back in the States, Dr Karchmer, was a world-renowned expert on endocarditis. Dr Ando was awestruck: 'Your home doctor is famous!'

Dr Karchmer confirmed that the ceftriaxone and ciprofloxacin treatment was appropriate and, two days into the antibiotic therapy, Dr Ando reported that the vegetation in my mitral valve had shrunk almost 40 per cent. David and I were overcome with joy; finally, our luck had turned. It wasn't my time after all. At this rate, I'd probably even be discharged early. I glanced around the tiny cubicle: it would only take a moment to pack my nightclothes and travel clock, the tube of cooling lavender body lotion a friend had sent. I told David I'd start planning a trip to help our family recover from all that had happened—maybe to Kyoto to see the autumn foliage at the old temples and eat the *nama yatsuhashi* sweet rice cake that Sophia and Henry loved.

Dr Ando was standing motionless at the foot of the bed, frowning deeply. At first, I attributed this to Japanese reserve or the professional caution that doctors naturally had to exercise. But the gravity of his expression made me shiver. 'When the vegetation appears to have shrunk rapidly,' he said, 'one possibility is that parts of it have broken off and embolized into the circulation.' The emboli might reach my kidneys, he went on, leading to renal failure. They might travel to my brain and obstruct a blood vessel, causing a stroke. Or they could block a coronary artery, resulting in a heart attack.

I took three sleeping pills that night instead of the prescribed two, but still I hardly slept. Hot spikes of pain radiated from my joints, and I was tormented by the usual feverish nightmares and my fears of the emboli that might be moving through my veins like time bombs. When dawn came at last, grey and dreary, blue-black crows cawing from the rooftops, I felt so grateful to be alive that the morning looked beautiful despite its melancholy.

I decided to try to eat some of the grilled tuna on my breakfast tray. As I took hold of the chopsticks, I realized I couldn't feel them against the tip of my pinkie. I tested it with my other hand; it was numb. There was also a shimmering at the edge of my field of vision, like heat rising from a road.

The doctor on duty, a quiet man with lank hair, poked his head through the curtains and smiled. 'How are you feeling?'

His smile vanished as I told him about the new symptoms. He excused himself, then returned a few minutes later: I'd be taken immediately for an emergency MRI and CT scan. This is how it was discovered that a piece of the vegetation had lodged in the occipital lobe of my brain, causing a large abscess, or pocket of infection, to form. If the abscess cut off blood flow to the surrounding tissue, I could suffer irreversible cognitive impairment or—the doctor paused, searching for the right words—'even more critical complications.'

He hooked up a bag of glycerol, a diuretic that might reduce swelling around the abscess. Then he left, closing the curtains around my bed like a shroud.

All that filtered in were the hoarse ravings of the elderly woman, who in her sleep kept calling out, '*Iya da* [It's not okay]!' The optimism David and I had felt when the antibiotics seemed to be working appeared childish and desperate now. I cast about for encouraging thoughts, a Buddhist principle to hold on to, but my mind was blank.

When David arrived with Sophia and Henry for their Saturday visit, he was lively as always, demonstrating basketball moves for the kids and making them laugh by squeezing into the top to the polar bear-print pyjamas they'd brought me. I forced myself to concentrate as Henry told me how many *dango* rice-flour dumplings he planned to eat at his school's upcoming *otsukimi* autumn moon-viewing celebration, the one we always went to together. Sophia showed me photos on her cell phone of possible outfits for a karaoke party that evening, and we debated the merits of a skirt versus a dress, then fell into a heated discussion of how short was too short. She insisted she was old enough to decide for herself: '*I'm the one who's going to be wearing it, not you!*' Her strong will was sometimes exasperating, but now I treasured her pluck and passion.

Henry had brought his *ondoku* Japanese reading-aloud homework, which he liked to do with me. I listened to his usual earnest and dramatic rendition, this time a story about two cranes flying south for the winter, one being killed by a fox and the other lamenting not having been nicer to his now-dead companion. At the end, Henry sighed with satisfaction. A gentle, thoughtful boy, he spent time pondering the workings of the world and liked stories that affirmed a moral order. He especially adored fairy tales, where problems had solutions, right triumphed over wrong, and loyalty and love were eternal.

When he was small, Henry told me, 'I'm going to like you forever. Are you going to like me forever?'

'Forever and ever.'

'A lot of evers?'

'That's right.

Now he pressed against my hospital bed and smiled, his blue-grey eyes radiant with love and trust. 'You'll be coming home soon, won't you?'

David and Sophia had been talking, but they stepped close to listen.

'It'll be just a little longer,' I said, struggling to push down the tide of grief and horror inside me.

Sophia fiddled with the braided strap of her shoulder bag and refused to meet my gaze.

Henry burst into tears. 'But you're going to get well, right?'

'You bet, buddy!' David said, clapping him on the shoulder.

* * *

Two days later, on the evening of September 20th, David and I had a consult with the neurosurgeon. We gathered in a cramped room down the hall with fluorescent lighting, a bare desk, and moulded plastic chairs. David and the surgeon chatted for a moment about the flash flooding caused by the latest typhoon and about the dispute that had erupted between Japan and China over control of a chain of islands in the East China Sea. Then the surgeon, a gracious man with slim, tapered fingers that looked well-suited to his speciality, opened his laptop to show us an image of the brain abscess from the MRI I'd had that morning.

As the computer booted up, David and I held hands, hopeful that the glycerol had reduced the swelling. But the foolishness of our optimism was revealed again.

'Quite a bit more enlargement has taken place,' the surgeon said, clicking open the file. As they'd feared, this had led to infarction, or obstruction of the blood supply, resulting in the death of the surrounding tissue.

I stared at the ghostly, grey ovoid on the laptop screen. At the lower left, a black orb was expanding, destroying my brain.

I thanked the neurosurgeon and started back to my room in the wheelchair. The sound of David pressing the doctor with questions faded as I inched past other patients' rooms, other lives and fears. The big stuffed Snoopy and Hello Kitty on the counter of the nurses' station looked forlorn, as though they knew what little consolation they could offer in this outpost of misery.

Flipping through some papers David had left on my night table, I found the syllabus for the course he was teaching on social identity in post-war Japan and a list he'd scribbled on a yellow post-it: 'sleepover party, bank, change ortho appt, parent-teacher conf, cucumbers.' Tucked in the back was my living will. It seemed responsible to read through it, but the words that had once made perfect sense now appeared to be written in a language I didn't speak: 'there can be no recovery . . . my death is imminent . . .'

I returned the will to the folder.

The cold hush of night descended on my room, on the hospital, on the encircling labyrinth of the dark city, its crooked alleyways and dead ends. What seemed to be happening to me couldn't be happening. I couldn't die. I was born in the Tibetan Year of the Ox, and not only that, I was a Metal Ox, strong as steel. At the age of eight, I could lift my 200-pound father, and the sole girl in fifth-grade judo, I threw and grappled my way to the top, beating all the boys and winning the championship. Speaking only classroom French, I moved to Paris by myself at eighteen and worked for a year as an au pair, zipping around the city in a beat-up Ford Escort I bought for a few hundred dollars. In my twenties, I travelled alone through India and Mexico and interviewed writers in Cuba while being followed by the secret police. I arrived in Japan with $800, no job, and not a word of Japanese, and became a university professor. I wasn't going to be struck down now by a random illness.

David returned to the room, his eyes red, his face drained of colour. 'The doctor says the glycerol still might work!'

I heard the despair but clung to his words.

'Did he say anything else?' I asked.

He said the doctors were considering drastic measures to relieve the pressure building in my brain. They might try drilling a small burr hole in my skull to drain the abscess. If this failed, the only hope might be a craniotomy, where they would remove a piece of my skull bone to expose and evacuate the abscess. But there was a good chance I'd end up paralyzed or a vegetable, or maybe worse.

I'd always imagined that if a moment like this came for us, we'd say what we didn't say in our ordinary, busy lives: *There has only ever been you.* We had important things to tell each other, now. But we fell silent, alone together in the beeping, hissing night.

Something long forgotten came back to me. In the late eighties, soon after we married and before we had children, we took a holiday to a volcanic island in Fiji. It poured rain all week, turning the dirt roads into muddy rivers, so we spent our time diving. One morning we did a drift dive, the kind where you descend holding on to a rope until you get below the strongest part of the current, close to the ocean floor. But we let go too soon and, unable to see the bottom or the surface, were lost together in the endless blue.

* * *

Tibetans believe that when someone dies, the surviving relatives may encounter obstacles. This was why, on a cold Darjeeling morning in December 2004, a few days after my grandmother's cremation, an obstacle-removing ceremony was held at the family home. Clouds wreathed Mount Kanchenjunga and the usual cacophony of car horns sounded from the lower part of town. The sharp scent of sacred burning juniper rose from a fire that had been lit in a corner of the back garden. Together with family members, I watched as long prayer flags tied to metal poles were erected for us on the hill behind the garden, where the household staff had arranged plates piled with sugar, curd, biscuits, *tsampa* barley flour, incense, butter, bananas, and apples as offerings for the deities. The guardian gods of the ten directions had been invited, along with those who had been in meditation for thousands of years.

A senior monk, who'd fled to India from eastern Tibet after the Chinese invaded in 1950, had come from a nearby monastery to perform the ceremony. He took his place at a low, brightly painted table in the garden and, turning the two-headed *damaru* drum back and forth, ringing a Tibetan bell and rotating a small brass double-sceptre *dorje* in the air, intoned guttural prayers for every wish to be fulfilled, every obstacle removed, every sentient being benefited.

As the ceremony ended, the sun broke through the clouds, and a golden ray fell on the assembled group of aunts, uncles, and cousins bundled in wool shawls and down jackets. A breeze unfurled my prayer flag, revealing the invocations written in Tibetan script next to an illustration of a parasol, one of the lucky symbols, for protection from evil forces, accidents, and disease. Although I didn't really believe in the ceremony, this did all seem highly auspicious. As if hearing my thoughts, the monk turned to me and said, 'You must have faith.' There was no need, he explained, for deep-mind analysis because the scriptures had already been dissected by scholars over the centuries. He added, 'It is the same when you visit the gold dealer. You don't analyse the gold yourself. You trust that it is real.'

I decided I would try to have faith in the ceremony. I didn't know how exactly to do this, but at least I could suspend my doubt.

After the meeting with the neurosurgeon, I returned again and again to what the monk had said. Buddhism had been a philosophy for me rather than a religion, but now I felt there might not be such a big difference between the two. I wondered whether I'd had enough faith—whatever this meant in my case— in the six years since that morning in my grandmother's garden. Because I'd at least been present at the obstacle-removing ceremony, I took solace in something else the monk had told me: even if your faith was insufficient, you could gain protection through the ritual, in the same way an ant could earn merit if it inadvertently circumambulated a temple on a piece of swirling dung in a flood.

* * *

The next day, David got the kids off to school and then rushed to the hospital to talk with my doctors about a corticosteroid called dexamethasone. He'd been up most of the night in frantic contact with Dr Karchmer, who'd recommended that, in addition to the glycerol diuretic therapy, high-dose dexamethasone therapy be initiated to try to decrease the brain swelling. The situation, Dr Karchmer said, required 'very careful following'. The new therapy was started that morning.

When Dr Ando stopped by on his rounds, David and I thought he'd say my chances had improved now that I was on steroid therapy. But there was only a grave discussion of neurological complications and additional tests; of the possibility of open-heart surgery to replace my mitral valve; of the danger of a stroke since the infection could weaken the blood vessels in my brain. I closed my eyes and listened numbly to their talk, to announcements on the public address system and the shrill sound of doctors' pagers, to the elderly woman in the next bed grumbling to a visitor about the minuscule food portions and asking him to smuggle in *tonkatsu*, deep-fried pork. The headache that still hadn't subsided after nearly a month pounded at the base of my skull, and my body felt stiff and cold.

Dr Ando said he needed to go and would keep us updated. 'But the remaining three weeks of antibiotics must be completed,' he told us, 'before we can evaluate what is required.'

The days passed slowly. I slipped into a dream within a dream, drifted into an eerily calm bend in the nightmarish river that had engulfed me. Clouds bloomed like surreal flowers in the azure sky; rain slanted across the cityscape. The sun rose and set over the tidy houses and streets, where somehow life was proceeding as usual. Girls in sailor-style uniforms walked to and from a nearby school; salarymen hurried to work, carrying their suit jackets in the early autumn heat; women rode past on shopping bikes with fat white *daikon* radishes poking out of the basket; vendors drove along in mini-trucks with loudspeakers on top, hawking things like laundry poles and buckets; fireworks from one of the city's festivals lit up the distant sky.

The curtains around my bed were usually closed—a relief since I felt too ill for small talk. But I was greatly cheered one afternoon when the elderly woman, who'd finally been discharged, stuck her wizened face through my curtains, hair pinned into a lopsided beehive and a smudge of rouge on her cheeks. '*Ganbatte, nee* [Hang in there],' she said in her creaky voice. I realized I'd felt a kinship with her as the other patients came and went. I was touched but not surprised—considering her illicit cell phone use and request for contraband *tonkatsu* pork—that she'd breached the barriers of patient privacy and my foreignness to encourage me.

I started to feel a little less afraid as my periodic echocardiograms and CT scans showed a gradual decrease in the mitral valve vegetation and brain swelling. The abscess began to scar over, and the dexamethasone was tapered. Dr Ando said I could try walking, so every couple of days a nurse disconnected the IV tube and I shuffled down the corridor to the bathing room. Exchanging my beige bed slippers for pink rubber bathroom ones, I showered wearing a plastic bag over the IV needle. The soap had the same fresh, clean smell as the soap we'd used to give Sophia and Henry their first baths as newborns in a hospital only a few blocks away. I could still feel their downy, wrinkled skin and the way their tiny bottoms and backs fit into the curve of my hand, the wild joy and hope that had overtaken David and me as our children's lives began.

David would come for lunch, bringing Starbucks lattes, my mail, and the laundry he'd washed for me. We talked about stories in the news and how his teaching was going, household matters, and how Sophia and Henry were doing in school. Later in the afternoon, Sophia would stride in, wearing the high-heeled black espadrilles she'd found in my closet, her long legs tan, her skin smelling of fruit-scented body lotion, her oversized sunglasses pushed up to hold back her flowing brown hair. Moving the IV stand aside, she would show me cell phone photos of her friends, ask me to test her on French verb conjugations or paint her nails with red polish she'd brought from my bathroom drawer at home. Henry would text first—'On my way, want anything?' with an emoji of a boy running—and zoom over on his bike, in his basket the ginger ale I'd started to crave, along with 'a little candy' he'd thrown in for himself at the store with money from David. A great foodie, he sat close, his breath smelling of gummy bears, and told me about the best ('yummy') and worst ('really gross') school lunches David was making, or his favourite dishes at all the neighbourhood restaurants they were getting to know.

Sometimes, Sophia and Henry stayed through the afternoon and to the amusement of the nurses, we lay in the bed together— the kids making it go up and down with the remote control—and watched movies on my laptop: *Le Divorce*, *Last Chance Harvey*, *Roman Holiday*. Careful not to dislodge the IV needle, the kids stretched out, draping their arms and legs on me, the way they'd done when they were little, and snacked on Japanese comfort food: *onigiri* seaweed-wrapped rice balls, salty *senbei* crackers, and cold *mugicha* barley tea. 'Let's go to France!' Sophia said as the Hermès Kelly handbag in *Le Divorce* sailed like a red balloon over the Paris rooftops. We made a pact to go together *en famille*, and I promised to show them the tiny maid's room in the Marais where I'd lived when I was an au pair.

After Sophia and Henry left, I would replay in my mind the movie scenes of daily life: Naomi Watts opening mail in her bohemian Paris apartment, Dustin Hoffman walking Emma Thompson along the River Thames to her writing class, Audrey Hepburn eating ice cream on a sunny day in Rome. The Buddha taught that only when we truly experience our impermanence can we perceive the profound beauty in everyday existence. Indeed, the ordinary now seemed sublime. If I made it, I would sew Sophia and Henry costumes for Halloween. I'd plant rosemary in the garden and buy plump goldfish for the moss-covered stone basin. After writing all day, David and I would go for walks, stopping to chat with friends and lingering over *aki-agari* autumn sake at an *izakaya* bar, with Miles Davis's *Sketches of Spain* or *Birth of the Cool* playing in the background. I would cook for my family: Moroccan chicken with preserved lemons and olives, spinach and fenugreek with Indian *paneer* cheese, tagliatelle with hazelnuts and prosciutto.

Nights were a journey through realms outside space and time, only the steady beeping of monitors reminding me that the hours were passing linearly. During the long insomniac darkness, I visited my grandmother's cozy house in the crook of a Darjeeling lane. Climbing the polished wooden stairs to her prayer room, I heard the happy shouts of children playing outside in the Himalayan twilight and the high-pitched whistle of the train as it eased into the station down near the bazaar. I sat on the silk brocade cushions before the carved altar and studied the framed photos of deceased family members, looking long enough to feel the thread linking us but not too long because I didn't want to see my own photo next to theirs. Breathing in the earthy odour of the burning butter lamps, I meditated on the golden statue of the fierce, wild-eyed Guru Rinpoche, the Buddhist sage my great-grandfather had prayed to when buried in the snow, who was believed to have hidden spiritual teachings under rocks, in lakes, in the mindstream, to be revealed to future generations in times of adversity. One of these teachings was the eighth-century *Tibetan Book of the Dead*, written to guide travellers on the terrifying journey through the after-death *bardo* and difficult *bardos* experienced in life, like accident and illness, to urge them to accept reality but not lose hope. Buried in the hills of central Tibet, the *Book of the Dead* was discovered centuries later; in the same way, I now felt, my great-grandfather's lesson about faith had been hidden in our family's mindstream, to be revealed when it was most needed.

* * *

On Wednesday, October 13th, the four weeks of antibiotic therapy, at last, came to an end. My temperature had returned to normal and the headache, nausea, chills, joint pain, and visual disturbances had almost disappeared. The echocardiograms showed that the vegetation in my mitral valve had shrunk from 12.7 mm to 5 mm; a reduction Dr Ando believed was due to the ceftriaxone and ciprofloxacin. The brain abscess had decreased from 53 mm to 47 mm, and my blood cultures were clear of *haemophilus parainfluenzae*. Yet another happy point, Dr Kondo said, cautiously hopeful, was that my mitral valve hadn't been damaged, so valve replacement surgery wouldn't be necessary.

I was still at risk for a cerebral haemorrhage. If the infection had created weak spots—aneurysms—in the vessels of my brain and one of the aneurysms ruptured, blood would leak out, putting pressure on the brain tissue and compromising its oxygen supply. Haemorrhagic stroke was, Dr Ando said, 'a catastrophic event' that often proved fatal or resulted in permanent brain damage. They now needed to perform a cerebral angiogram to check for impaired vascular integrity. A catheter would be inserted into my groin and up into one of the neck arteries, which supplied blood to the head; contrast dye would then be sent through the catheter into the blood vessels of my brain. Watching animated images, the radiologist would study the movement of the dye through the blood vessels. If aneurysms were detected in the vessel walls, I'd have to stay in the hospital for two more weeks of antibiotic therapy and, possibly, brain surgery to try to repair the weakened areas.

I set my sights on making it to Henry's cross-country final that weekend. This was the first season he was competing and I had missed all his races. I would, I decided, make it to that last one.

On Thursday afternoon, I was given a sedative and a local anaesthetic and then wheeled to a brightly lit room. Two nurses lifted me onto an examining table, positioned me under a camera, and dimmed the lights. The radiologist, a middle-aged man in blue scrubs and white running shoes, chatted with me about the time he'd spent studying in Los Angeles as he observed the flow of the dye through my brain on a big screen along the wall. A strap held my head in place, but I could see the image: a tangle of gossamer branches anchored by a thick, dark trunk, like an Ansel Adams photo of a California oak in fog. 'I'm from the San Francisco Bay Area,' I told the doctor, and we talked about how beautiful the city looked from the Golden Gate Bridge, the lush green of the Marin Headlands above the blue Pacific. Lulled by the sedative, the memories of where I grew up, the hum of the machinery and the warmth of the room, I felt safe for the first time in many weeks and wished the exam would never end. But in only an hour, the doctor had finished.

'There's no problem,' he said, patting me on the arm.

It was finally over.

The next morning, the October light golden on the ginkgo trees, David came to take me home. I could hardly believe that at long last I was walking out of the sterile, airless room where I'd been suspended in *bardo*, the room I might very well have left on a gurney, covered by a sheet.

I was filled with gratitude towards my great-grandfather. His faith no doubt sustained my grandmother as she approached death, and it had sustained me. In *bardo*, *The Tibetan Book of the Dead* says, we are pilgrims in search of a lost harmony. I'd thought this meant we seek to restore our old life, but I understood it differently now: it was about the harmony we lose when we forget that impermanence is the central truth of existence.

Some nurses helped David and me pack, exclaiming over and over, '*Yokatta desu nee! Yoku ganbarimashita, nee!*' It's great, isn't it? You really hung in there!

We gave the nurses a tin of chocolate chip cookies the children had baked and a note they'd written since they were at school:

Thank you for taking care of our mother.

Sincerely,

Sophia and Henry

Dr Ando and Dr Kondo stopped in to say goodbye.

'Your case was very difficult,' Dr Ando said, his worry lines softened by a relieved smile. With typical Japanese humility, he added: 'We learned a lot.'

We thanked them again and again, but no words seemed adequate. How could you just say thank you and goodbye to people who'd saved your life? Would I never see them again? Part of me wanted to clutch on: *Let me stay!* What if they'd missed something and I had a heart attack or a brain haemorrhage? I could be dead by the time I reached the emergency room.

After more thank-yous and goodbyes and lots of bowing all around, David and I left. We dropped my things at home, where Mac launched himself at me, barking with joy, and then we went to lunch at a neighbourhood trattoria. After so many weeks in the hospital's beige and white, I felt like I was in *The Wizard of Oz* at the moment when everything turns to colour: the trees, the flowers, the signs, the cars pulsed in a dazzling array of greens, oranges, pinks, and reds; the sky was a brilliant turquoise. I'd lost ten pounds, my hair was thin, and I had track marks on my arms from the IV needles. But I was eating tomato-and-tuna pasta with my husband on a sunny fall day, my dog at my feet, people talking and laughing at the tables around us, a baseball bat pinging in a nearby field.

My Journey to Lhasa

Jamyang Norbu

I was born on 14 April 1949. Four months later, wrapped warmly in soft woollen blankets and strapped to the back of a sturdy manservant, I crossed the Nathu-la pass from Sikkim to Tibet. My old nanny, Pema Tsewang (who later died of starvation during the Chinese occupation), rode beside us on a pony, while my mother and father rode on ahead.

My mother's family, the Tethongs, had yet to make their decisive move to leave Tibet (which they would in the next year) as my mother had to return to Lhasa to make arrangements for the wedding of her younger sister, Tashi Chodon, to the son of Changoepa aka Ringang, one of the four young Tibetans sent by the Thirteenth Dalai Lama to study at Rugby in England. He had graduated in electrical engineering from what is now the Imperial College of the University of London, and as the writer, Dundul Namgyal Tsarong, wrote, '. . . single-handedly took on a plan to build a hydroelectric plant at Dodé, three miles from Lhasa behind Sera Monastery . . . providing all of Lhasa City with electricity for the first time.' Of course, my mother had to show her new husband and baby around to her many relatives and friends, but she had mixed feelings about that. She had been a nun since childhood and had not quite gotten over the discomfort of having given up her spiritual vocation.

The journey from Kalimpong to Lhasa took around eighteen to twenty days, in easy stages of about twenty miles a day. Tibetans like to start early, preferably at the crack of dawn, ride briskly till noon, after which you found lodgings in a village or nomad encampment or, lacking that, select a good campsite and settle down for the rest of the day and for the night. The only memento I have of the journey is a photograph of my nanny at Gawu or Gautsa, a name that British Trade Agent David McDonald translates as the 'Meadow of Joy'. She is holding me on her lap, while her nephew Tsering Phuntsok is sitting beside her. Our ponies graze peacefully in the background before a distant waterfall.

Gawu is a fifteen-mile trip from the trade mart and customs post of Dromo or Yatung, which in Chinese means 'eastern trade-mart'. You ride up a valley of 'extraordinary steepness' on a stone track that follows the eastern tributary of the Amo River, '. . . a rushing mountain stream overhung with thickets of wild rose, daphne, and jasmine', till hours later you come up on a broad level tract of a meadow surrounded by fir-clad hills with snowy peaks beyond. The stream now meanders peacefully, '. . . through the verdant pasture which in most parts is carpeted with the cowslip-like blooms of *Primula Sikkimensis* and other flowers', as Spencer Chapman (who was part of a British mission to Lhasa) wrote. Phari, our next stop, was twenty-three miles away.

We arrived at Shigatse just when the barley fields were being harvested. We also attended the *Sigmo Chenmo*, or the 'Great Spectacle' at Tashi Lhunpo, the famous monastery of the Panchen Lamas. We stayed for a couple of months at the family estate of Kharag, about ten miles from Shigatse town with my uncle Tomjor, the head of the Tethong family, after which everyone departed for Lhasa—a week's journey from Shigatse.

We stayed at the family mansion at Banakzhöl, the eastern suburb of Lhasa. I was made much of by relatives, and taken by my nanny to all the many places of worship in and around Lhasa. Tibetans are diligent subscribers to auguries and omens, so my mother and nanny were pleased when a number of my visits to these holy sites, such as the Tashi Lhunpo monastery and Sera monastery, coincided most auspiciously with occasions of sacred food being distributed after special services and encounters with congregations of monks carrying bowls heaped with rich rice and raisin pudding; nothing extraordinary enough to warrant an investigation of my possibly being an incarnate lama, but sufficient to reassure our nanny and my mother that I was a blessed child.

I am told that I also attended the *Shoton* opera festival the next year at the Norbulingka, the Jewel Park and the Dalai Lama's summer palace. Tibetan operas are relaxed affairs lasting the entire day, from which babies, pet *apsos*, food, drink, and intermittent conversation (during the boring bits) are not prohibited. They are usually held in the open under an ornately decorated canopy, in August or September, when the flowers at Jewel Park and the Lhasa weather are both at their delightful best.

But dark storm clouds were already gathering at the far horizon of the arcadian Tibetan world. Though most people carried on with their regular lives in the same blissful ignorance as my burbling self, more astute individuals were beginning to hear disturbing accounts of the *Ulang Marpo*, or 'the Red Ulan' (an inadvertent tautology, '*ulan*' being the Mongol word for red). The Communists were winning the civil war in China and were making clear their intentions of 'liberating' Tibet.

In 1949, the Tibetan Foreign Bureau responded by sending a letter (with typed English translation) to "The Honourable Mr. Mautsetung" (sic), pointing out that "Tibet has from the earliest times up to now, been an Independent Country...(who) also defended her own territories from Foreign invations (sic) . . . and we would like to have an assurance that no Chinese troops would cross the Tibetan frontier.' The Foreign Bureau did not forget the Chinese-occupied regions of Kham and Amdo: 'As regards those Tibetan territories annexed as part of Chinese territories some years back, the Government of Tibet would desire to open negotiations after the settlement of the Chinese Civil War.'

In 1947, the creaky Tibetan government had sent a trade mission to India, Britain and the United States, to drum up some international support. A Washington journalist had dubbed it 'The Yak-Tail Mission'—it being one of the items of Tibetan export and used in the manufacture of Santa Claus beards and also as ceremonial whisks in Hindu and Sikh temples. In spite of the facetiousness of the Washington journalist, America did regularly import a substantial quantity of Tibetan wool.

Breaking further with its isolationist tradition, the Tibetan government also invited the journalist and radio commentator Lowell Thomas and his son for a visit. We encountered the Thomases on our way to Lhasa from Shigatse. Thomas senior had fractured his hip falling off his horse and was being carried by Tibetan porters on a makeshift stretcher on a long and somewhat painful journey back to India. They later made a documentary film (*Out of This World—My Journey to Lhasa*, in the brilliant Technicolor of yesteryear) which is now chiefly memorable for some achingly haunting scenes of old Tibet on the eve of its disappearance. The commentary has a very 'fifties' flavour to it, with lines about 'godless Communists' and the like. My favourite is the effusive description by Thomas junior of the Potala Palace as 'the penthouse of the gods'.

Around 8 p.m. on 15 August 1950, a year after the Thomases had left Lhasa, my nanny, Pema Tsewang, began crying out in her sleep that she was dying. I woke up and started howling as well. My mother rushed into the room and tried to reassure Pema Tsewang that she was all right and that we were only experiencing an earthquake. My mother picked me up from my cot and ran out on the terrace where her younger brother, Rakra Rimpoché, an incarnate lama, joined us. From the east of the city came loud detonations. My mother counted fourteen. A huge red glow became visible in the cloudless dark sky from the hills to the east of the city. The cooks and other servants had come out into the courtyard below and were all staring in the direction of the explosions. The earthquake had been entirely unexpected and violent, without any premonitory tremors. Everyone was terrified. People began to whisper about 'Lha-mak', a Tibetan Gotterdammerung or Ragnarok. The gods of Tibet were battling the Gya-dré demons of China, and the frightened Lhasa folk dared not presume as to the outcome.

Tibetan fears were magnified by the fact that no one had really seen a Communist before, and the more unsophisticated speculated whether such creatures would have fangs or horns. Simple Tibetans have never wavered in their belief that fabulous beings existed beyond the frontiers of their land, like those grotesques and monsters reported by such Greek travellers as Herodotus and Cteseas and which appear in the Liber Chronicarium and the Collectanea Rerum Memorabilium of Solinus. One such race with enormous ears, illustrated in their treatises, is familiar to Tibetans. It turns up as well in the Chinese Shan Hai Ching (Classics of the Mountains and Rivers), possibly the earliest travel book in the world (circa 500 BC). In the Tibetan description of this unique race, their ears, besides performing their usual auditory function, served their owners in other useful ways. One ear could be used as a sleeping mat and the other as a blanket.

The titanic scale and destructiveness of the earthquake certainly had an apocalyptic feel to it, though in Lhasa city itself, there was little damage done, only to an old public toilet collapsing in the Bharkor Circle. The epicentre was in southern Tibet, on the outskirts of the village of Rima, where mountains and valleys were displaced. Large rivers had their courses changed. Many villages and monasteries disappeared altogether. The plant hunter Frank Kingdon-Ward was in the area when the earthquake struck. In a *National Geographic Magazine* article, he wrote that the earthquake started exactly at 8 p.m. and also mentions the succession of detonations, which he thought '. . . sounded like *ack-ack* shells bursting'. The magnitude was 8.6 on the Richter scale. 'No stronger earth shock has been recorded since the use of seismographs for measuring them became general about the turn of the century.'

Evil portents were seen everywhere. An old family retainer on a trip to Phari claimed to have encountered a long caravan of silent, spectral people and animals leaving the country. Such stories became common. In one account, a person even saw a recently deceased relative in one of these phantom caravans. People gradually began to interpret such ghostly phenomena as a sign that the gods of Tibet had lost the great battle, and that our entire multi-dimensional world of men, gods, animals, phantoms and wraiths was now at the mercy of the evil from China. Ghosts being the most pathetic creatures in the realm of existence, they were, like rats from a sinking ship, deserting the country first.

Many people began to have strange dreams and reported unusual experiences, and fortune-tellers and mediums were in great demand. Before a nation or a community undergoes a devastating catastrophe, they sometimes seem to receive a premonition of their common fate, an experience that does not necessarily seem to be exclusive to primitive or ancient societies and individuals. A decade before Hitler came to power, Franz Kafka recorded a dream in which he and four others were dragging and pushing a giant naked man into a red-hot oven with an '. . . extraordinarily large cast iron door . . . I awoke not only in a cold sweat but with my teeth actually chattering.' Another entry from Kafka's diary: 'a faint greyish-smoke was lightly and continuously wafted from the chimney.'

The 'Smokey Long-Tailed Star' (as Tibetans call a comet) of 1949, a year before the earthquake, was the first sign for Tibetans that their future was becoming uncertain. It made its appearance at the time we arrived in Tibet and could be seen around dawn in the direction of the Mindruzari Mountain south of Lhasa. Like ancient Romans, Tibetans believed that the advent of a 'long-haired star' (as Suetonius describes the comet that presaged the death of Emperor Claudius) augured a national calamity. The fact that the earlier Chinese invasion of 1910 had been immediately preceded by the appearance of Haley's comet did not help matters. Besides, there were so many other omens—a glut of them, to drive home the point, as it were—that fear and uncertainty crept into the stoutest of hearts.

The well-known incident of a gargoyle on the roof of the Jokhang, the main temple in Lhasa, dripping water on a blazing hot day, also occurred around the time of the appearance of the comet. My uncle Sonam Tomjor, the head of the Tethong family, was a member of the commission sent by the Kashag, or cabinet, to investigate this phenomenon. Setting up ladders and scaffolding (used for the annual butter sculpture displays), the commission checked the roof and the guttering around the particular gargoyle—more properly a *chusing* (in Tibetan) or *makara* (in Sanskrit), a fabulous sea monster—and discovered everything to be bone dry. The head of the beast, fashioned of gilded copper, had not the least bit of condensation around it and the drops of water appeared only at one point directly under the chin. The hollow inside of the head was also bone dry. The commission dried the head a number of times with towels, only to observe the phenomenon occurring again. They collected three full buckets of water before the monster finally let up. My uncle was convinced that there was no rational explanation for this *lusus naturae* [a freak of nature].

Soon after fulfilling this official duty, my uncle, with his entire family, departed for India. My father also left with them. He had to travel to England that year to study for an engineering degree at Leeds. My mother stayed behind with her younger brother Rakra Rimpoché to wrap up the family business. The next year, a little more than a month after the great earthquake, my mother received telegrams from my father in England and my uncle in Kalimpong, urging her to leave Lhasa as quickly as possible. A year earlier, Communist China had begun to announce its mission to 'liberate' Tibet from British and American imperialism. Then a Chinese radio broadcast in May 1950 made it clear that military force would be used by the Communists to achieve their goal. My mother, my uncle Rakra Rimpoché and I left Lhasa on 10 September 1950.

A month later, on 7 October, the Chinese Communist army crossed the Dri-chu, the Upper Yangtse River, and attacked the Tibetan military headquarters at Chamdo and other defence outposts along the ceasefire line (known as *mentsam shagsa* in Tibetan) in Eastern Tibet—negotiated by my grandfather, Tethong Gyurme Gyatso (then Governor General of Eastern Tibet), in 1933. It had begun.

An Amcho's Recitation

Pema Bhum
Translated by Tenzin Dickie

In 1970, when I got into Malho Trik National Teacher's College, there were about sixty students in my class. To separate us into two sections, upper and lower, the school tested our Tibetan language and mathematics. I found the math test easy because it only tested addition and subtraction, multiplication and division. But I had trouble with the Tibetan test. There was only one part to it, a dictation of Lin Biao's introduction to the *Quotations from Chairman Mao Zedong*. We carried *Quotations from Chairman Mao* on our person at all times, no matter what we were doing. We needed to study the Little Red Book at least once every day and I could even recite many of the passages from it, word for word. But I had never read the introduction. During the test as soon as I heard the word 'introduction', I was totally confused. I still remember struggling to write 'introduction'. The teacher began, 'Comrade Mao Zedong is the greatest Marxist-Leninist of our era . . .' I tried my best to write down the words as I heard them.

The results were posted the next day. I had made it to the upper section. At the time, I could hardly believe that I had made it to the upper section when I couldn't even spell the word 'introduction' properly. Now, when I think back on this incident, it makes sense. All the students who sat for that test were around thirteen or fourteen years old. It was just as we were learning to read some Tibetan that the Cultural Revolution had begun and put a stop to our education. Most of us who were taking that test could barely get any words down on paper, let alone spell them correctly. The ones who could scrawl something must have made it to the lower section.

A few days after this test, we began our classes. But we had no textbooks for any of them. All the compositions of the great Tibetan scholars had been classified as 'poison'. Even the Tibetan-language textbooks compiled under Chinese government supervision before 1966 could not be used. Once again, the text that we used for our Tibetan-language class was *Quotations from Chairman Mao Zedong*. Soon after, the campaign to study Mao's three great essays was launched; these essays were titled 'Serve the People', 'Yugong Moves the Mountain', and 'In Memory of Norman Bethune'. So, we had to study these essays for a while in our Tibetan-language class. As soon as this campaign was over, the campaign to study Chairman Mao's *Five Essays on Philosophy* swept the country. The essays were as follows: 'On Practice', 'On Contradictions', 'On the Correct Handling of Contradictions Among the People', 'Speech at the Chinese Communist Party's National Conference on Propaganda Works', and 'Where do Correct Ideas Come From?' The school began using these essays as our textbooks for the class. The school had three different grades at the time but students in all three grades used the same textbook. The first essay, *On Practice*, was the text that we had to study and our teacher was to be Sir Dorje Tsering.

It was Sir Doring who taught us Tibetan for the first time. My memories of that first day when he came to teach our class are as vivid as if it were yesterday. When he stepped inside the classroom, we collectively sucked in our breath and stopped breathing, so awed and intimidated were we by his fame and his majesty. We all sat up straight in our chairs and waited breathlessly for his first words to us. Sir Doring put down his copy of Chairman Mao's *Five Essays on Philosophy* on the desk, looked at us and said,

'It smells of shit in here. Open the windows.'

Not sure what he meant, some of us just looked at each other. Others stared at him, waiting for him to say more.

'Did you all hear me? Open the windows,' repeated Sir Doring. The students who sat near the windows quickly opened them.

'If you must smoke, go and smoke in the toilets, inhaling the smell of piss and shit as you do so. Cigarette smoke in the classroom stings my nose and mouth, and I can hardly read a book in here.' Then we understood that by the smell of 'shit,' he meant the smell of cigarettes.

A few students in our class smoked, sneaking in their smoking inside the classroom between breaks. As it were, students weren't allowed to smoke in school. The other teachers, when they found us smoking, punished us by giving us a long lecture. Of course, the teachers had gotten used to giving this lecture and the students had gotten used to hearing it. Sir Doring's way of scolding the students who smoked was so novel that it confused us at first.

Now Sir Doring called out some names and had these students read out a few lines from 'On Practice'. One or two of them, thinking that a quick reading would impress the teacher, read hastily, tripping over some words and mispronouncing others in their nervousness. If it were another teacher, they would have stopped the student, corrected them and given them a scolding all in one go, but not Sir Doring. He listened to all the students one by one without stopping them.

Then he asked, 'Do you guys know what an *amcho* is?'

Maybe the other students didn't know what an amcho was. They just looked at each other and no one said anything. I knew that an amcho was a monk who went to people's houses to read scripture, but was that the answer Sir Doring was looking for? I wasn't sure so I kept quiet.

No one answered. Sir Doring said, 'An amcho is a monk who reads scripture in people's houses.' I felt very sorry that I had not given the answer when I had it. Sir Doring continued, 'When the amcho reads a scripture at people's houses, it is not necessary for the host to hear and comprehend the words. Often, it is not even necessary for the amcho himself to hear and comprehend what he is reading. In fact, the faster an amcho reads, the more skilled he is considered to be.' Now we understood what he was saying—we read like amchos.

Next, Sir Doring wanted to give us a dictation. He told us to mark the words we didn't understand. After he finished dictating, he wanted us to tell him all the words we didn't know.

He read very slowly. His voice wasn't loud, but he spoke each word very clearly, as if he wanted us to hear that this was the way to read and not the way of the amcho. As he read, his voice sounded dewy and full-throated, as if a lump of saliva had lodged in his throat. I kept wondering why he wouldn't just swallow the saliva and then read.

After Sir Doring finished reading several passages, we gave him some words that we didn't know like 'explanation' and 'retinue'. Then he said, 'These are the only words that you don't know?' Nobody answered him, and the classroom went very quiet.

'I don't know more words in this essay than you guys,' said Sir Doring. 'Who can explain these terms to me?' He listed a bunch of revolutionary terms—society, economy, class, production. We came across these terms at least once every day, either in our books or in our lives but there was not a single one of us who could explain what they meant. We sat there dumb and silent.

Garpon La's Offerings

Tsering Woeser

Translated by Dechen Pemba and Fiona Sze-Lorrain

I didn't know him personally, but I've heard many stories about Garpon La. There are even more that I haven't heard, and in fact some people emphatically and even angrily say that the Garpon La I've heard stories about isn't the one who went to Dharamsala and the Garpon La who did go to Dharamsala isn't the same Garpon La I've heard about. A bit like a brain teaser, it's enough to make you dizzy.

Added to this is the fact that I'm using the honorific term *La* to refer to the person whose story I want to tell, though I don't actually know if I should, and the question doesn't really matter to me anyway. Honestly, I am not even that interested in sorting out one Garpon La from another. This is probably a mistake. By not doing much research, I have to rely on my memory. However, while the obstacles I've created for myself are troubling, I don't intend to talk about Garpon La's life and achievements anyway; they aren't important. That is, they're not important to this story. After all, I'm not writing his biography; I just want to talk about one incident.

I should also say that these events occurred during a confusing time. That doesn't mean I've forgotten things, but it's possible that the story has become muddled. I've told and retold it on ten or more occasions. Every time I tell it, the regret that weighs on my heart becomes heavier.

I remember the bright, summer afternoon sunshine two years ago and the homey atmosphere of a certain Tibetan restaurant in Unity Village. Flowers in full bloom lined the windows, and through the flowers, I could see people outside playing music on the *dramnyen* (Tibetan lute) and singing *Jha Dhey Karpo* (White Bird).' They played very loudly, which at first didn't seem to fit this nostalgic scene, but that's all right. Garpon La's disciples were robust, and their big voices clanged like a huge bell, just the way slow Gar music (music composed for the Dalai Lama) is supposed to sound. At that time, Garpon La was no longer young: his hair was greying, and he had retired. Thinking of him now, I feel regret because I promised him I would write down the stories he told me about incidents in Lhasa. But I've procrastinated until many of the stories seem like floating clouds at the end of the world, gradually fading into a mist.

Not so long ago, a dusty book fell from my bookshelf and practically landed in my hands. I took it as a sign that, no matter what, I must finally write down this story. That book was crudely manufactured, with no serial number or publisher's markings except for one line in Chinese, on the back: printed by Tibet Xinhua Publishing House. Everything else was in Tibetan. The cover had been designed using Tibetan colours and patterns, which, like the Tibetan script, appeared to be dancing. Because of the story I'm about to tell, I now recognize that the eight-petal, red-and-blue lotus flowers on the book's cover are bunched together to represent a *damma* drum. And below the figure of the eight auspicious signs and what looks like clouds are two Tibetan *suna* [oboes]. The damma drum and suna were brought to Tibet a long time ago and used in Gar court songs and dance performances.

This book, titled *Songs and Dances for Offerings*, was published in 1985 and contains musical scores and lyrics for fifty-eight Gar performances. It had belonged to my father's collection of Tibetan books. He had served in the army all his life—as would be expected, given the period in which he lived—and he loved Tibetan revolutionary songs in the style of *toeshey*, *gorshey* and *nangma*, as well as Gar and all popular folk and love songs from Ü-Tsang Province. Among his books were numerous musical journals, all of which still exhaled the atmosphere of the times. I brought all of them to Beijing with me, where they took up over a meter's worth of space on my bookshelf. *Songs and Dances for Offerings* was one of the volumes I hadn't gotten around to browsing.

As soon as I opened the book, I was enormously excited to see a photograph of Garpon La. Yes, it really was Garpon La, sitting on a simple chair and holding a suna in his hands. Behind his glasses, his eyes looked old and somewhat anxious. From the surroundings, I could tell that the photograph was taken in the People's Stadium of Lhasa. Situated near the banks of the Kyichu River, the area had once been verdant and lush. From the 1950s, it became the place where tens of thousands of people gathered for political assemblies—to celebrate the Cultural Revolution, for instance, which was then sweeping through Lhasa. It was also the place for big demonstrations denouncing the American imperialist invasion of Vietnam, and for the noisy public trials of 'anti-revolutionary elements', people who were counter revolutionary criminals.

Of course, in the photograph, the stadium was silent. The grounds were empty and overgrown with weeds. Garpon La appeared to be sitting alone. He was smiling in an elegant, very Lhasa way that belonged to the Lhasa of times past. I could tell it was a smile from Lhasa's past, even though the photograph was taken before I was born—it expressed an old-fashioned, illusory gaiety. The impression of the past was emphasized by the ornate clothing Garpon La was wearing: the flat, round cap, the long earring dangling from his left ear, the golden-yellow brocade gown over pure-white collar and sleeves, and the red boots with blue soles. The clothing had been specially made, but when I first saw the photograph, I knew nothing about the reasons he was dressed in such a way. For example, it appeared to me that he was wearing the gold-and-turquoise earrings called *sochen*, even though such jewellery was only worn by aristocrats, high officials and, occasionally, wealthy businessmen. His outfit seemed to come from a time long before the 1980s—when the photograph was taken—and of course from long before 2009 when I first saw it. Nevertheless, Garpon La looked stunning beyond compare—an impression that is hard to describe. Behind him on the rostrum, bulky blood-red pillars had been pushed together. They struck me as rude and inappropriate. I felt them stabbing at my eyes, and I was suddenly overcome by sorrow.

Even a short introduction in a book can reveal a lot of information. This was the case with *Songs and Dances for Offerings*, with its brief introduction to the Fourteenth Dalai Lama's eleven-member dance troupe. After a few pages, only bits of information about the troupe emerged, such as the number of members and their ages. There wasn't a lot, but at the time it probably wasn't safe to write much more. The introduction seemed to be quite ordinary, even mediocre. Nevertheless, much information was hidden between the lines. These nuances could only be understood by another Tibetan, who would discern from just a glance what was really being said, what happened when and where. Many Tibetan readers experienced the hardship and torment the troupe endured before they had at last survived the disasters in their lives. Anyone who hasn't experienced similar torments will find it hard to read between the lines of the writing and know what the men went through. That's why a narrator like me is needed, who is at some distance from the incidents but is sympathetic to their reality and able to retell the story. I must say, though, that the only reason I am able to enter, even temporarily, the collective memory of these events is because of the help I've received from those who survived.

Take, for example, what the introduction says about Garpon Pasang Dhondup. He joined the Gar Song and Dance Troupe at age nine. At twenty-one, he served as a Gar musician, having mastered many instruments. At thirty-two, he became the head Gar musician and was given the title Garpon (Master). At forty-three, he upheld the 'Democratic Reforms.' At that point, the introduction doesn't reveal that the year was 1959, or say what happened next. Twenty-two years of his life are omitted without comment. Suddenly the year is 1981, and we learn that Garpon Pasang Dhondup participated in the first TAR (Tibet Autonomous Region) Conference on Literatures and Arts, reintroducing Gar to the agenda. The section on him concludes by saying that at the age of sixty-four, in 1982, he was absorbed in saving the Gar tradition, whose transmission had almost come to an end.

So, where was Garpon La during those twenty-two years? And what about the other members of the Gar Song and Dance Troupe? It seems as if each of them was also lost for twenty-two years as if they had all evaporated, disappeared without a trace. I don't know if the others in the troupe shared a similar experience, but according to what his students told me on that summer afternoon in Unity Village, Garpon La was arrested by the People's Liberation Army, charged with being an 'insurgent', imprisoned and later sent to the 're-education through labour camp' in Gormo. Prisoners in that camp constructed railways and the Qinghai–Tibet Highway. But how many years was he there? How many other people were in the camp and how long were their sentences? History becomes very murky here. Nobody seems to have any answer. We only know that Garpon La was amongst the very few who—old, weak, sick, and injured—came back from the Gormo labour camp alive.

Before going on, I should explain a little about what Gar is. As I mentioned earlier, Gar is a form of Tibetan court song and dance performance. Over four centuries ago, it came directly to the Tibetan court from the kingdom of Ladakh, when the Fifth Dalai Lama was enthroned. Gar was thereafter regarded as sacred music dedicated to the Dalai Lama and performed only during special, high ceremonies. According to the book, *The Auspicious Banquet for Heart, Ear, and Eyes*, the most important score in Gar music is 'Lucky, Happy, Plentiful'. The lyrics go roughly like this:

> The vast beautiful empty sky of today overhead,
> the fortunate earth is happy,
> here is a lucky, happy, and plentiful time,
> beginning songs and dances of offering,
> dedicated to the enlightened sage,
> all-knowing ocean of wisdom,
> field of happiness, King of Dharma,
> respect and admiration for the sacred ruler.

Other important musical scores include 'Sacred Land of Lhasa,' 'Rays of the Sun,' 'Reverent Prostrations,' 'Cloud Offering,' and 'Star in the Sky.'

The Gar court troupe consisted of thirteen boys, chosen from very good backgrounds, who were trained from a young age with meticulous care. People from Lhasa speak of their having 'an honourable and glorious obligation' because they performed for the Dalai Lama at all kinds of ceremonies, celebrations and meetings. They praised the deities and Gongsachog (Dalai Lama) with sparkling, clear songs and regal dancing. Each artist wore beautifully-coloured costumes, resembling those worn by the celestial beings depicted in the murals. Lhasa people said, 'It's only those fortunate women who can win the hearts of performers with Changdi clothes.' Of course, they had to wait until the pure children had been transformed by their training into splendid and good-looking performing artistes. When the boys reached the age of eighteen, they would have to return to society and assume a role in the secular world.

All that belonged to Old Tibet, however. People in New Tibet, such as myself, have only heard songs and seen dances performed by the Tibetan opera troupe or by performers in nangma. Unfortunately, these performances are too embedded in secular values and influence to be pure. The earliest nangma emerged around the 1990s. At the time, it was still worth going to see them. Many old people performed traditional toeshey, gorshey and nangma, and people in the audience were allowed to go on the stage and dance. I've taken my mother and aunts to the nangma performed today. My uncle, who trained as a dancer, came along with us once, examined everything with a critical eye, and said in a dissatisfied voice that things had already changed for the worse. I wouldn't know what the real thing was like, but it was still enchanting when my mother and aunts were gracefully singing and dancing. It's true, though, that you don't need to be an expert to see that today's nangma dances are simply a nauseating mixture of Chinese and Tibetan pop music, performed by degenerate men and women—nothing more. Fortunately, the nangma dances do not attempt to include Gar. Reduced to such circumstances, Gar would be an omen of catastrophe.

But I must return to the Garpon La story. I'm always like this: I mean to say one thing, but then start going on about something else. It's really a bit embarrassing.

After Garpon Pasang Dhondup La survived the hellish Gormo labour camps, he returned to an unrecognizable Lhasa. The sight was terribly disheartening. At the time, the popular saying was, 'Many things are waiting to be done.' This meant that the catastrophe was over, everything could start anew, including the recovery of things—such as Gar—that had been treated as 'feudal superstition' and swept into the dustbin of history by the Cultural Revolution. However, even in the big city of Lhasa, Gar had disappeared. Feeling guilty, the Party and the government repeatedly asked Garpon La to come out of retirement and restore Gar. But he refused. People say that Garpon La pointed to the scars on his body and very politely said, 'Sorry. Because the "re-education through labour" I received at Gormo was so thorough, I've completely forgotten Gar.' Listening to him explain this repeatedly, with his scars looking ever more shocking, the Party and the government became too embarrassed to continue bothering him. They were trying to improve their image around this time.

In the 1980s, the first official contact began between Beijing and Dharamsala. Separated for twenty years, Tibetans inside and outside the country gained a little more freedom of movement. I don't know what brought luck to Garpon La, but when he applied for a passport that would permit him to visit relatives in Nepal or some other country, it was granted to him. I should note that India was not among the countries Tibetans were allowed to visit—a strict rule that continues today. Nevertheless, when Tibetans wish to travel abroad, their final destination is usually India—Dharamsala, in the northern part of India, to be exact. There is only one reason for wanting to go to Dharamsala: to meet the Dalai Lama. Actually, this is hardly any big secret.

Summarizing all the details, I'll just say that Garpon La eventually went to Dharamsala and saw Kundun (the Dalai

Lama). Coincidentally, that was Kundun's twenty-fourth year in exile, his *ka* year—when one is prone to bad luck. Garpon La was past middle age and had dedicated splendid Gar to Kundun numerous times. With deep respect, he had watched the challenges that the God-King had faced during his life. And now he was in a foreign country where he hoped once again to see him; to Garpon La, there was no miracle more impermanent than meeting Kundun. My own Buddhist master used to tell me, 'Suffering is impermanent, happiness is impermanent.' What an honest and true saying.

Once he was before the Dalai Lama, Garpon La couldn't help bursting into tears. People say he sobbed and pleaded, 'Kundun, please give permission to this troupe-of-one to make offerings to Kundun with Gar. For more than two decades, this body hasn't been used to express Gar. It has been waiting for this day to once more be used in dedication to Kundun.'

I don't know whether the Dalai Lama, during his long years of exile, was likely to have an appreciation for Gar, once called 'delightful to the eye'. After all, when the Dalai Lama departed Lhasa, the Gar troupe was shut down within days. What the Chinese could seize was seized, what could be shut down was shut down and what could be scattered was scattered. Had there been another Gar troupe that could follow Kundun into exile to Dharamsala? At this moment, the ageing Garpon La—who for more than twenty years had been cut off from Gar—was alone, surrounded entirely by exiles. And yet he wanted to make traditional offerings to His Holiness.

People say that when Garpon La started tapping the damma drum and singing with his desolate voice, the sounds of crying and weeping filled the house, enclosing the air of a foreign country but smelling of the incense of Lhasa. And His Holiness also quietly shed tears. Afterwards, people say, Garpon La announced, in effect, that by having dedicated Gar to Kundun for the final time, he had been granted the wish that kept him alive during his many years of hard labour. So from then on, he would only perform Gar songs in the heavens, even if it meant allowing Gar to disappear from the earth. He would rather risk the danger that Gar would become a lost tradition than perform Gar again in the secular world.

His Holiness closed his eyes slightly, seeming to quell the flood of his emotions. After remaining motionless for a while, he slowly began speaking. He said that he did not quite agree with Garpon La. Not only did he disagree, but he also obligated Garpon La to return to Lhasa and to transform Gar into a ceremony for the public to see. 'You have to perform again,' Kundun said. 'In fact, you will go back to Lhasa and accept the invitation of the Party and government to restore Gar. You will also recruit a number of Tibetan boys and teach them. You can make reforms by teaching Gar to Tibetan girls. In short, no matter the obstacles, you must not let Gar disappear.'

I've quoted His Holiness's statement to Garpon La as if I were present at the scene. I did this in order to make the story more dramatic. In any event, according to Garpon La, he regarded what was said to him as a perfect teaching that effectively changed his life. When he returned to Lhasa, it was like a miracle. Almost overnight, the entire city knew what had happened: that, unexpectedly, the nearly forgotten Gar had been recalled into existence; that Gar, once banished like Garpon La, was returning to Lhasa. This news was a source of joy. This return of Gar made Garpon La so happy that he let bygones be bygones. The stigma of 'insurgent' given to him by the Party was washed from his records. He received awards and became a famous court musician. As a celebrated expert in Gar, he was also given the title Professor of Music by Tibet University. How dramatic all this was! Having suffered torment for so long, in his final years, he radiated with glory in the brilliance of 'New Tibet'.

People say it was as though a tree made of iron had suddenly blossomed with flowers, as though a mute had begun to speak when Garpon La gathered his troupe in front of the Party's cultural officials and began to beat the damma drum. That voice of desolation sang without hurry:

> Beginning songs and dances of offering,
> dedicated to the enlightened sage,
> all-knowing ocean of wisdom,
> field of happiness, King of Dharma,
> respect and admiration for the sacred ruler.

I'm absolutely certain that nobody in the audience had ears in the least bit qualified to listen respectfully to Gar. During the previous decades, their ears had become tarnished and stuffed with earwax. How could they appreciate this devotional, beautiful, splendid music of compassion, of *nying-je*? Consequently, Garpon La turned his gaze inward, into the centre of the void, as though he hoped to see the Dharamsala in his mind, with Kundun nodding his head and smiling, intoxicated by the spiritual music coming from Lhasa. Garpon La couldn't help but shed tears.

Music from suffering, the true meaning of impermanence in *dharma*, was once again heard in the world. No doubt Garpon La had mixed feelings. He became more meticulous and devoted to his work. In the last years of his life, on the eve of leaving this world and rushing towards rebirth, he turned to modern science and technology. He recorded dozens of Gar songs on compact discs (CDs), which could be reproduced countless times. Heavenly music for the benefit of all sentient beings, including me, a lost sheep. Nowadays, having transferred all these Gar songs on my iPhone, I can listen to them whenever and wherever I want. Sacred Gar music has joined a myriad of other songs to last forever in the secular world. For this reason, I want to pay tribute to Garpon La. Because of Gar, he may have already been reincarnated into a deity, his thousand arms extended, and a thousand bright eyes looking over Avalokiteshvara's pure earth as he continues to make his indescribably beautiful offerings. *Kunchok Sum!*

Calcutta Evening

Ann Tashi Slater

My mother and I get take-out momos and chow mein from a restaurant near my aunt's apartment by the old Theatre Road renamed Shakespeare Sarani after Independence in 1947. We eat at the polished mahogany dining table, just the two of us because my aunt and uncle left for London this morning. Geckos click and the all-day cacophony of car horns subsides as darkness falls. Wearing a red tank top and jeans, my mother looks far younger than her almost eighty years. She's quiet, gazing downward as she eats; watching her, I feel the ache of the loss her presence promises. There won't be so many more meals like this—my mother and I on a quiet evening. Maybe this will be the last time we're together in India.

I attempt a conversation. 'How are the momos?', 'Is the weather usually this hot in Calcutta?', 'Do you feel ready to go to Darjeeling tomorrow?' But my mother's replies are monosyllabic. She seemed especially exhausted today when we visited the eighteenth-century mansion of poet and 1913 Nobel Laureate Rabindranath Tagore. We examined photos of Tagore with Einstein, Helen Keller, and Gandhi; strolled through a courtyard where musicians once played ragas on moonlit nights. My mother grew tired and sank into a chair in an alcove, fanning herself with her guidebook. 'I'm melting in this heat,' she sighed. 'You go on without me.' Leaving her to rest, I continued touring the house. I learned of Tagore's connection to Japan: in 1908, he met Ekai Kawaguchi, a Buddhist monk who was the first Japanese known to have travelled to Tibet and Nepal, and Tagore visited Japan often, exchanging ideas with fellow intellectuals and artists. 'The finest revelation of Japan,' Tagore proclaimed, 'is not of pride and vainglory, but of renunciation.' This reminded me of the Jain festival we had happened upon the previous week in Delhi, of the woman at the festival who had fasted for eight days. It made me feel that on this pilgrimage with my mother back to her hometown of Darjeeling, renunciation is the task before me, and I wondered what I'm meant to give up. When I returned to the alcove, my mother was still in the chair, her head against the wall and mouth open. I hurried towards her, but coming close, saw she was breathing, sweat glistening on her face. Gently, I shook her awake. 'This heat is enervating,' she said.

'I thought you'd be used to it since you grew up here.'

'Not anymore. And Darjeeling is much cooler because it's up in the mountains.' This partly explains why she settled in northern California so many years ago and loves living there. As in her Himalayan hometown, the Bay Area mornings are often cold and misty, moisture dripping from the trees.

My mother finishes her last momo and stands. 'I'm going to retire. It's been a long day.' Slowly, she walks down the hall to the bedroom.

I take the dishes to the kitchen and start washing them. Air conditioners hum and there's the clink of China as, two stories down, a sinewy man in an undershirt, a plaid sarong knotted at his waist, rinses plates in the alley. Above, in the blue-black sky, a waxing, three-quarter moon bobs next to a solitary star.

The sorrow of things seeps through me. Somewhere here in this city is the hotel where, in 1980, my grandfather had a heart attack, after he and my grandmother had gone out for dinner with friends. He drank too much that night, my grandmother told me, his sadness about the children—all five of them settling abroad, the recent death of their youngest daughter in her forties—overcoming him in old age. Determined that if it was his time, he pass away in Darjeeling so the proper Tibetan rites would be carried out, my grandmother rushed him home and he died a few days later.

I see California's fog-shrouded hills, grey waves rolling in endlessly on the wide, empty beaches where my mother used to take us after she and my father split up; see my mother walking down a Calcutta street in her Eddie Bauer sun hat, looking like a stranger in her own land. I feel the melancholy of this city that, with its dilapidated buildings and raucous crows, its dusky tropical air, embodies absence and memory. I see my mother in the bedroom, the overhead fan whirring, the mosquito net swaying like a wraith in the dim light. What would she have thought if someone had told her as she set off for medical school in America that almost sixty years later, she'd be a divorced, retired doctor living in California, back in India on this hot, still night with her American daughter?

In the living room, I switch on the British Broadcasting Corporation news and flop down on the couch with a bag of chilly-spiced potato chips. The BBC programme is relaxing in a way American news shows are not, the reporters' crisp accents and no-nonsense delivery making it seem as if all is, if not well, at least being taken in hand. It was the same when I stayed with my Tibetan grandmother in Darjeeling after college and we'd listen to the BBC on the radio after dinner, the crackly, reassuring voices bringing news of the world's upheavals into the cosy room high in the Himalayas. Propping her short, wide feet on the wall next to the coal fire, my grandmother followed the broadcast intently, frowning with concentration. Did I think Reagan was going to be a good president, she wanted to know, and what was my view of Thatcher? It was terrible about all the people starving in Ethiopia—as a Buddhist, she wished she could do something to help.

Tonight, there's a story about Australian cricket and a hurricane bearing down on Haiti. Poland's last Communist leader is in court, a fire has broken out in the Chunnel, and a new government is taking shape in Zimbabwe. There's trouble in Thailand: the Prime Minister is being forced to resign for hosting some cooking shows. Is this such a dreadful crime? It seems it is: the anchor briskly points out that it *does* contravene the Thai Constitution.

Relieved to just stare at the screen, I watch ads for shiny hair, glowing skin, and credit cards; channel surf to a Paris fashion show and Snoop Dogg's *Singh Is King* music video. My mother isn't the only one who's tired. She keeps waking me: snoring, rummaging through her bags in the middle of the night (what is she looking for?), starting conversations with me in the dawn hours while I'm still asleep. And my feet are sore from walking day after day in the heat and monsoonal rain through Delhi, Dharamsala and Calcutta. Will I have enough energy left for Darjeeling? I miss my husband and children, the peace and order of my life in Tokyo, the quiet hours in my study reading and writing. And this trip with my mother is reviving long-forgotten memories of childhood: my frustration over the distance between us, the fallout from my parents' bitter divorce, and the ethnic and racial isolation I felt growing up in predominantly white communities in the US.

Why did I decide to accompany my mother on this journey? There's a reason I've spent most of my adult life in Japan, far from our complicated relationship and my girlhood miseries. But when my mother asked me to come with her to India, I worried I'd regret not helping her make one last visit home. And even though she frets that I've turned out 'too American', she's managed to instil in me an Asian filial piety that made me feel it was my duty to go with her.

East West masala, Singh is the king, so you all have to follow . . . Snoop Dogg and a stunning Indian woman are dancing against a Taj Mahal backdrop.

I make myself a gin and tonic and stroll around the apartment. The Italian marble floor is wonderfully cool under my bare feet. My aunt and uncle have exquisite taste: there are painted Chinese screens and carved cabinets, beautifully detailed Tibetan *thangka* scroll paintings and plush Tibetan rugs. Framed lithographs of eighteenth-century Calcutta adorn the walls, depictions of the East India Company building in Leadenhall Street; a woman and child squatting next to a hut under a palm tree; a black elephant caparisoned in red and gold, bracelets around its ankles. And there are maps: 'Northern Hindostan, India—the Eastern Provinces (with The Island of Ceylon),' 'Nepaul' 'Bengal—Mouths of the Ganges'.

I study the rivers emptying into the Bay of Bengal and the Indian Ocean; envision the dark, silent tide of the waters flowing down from Tibet. After my grandparents were cremated, their ashes were scattered in the Teesta River near Darjeeling, to float down to the Brahmaputra and the Ganges, and then to the sea. I feel the rivers coursing from the north, from the Himalayas and the Tibetan plateau, their primaeval, ceaseless current like the flow of the blood of the ancestors, the blood in the veins of a deity overlying this ancient landscape. The rivers are roads emanating from the centre of a mandala in an intricate geography that, like the inner architecture of a mandala, is only accessible to those in the right frame of mind.

Why do we become fascinated with rivers and, even more, with their origins? We feel an atavistic impulse to know where they—and we—have come from, to push towards the source. And the ineluctable being-ness of a river draws us, the tension between fixed presence and constant flux.

The glass-fronted bookcase in the living room holds volumes on Asian history, economics, and politics. There's William Dalrymple's *City of Djinns*, Pico Iyer's *The Global Soul*, Geoffrey Moorhouse's *Calcutta*. I leaf through Sudha Koul's *The Tiger Ladies*, her account of growing up in Kashmir and emigrating to the US when she married. In her elegy for a vanished way of life, Koul writes, 'We come from a place (Kashmir) where people hardly think of even their grown children as separate persons, with different goals for their well-being. Here (in America) every new baby is an individual, and we have to explain ourselves to our children. They think they are free and don't know that eventually, they will come looking for us, and for those before us. No one is really free, and it has nothing to do with being Indian.'

I have indeed come looking for my mother, and for those before her. Instead of moving to Paris after college as I'd intended, I set off for Darjeeling. Then, as my mother did, I travelled to a new land—Japan—and never came back (did I think that following in her tracks would help me better understand her, or myself?). I've spent years of my adult life researching and writing about my Tibetan family history, caught up in a slow archaeology of interviewing and reading, of unearthing files and letters and photographs. Moving forward through the years, I've travelled back in time and memory—my mother's, my grandmother's, and my own. When I was a girl, I often wished I'd sprung spontaneously into existence, unburdened by the family sadness and the alienation I felt as a Tibetan American in 1960s and 1970s America. But growing older, I'm starting to understand. In America, the land of freedom and reinvention of self, we're taught we are *tabula rasa*: we can be anything or anyone we want. We learn to go outward, not inward. This makes it easy to forget we're already shaped— and being shaped—by our parents and grandparents, by all our ancestors.

I want to know my mother's story so it, and she, won't be forgotten. I want my daughter to know where she comes from, to inherit my mother's strength and passion for life, as well as grow up free of the inheritance of emotional distance that's been handed down. But here in Calcutta, as I've asked my mother about her girlhood days—over coconut prawns at Oh! Calcutta restaurant, while shopping at New Market—she's grown increasingly quiet. I feel a mounting dread: when my mother dies, everything I don't know about her will be lost.

When I left for college, my mother gave me a tear-shaped turquoise pendant that her father gave her when she flew to America. The pendant is the cyan blue of the sky arcing over the Tibetan plateau, over the snowy peaks of Mount Kanchenjunga that tower above Darjeeling. Turquoise symbolizes the sea and the heavens, and, because it can change colour, the circle of life. It's said to lend protection on a journey. I imagine my grandfather picking it out in one of the old shops at Darjeeling's Chowrasta town square. I see him giving it to my mother, the first of his children to go abroad, on a cold December evening in Calcutta, the moon setting over the Hooghly River. On the desk in their room at the Great Eastern Hotel was a telegram from my mother's brother Kesang: 'BEST OF LUCK SAFE JOURNEY'. My mother's Samsonite suitcase lay open on the bed, packed with long Tibetan *chuba* dresses and Kashmiri shawls, Darjeeling tea and *khata* blessing scarves to give as gifts to her American sponsors. Winter was the pilgrimage season and she was about to undertake a new journey that was also one of the oldest, the voyage made mythic by all who had set out from home in search of a different life.

The next morning, my mother and her parents headed for the airport in the pre-dawn fog, my grandparents dispensing last-minute instructions and advice. My mother was to purchase air tablets when she arrived in Bombay if she experienced motion sickness and warm socks if she found the airplane cabin chilly. She must write as often as possible and if there was any matter for which she required guidance, she must let them help from their end. At 8 a.m., the Trans World Airlines plane lifted off into the clearing sky and my grandparents waved from the aerodrome as their daughter was launched into the wider world. They never dreamed that they wouldn't see her for twelve long years, and only then when she returned with her American husband and two little girls for a visit.

In giving me the pendant, was my mother entrusting me with her story? I had been a difficult child, always ready to argue with her. Yet, somehow, she knew I would care—more than my siblings, and maybe even more than she herself. Perhaps it was a way of giving me what she had no other way of giving me and what she herself didn't want to hold on to. Not only was she happy to leave behind Darjeeling's antediluvian ideas about girls (though she'd find it hard to break this legacy with her three daughters), but as a divorced mother of four and the sole breadwinner, she had neither the time nor the energy to look into the past.

What might my life have been if I weren't the excavator and guardian of the family stories? For me, it's been a push and pull: the urge to escape all the little and not-so-little crimes and tragedies of family and childhood life and, at the same time, find my way to the source.

I walk over to the tall windows. In the apartment building across the way, lights go on and off as people move about. A man enters a room, sits on the sofa with a drink, and contemplates a floor-to-ceiling painting of a woman's face. Down at street level, laundry hangs outside a shed next to the building; on the roof of the shed, a ginger cat lounges, tail flicking. Like the cat, I watch and listen, alert for a shift in the terrain, for signs and openings in the night.

The Prince of Tibet

Chhimi Tenduf-la

It is June 2009 and the civil war in Sri Lanka has just ended. I am nursing a cool beer at the Colombo Swimming Club bar when I see a notorious gangster's son speaking to my brother. He moves on, and I think nothing more of it. Two beers later, the gangster's son approaches me.

'Where are you from?'

I stand to attention through fear that anything less may lead to certain death. 'I am half Tibetan and half English,' I say.

The gangster's son slaps my back. 'No way.' He points to my brother. 'That dude is also from Tibet and England. You should meet him.' He bows to me and lifts his hands in prayer, a sign of reverence for a Tibetan Buddhist culture even the underworld admires. 'Give me your phone number and I shall visit you there.'

I jot down a made-up number without bothering to explain that I do not live in Tibet. I do not explain that I, like my late father, who was commissioned to write a book called *I am a Tibetan* many years ago, have never been there. I do not bother to explain that my Tibetan family moved to Darjeeling long before I was born and that I, like the gangster's son, have not met many other Tibetans at least in the last twenty years.

I was born in London, moved to Hong Kong, moved back to London and then to Delhi before settling in Colombo. I went to Eton College, a boarding school in the United Kingdom, where I was a year junior to the prince of Nepal, who went on to gun down his entire family many years later. Word spread that I was the prince of Tibet because Eton attracted that sort; as a Tibetan, I was much rarer than a prince at that school. My denials only built up the façade. 'He is undercover,' some said. The history geeks would suggest that, because of the Chinese rule, I was a prince in exile. When I went to stay at friends' houses for half term, their parents would bow to me and call me, 'Your Highness'. My best friends knew I was far from a prince, but they loved telling their parents otherwise and the joke was often too far-developed for me to ruin the punch line with the truth.

As far as I am aware, there is no royalty in Tibet, but no one bothered to look that up. It seems my Tibetan family was privileged and well-known, but that was nothing out of the ordinary for Eton. I was surrounded by the offspring of royalty, aristocracy or the famous—Jeffrey Archer's son took a particular interest in my background. Introducing myself as half Tibetan, half English, and living in Sri Lanka sounded rather glamorous, especially when people whispered that I was also a prince. You would think this might make me a hit with the girls at Eton, but sadly there were none.

I was in the same year group as all of the most well-known English establishment families, so I might have felt out of place. However, the mystique of Tibet held me in good stead there and has continued to do so wherever I go. Saying my late father was from Tibet is one hell of a conversation starter. People always have so many questions. I, however, have few answers.

* * *

It is January 2015 and my first book, *The Amazing Racist*, has been released in India. I am being interviewed by various news outlets and soon my Facebook account is flooded with new friend requests from people with names I recognize, even though I have no idea why. These are Tibetans, seemingly happy to see one of their own getting a fair amount of press.

It is June 2016, and I am at a kid's party with my daughter when I am introduced to a lovely couple. The father is clearly German and the mother is a bubbly, charming Asian lady. She asks where I am from and I give her the standard, 'I am half English, half Tibetan' line.

'No, you're not,' she says. Everyone around us seems to stop talking. 'You are half English, half Chinese.'

I look at her husband, who shrugs his shoulders and mouths, 'Sorry.'

'Anyway,' his wife says with her knockout smile. 'I am from China, too.' With that out of the way, we go on to have a jovial conversation about our kids. She is one of the warmest, most compassionate people I have met recently, but she cannot accept my reluctance to say I am Chinese. Later, while I have a moment to myself, I think about this. In post-war Sri Lanka, we never want to hear people say they are Tamil, or Sinhalese, Muslim or Burgher. We want them to say they are Sri Lankan. Maybe she wants China to have that same unity of spirit. Yet, I am forty-two years old, and I have never, for one second, considered myself to be Chinese. I have always been Tibetan, even though I profess to know embarrassingly little about what that means. I know enough about our history, however, and I have read about too many Tibetan refugees and activists to be able to identify myself in any other way than I do. In the many countries I have worked or studied in, I have had many Chinese friends, colleagues, students, and teachers, all of whom I have got on with exceptionally well. I admire the Chinese work ethic, their contribution to global culture and I absolutely love Chinese food. Yet, I am not Chinese.

China is beginning to build up a presence in Sri Lanka. When the government here was accused of perpetrating war crimes, China stood up for them. While a post-Iraq-war America criticized Sri Lanka, coming across as thoroughly hypocritical, here was a foreign superpower, China, which seemed keen to defend this country and help them to develop. Chinese money poured in, but there were strings attached. High-interest loans were not the only thing that would restrict our freedom here.

It is September 2017 and as I struggle to think of a plot for what I plan to be my fourth book, I happen to chance upon my father's manuscript, *I am a Tibetan*. He had a powerful US literary agent and a contract, as I understand it, with the John Day Company, but the book was never released. My father wrote as an outsider to American culture. This interests me because I feel like an outsider wherever I am. As a Tibetan, I have been welcomed wherever I go with open arms, but I am still essentially a foreigner, and since I am not sure I will ever live in Tibet, I always will be. Yet, I see this as a good thing. I write about Sri Lankan culture, and I am more observant because so much is new to me—much like it was to my father when he first travelled to the United States. He had not known about prostitutes, for example, and thought that women who walked the streets there were very friendly. His exposure to American culture made him question his own religion and beliefs, but he always remained a Tibetan. I wonder, now, how I can use his book in my new novel.

Two stories my father would often repeat have stayed with me. Firstly, he claimed that he was brought up by his Tibetan parents to always turn down any offers the first couple of times, and only accept once his host insisted. In America, he found, there was only ever one offer. So, when he first stayed with a family there, he went days without food because he would always decline an offer the first time. Soon, he found himself having to sneak out of windows in the middle of the night to buy chocolate bars and the like, and it was at these times, I am guessing, that he bumped into these 'friendly American ladies who walk the street'. Luckily for him in this case, thanks to his upbringing, he was skilled at turning down offers.

The second story concerns my grandfather. My father used to say that, as a family back in Darjeeling, they were brought up listening to the BBC World Service on the radio. My grandfather became obsessed with English culture and, when he finally visited London for the first time, he did so in a three-piece suit and bowler hat. On his second visit, he took my father's dog for a walk in Regent's Park and all the way he would stop, doff his hat, and say, 'How do you do?' to passers-by. Eventually, when my grandfather returned to the house, he did so alone. When my father asked where his dog was, my grandfather said, 'He had to stop to do number two, which was rather embarrassing, so I left him there.'

It is October 2017 and as I am pushing my son around in his pram, I pass an old school friend in the lobby of a five-star hotel. She is excited because with her is a beautiful model who, my friend tells me, is half Indian and half—wait for it—Tibetan. I am absolutely thrilled to meet her, as it is perhaps the first time that I have met a Tibetan in Sri Lanka who is not family. The young lady plays with my son, who takes an immediate liking to her. As he is yet to turn two, he has no idea he is Tibetan, like her, but still I like to think there is a special bond.

To this day, that remains my one sighting in Sri Lanka of a Tibetan not related to me.

It is January 2018, and I have just done a panel at Kolkata Literary Meet. In the queue of people who want to get books signed by me are a couple of tough-looking young men. I ask for their names so that I can make the book out to one or both of them. When they write a name down for me, I immediately recognize its origins.

'Where are you from?' I ask.

'We live here,' one of them says.

'But your name . . .'

'We are Tibetan,' he says.

'Oh, wow,' I say. 'I am also . . .'

'Yes, we know you are Tibetan, and that is why we came. We are very proud of you.'

This is one of the most touching moments of my life and I am thrilled, a few days later, when the gentlemen in question reach out to me on Facebook. Perhaps they see me as being more successful than I am. Perhaps I should be proud that I am a writer, and maybe I am just a little bit, but I am much prouder that I am a Tibetan.

I am not a fan of overt nationalism. I have seen the problems it has caused in India and Sri Lanka. I like the idea of global citizens who can see beyond borders and boundaries and often I do not care where people are from and do not bother to ask. My father died in 2001 and since then I have had very little exposure to Tibetan culture. We have an ancient *thangka* in our house, but I have been in Sri Lanka for so long that I know much more about this country than I do my own. Yet, like the title of my father's proposed book, *I am a Tibetan*, and I always will be.

Lost in Lhasa

Tenzin Dorjee

The first time I laid eyes on Lhasa, what surprised me most was how it looked just like I had imagined it all my life.

The mountains and the lakes, the streets and the shops, the temples and the taverns, the pervasive incense smoke drifting and disappearing into the bluest possible sky, the men and women strolling unhurriedly but not aimlessly in their spacious *chubas*, their faces permanently tanned by the scorching sun of the plateau—each of these scenes, like unmistakable pieces of a jigsaw puzzle, fell perfectly into the vision of homeland I had carried in my mind all these years.

* * *

Sitting next to Kirsten Westby, my American companion who had deployed all of her wits and charm and tenacity to help smuggle me from Chengdu, I leaned against the window of the bus that was carrying us towards Lhasa, the centre of the Tibetan world. Having been born and raised in exile—a permanent state of diminished existence where we learned to tame our ambitions and lower our expectations early on in life as a technique of survival, where the prevailing philosophy was the *survival of the humblest*—I could barely believe that one of my wildest dreams was finally within reach.

Lhasa is a forbidden city in the true sense of the word, hidden from the world by an eternal conspiracy between geography and politics. In the past, the isolationist government of Tibet, suspicious of foreign ideas and influence, kept visitors out with a little help from the friendly Himalayas. Today, so does the Chinese government, fearful of what Tibetans might tell the world if given the opportunity.

Around the turn of the millennium, the Chinese leaders began drawing the curtain on Tibet, giving the occasional permit to starry-eyed travellers, as long as they did not peer too closely behind the curtain. A friend of mine, a Tibetan exile with Swiss citizenship, was one of the rare exiles to secure a visa to China and a special permit to Tibet. Her eyes had welled up with tears when she saw the Potala palace, the historical residence of the Dalai Lamas and the seat of the Tibetan government, floating above the city.

'If you ever saw the Potala with your own eyes,' she said to me, 'its magnificence would make you cry too.'

Well, thanks to my newly acquired American passport, here I was, on a bus that was hurtling down the highway towards Lhasa, the city that had served as the Tibetan capital ever since the emperor Songtsen Gampo made it his home in the seventh century. Would I really be moved to tears? If so, would it feel somehow contrived, as if I were enacting a plagiarized role that I had scripted for myself? And what if I didn't even make it to Lhasa? There might be informers on the bus who already knew that Kirsten and I were on a secret mission to stage a protest at Mount Everest base camp. There might be Chinese authorities waiting at the bus station in Lhasa, ready to greet us with handcuffs.

I was still lost in these thoughts when the bus suddenly made a turn, and without any warning, the Potala palace burst into full view. A collective gasp passed through the bus. I felt hot and then very cold, almost at the same time. My whole body had broken into a sweat. Well, I thought, no tears but close enough.

* * *

Kirsten and I stayed at a Nepalese-owned hotel, passing as a tourist couple. We had created this cover story—in hindsight, it was a rather thin cover story—to give me a measure of protection from the 'eyes' whose job it was to report on persons of interest. Lhasa, as much as it is a city of faith and worship, is also a city of spies and informers, and any Tibetan who comes from exile attracts immediate suspicion. So, I passed as a Sikkimese-American tourist visiting Lhasa with my 'girlfriend'.

By day, we meandered in and around the Bharkor, clicked pictures of landmarks, and drank gallons of butter tea in a rooftop cafe with a breathtaking view of the Potala. I ate momos, while Kirsten ate salad.

By night, we met up with the rest of the team—altogether there were five of us, sent in by the activist organization Students for a Free Tibet, where I was working as a staff—and prepared the logistics for our planned protest. It took us two days to assemble a banner that read: *One World, One Dream: Free Tibet*. The slogan was meant to subvert China's Olympic motto: *One World, One Dream*. We painted it on a banner several meters wide, word by word, letter by letter. When day broke, our sharpies had run out of ink and we were too high to sleep.

In the shops and restaurants, I spoke to people only in English, never in Tibetan. In a few days, we would be arrested for our protest and the Chinese authorities would retrace our steps and interrogate anyone who had been contaminated by contact with us. So, part of Kirsten's job was to ensure that I did not accidentally slip into Tibetan, to prevent me from unwittingly making friends with people and putting them at risk of guilt by association.

English is a cold language, sharp and precise. Every word has a function; words are self-sufficient and capable of travelling alone. 'Help'. 'Understood'. 'Worried'. In Tibetan, words hardly ever travel alone; to get anywhere, they must go in pairs at the very least. Each word is dependent on the other to achieve its purpose. '*Rokpa jeyrok.*' '*Go tsoe pa.*' '*Semdre lang pa.*'

You can converse with someone in English for an hour and not feel any closer to them. That would be impossible in Tibetan. The minute you speak with someone in Tibetan, the structural warmth of the language and the constant need to improvise begin to melt the walls that separate you from the other.

Under Kirsten's watchful eye, I spoke only in English everywhere we went, even when people insisted on speaking to me in Tibetan. At one point, I overheard a tall and giggly waitress exclaim to another, 'What a strange guy, that one. He swears he's not Tibetan, but he's been drinking pot after pot of butter tea!'

* * *

On our last day in Lhasa, I had one task left, perhaps the most important. I needed to find a torch.

Since we were going to protest China's plan to carry the Olympic torch to Mount Everest, we fell upon the idea that we should have a torch of our own to represent the Tibetan people's desire for freedom, a 'torch of liberation' that would stand in contrast to Beijing's 'torch of repression'. I left the hotel in the morning and spent all day combing the shops for anything that might resemble a tiki torch . . . something that would be easy enough to carry yet sturdy enough to hold a flame at 17,000 feet. I could find nothing that would do.

By evening I began to worry. I was beginning to suspect there were no torches in all of Lhasa. But I was so exhausted that I did not have the mental energy to give up. So I kept looking, walking, hoping, and searching.

And then my eyes fell on a stall with a table full of butter lamp bases. I stopped and walking over to the table, picked up what appeared to be the largest. I lifted it above my head and imagined a righteous flame in it. A sense of relief washed over me. Why, this brass lamp could take the place of a torch!

The vendor took out a calculator and typed in the price of the item. I gave him the bills without haggling. The lamp I was holding in my hands, and the mission it was to serve, was priceless.

I headed back to my hotel, which was located behind the Jokhang, but found I no longer knew which way to take. In my exhaustion and excitement, I lost my way in the winding alleyways of the old city, walking in circles and ending up precisely where I had been standing just a few minutes ago. I tried asking a vendor for directions and even accosted a few pilgrims, but none of them understood English.

At last, I stopped by an old lady selling trinkets on a makeshift bed. Seated on a low stool, she was not the type you would expect to speak a word of English. By now it was about to get dark and I was too desperate to waste any more time. Speaking in Tibetan, in the mixed dialect of the exiles that I had spoken my whole life, I asked her, '*Jokhang drosa lam ghaney rey* [Amala, which way would take me to the Jokhang]?'

'*Di ne yaa rey* [It is up this way],' she answered softly, using her hand to point me towards the temple. And she went back to her own business, without waiting for me to thank her or acknowledge her help.

She didn't look at me with curiosity. She didn't treat me like a tourist or a foreigner. As far as she was concerned, I might have been just another pilgrim from Kham or Amdo, temporarily out of place in the city but permanently at home in the country, among my own people.

In a way, the old lady was right. I was a pilgrim. A political pilgrim looking for a different kind of salvation, but a pilgrim nonetheless.

Catch and Release: Brushes with the Amorphous Uncomfortable

Chime Lama

'And is it fitting to regard what is inconstant, stressful, subject to change as:

"This is mine. This is my self. This is what I am?"'
'No, lord.'

—*The Buddha and his disciples, Nadi Sutta*

'I would like to give shape to the "amorphous uncomfortable."'
—*Claudia Rankine,*
In Our Way: Racism in Creative Writing

Throughout my life, I have had the fortune to hear Buddhist teachings that try their best to steer me away from misguided clinging. All the while, I try to deeply understand my place in the world and the circumstances that surround me. A part of this has been to find my place in the US as a child of Tibetan immigrants and the first natural-born US citizen on either side of my family.

I am one of many Tibetan-Americans who did not grow up in a *shija* settlement around other Tibetans. I never watched

Bollywood movies in theatres or mixed Hindi and Nepali into my Tibetan. In fact, I hardly had anyone to speak Tibetan with. Still, I look Tibetan, I 'feel' Tibetan and my Tibetan-ness is a fundamental part of my identity. So, I tried to embrace it in the most logical way available to me: Western academia. However, the more I learned about Tibet in American universities, the more I learned about their Western values and methodologies. I became trapped like Achilles in Zeno's paradox, and I could not catch the turtle of Tibetan-ness (see what I mean?). Ironically, the more I studied Tibetan and Buddhism in these institutions, the more I was alienating myself from my own culture. Though I tried to catch my Tibetan-ness, it seems that culture is not something you can learn by reading; you must be steeped in it.

My American-ness won't leave me. I can't get rid of it. Therefore, I will always be an approximation of a Tibetan, or at best, a fusion variation. Likewise, my older cousins who were born within Tibetan communities cannot get rid of their Tibetan-ness and seamlessly integrate into American culture. There is some subtle 'filter' that remains, however small, hinting at our foreignness to each other. For the most part, it doesn't matter. Yet, it points to the futility of my attempts to capture my Tibetan-ness, and I ask myself, 'What am I really trying to capture?'

I hoped to strengthen my Tibetan identity through creative writing, and I found myself defending it, perhaps unnecessarily, during an admissions interview for a Master of Fine Arts program. It was the winter of 2018, and I was wrapping up my applications when I was invited to meet with the faculty of a prestigious MFA. I entered a starkly furnished room of professors, mostly white, middle-aged men, and one white older female professor with whom I was to discuss my suitability for the programme.

I introduced myself and my interest in Tibetan creative writing, explaining how I wanted to promote Tibetan literature, hopefully, as a translator and maybe as a writer. 'Here are some books I really admire,' I offered, and rooted around in my bag to find *Burning the Sun's Braids* and *Old Demons, New Deities*. I can only imagine that it was an unimpressive display because it prompted the female professor to ask if I could write about other things, things *not* related to Tibet. How did she put it . . . could I write to a *wider* audience?

Now, this is not the first time a person of colour has been presented with that question, and though seemingly innocuous, it still lingers in my mind. What exactly did she mean by a 'wider audience'? What was I to assume about her ambiguous request? Well for one, it was certainly not an audience of Tibetan or Himalayan people or Tibetan enthusiasts. Did she perhaps mean an audience of European descent? Or did the wider audience that she has in mind contain a mixture of diverse peoples? I will never know. The next assumption I was to understand was that this wider audience would not be interested in my poems related to Tibet, and therefore, I had to prove that I could indeed write something that would appeal to them.

At first, I didn't know how to respond. In fact, I was shocked into silence. Never before had I met with anything but enthusiasm and support for my interest in Tibetan literature. So, like a jostled colt, I had to regain my balance to reply, 'Yes, I can.'

I think about this moment. I think about the struggle I put into reclaiming my heritage—the Bachelor of Arts (BA) in Buddhism, the Master of Arts (MA) in Tibetan translation, and the years of Tibetan language study in India and Nepal. It's not easy for Tibetan-Americans to speak and write Tibetan. All this effort was a part of my writing, my poems, and I was being asked for something else, something other, something *more*. This was my first real brush with professional racism, and I was very vulnerable. I was being asked to affirm that I could write in a way that would suit the tastes of this 'wider audience' or at least make my cultural references and perspectives more palatable to them. After all I had done to embrace my heritage, I felt like there was no way for me to win, like I was being cut by a double-edged sword.

Not feeling Tibetan enough, I tried to catch and embody that ever-elusive Tibetan-ness. Not appearing white enough, I had to put the Tibetan-ness aside to fit in and be accepted, quite literally. For, as Toni Morrison gracefully stated on the 1992 British TV show *Fin De Siecle*, 'In this country, American means white . . . Everybody else has to hyphenate.' Legally, I was American, but if American is taken as white, I would never be. I came face to face with what Morrison identified as 'whiteness as ideology and the first requirement of that ideology is to assume and assert its normalcy'. White is normal and I was not that, it seems the professor was trying to tell me. Therefore, my poems were not normal. Can I make my poems more normal? Can I make my poems more white?

Although years have passed, I believe one thing firmly: I should have asked for clarification. I should have asked her to tell me what she meant specifically by 'wider audience' and why she believed that they could not relate to my poems. At the time, I didn't have the courage to push back against the preferences and presumptions she took for granted and expected me to accept. By failing to assert my views and accepting hers, I failed the conversation and myself. Moreover, I lost the opportunity to have her clarify her statement to me, her colleagues and herself.

I think about the silent professors who sat beside her, witnessing. By virtue of their silence, they upheld her questions, quizzically looking at me like some foreigner they could not relate to, though I was born in this very country. Dismally, my silence in return made me complicit in my own othering.

I have tried to ease the discomfort of this interview by writing poems. They allow space for my imagination to take form. Humour has helped me to both digest and exaggerate the absurdity of this experience. Here is its poetic aftermath.

Become a Ball

> The old white female professor asks, 'But do you think you can write to a wider (*whiter*) audience?'
> She continues, 'How about walking with an upturned teapot on your head? Could you do that?'
> I don't respond quickly enough, and she takes the floor, 'You'll have to become more eccentric to fit in with this student body . . . I see you look a bit dowdy . . . I'm not trying to criticize, I just think we're looking for a more, how should I put it, *universally edgy*, applicant and I'm afraid you're not it . . .'
> [The other faculty members sit in their chairs in silence.]
> 'You know, I really don't think *you* have a place here. *No one wants to read about your whatever-it-is culture.* Do yourself a favour and give up that "angle".'

In the fall of 2020, I'm in an MFA poetry programme at a college with a truly diverse student body. Yet, our graduate cohort is less so. Due to the limited class size of ten students, I am one of the only two people of colour. While working for our programme's literary journal, we meet with a senior student to learn how to operate our website. He requests a poet's name to upload as a trial. 'Any poet at all,' he urges. My white male classmate shouts, 'Mao Zedong!' Again, I am speechless, but at least it's easier to hide that on Zoom.

There are some who consider Mao Zedong a hero despite his causing the deaths of over thirty million people and committing genocide in the country of Tibet. Perhaps my classmate is one of those people, but I sincerely hope not. Maybe he is ignorant of the atrocities that Mao committed, but I doubt that as well. Could this be a display of historical amnesia or, worse, indifference? Perhaps. But if an art teacher asks her students to name a painter, would anyone shout, 'Hitler'? No, that would be considered offensive because we are sensitive to the great suffering of Jewish people. Even if said as a joke, it would not be tolerated since it is reprehensible to joke about the suffering of others. Furthermore, the speaker may face social reproach, which might make them reconsider before making such odious comments. Regrettably, this event proves that the suffering of my people is neither acknowledged nor respected but is as invisible as I am silent.

Sitting at my computer, I try to convince myself that it's not a big deal: *So what? He can say that, right? I shouldn't say anything. I don't want to make things weird.* I fear straining my relationship with my classmate by objecting to his comment, just as I feared jeopardizing my chances of acceptance by disagreeing with the values of the professor. That both these individuals are white Americans is not lost on me. And I wonder if white Americans consciously or unconsciously know that they are shielded from censorship, and therefore do not have to think twice before speaking. Again, I turn to poetry to hash out my feelings, to help me better understand what was so wrong about the situation, and why exactly it felt so unsettling.

When My Classmate Nominates Mao Zedong

'Any poet, any poet at all . . .' —the instructor
'Mao Zedong!' —my classmate
Silence —me only
The rest of the class falls in line, and proceeds to pick a piece of writing by the Chairman.

Silent like a nation killed, I am,
Silent like my dead grandparents buried beneath snow.
Maybe I have no right to speak on my family's behalf
Since we're all progressive liberals here
And we're beyond condemning mass murderers as such
Since their writing is so chic, proletariat, and harmless.

Silence can precede a response. My silence did not signify that I had nothing to say. Rather that I could not respond in the moment. I had to understand what I was witnessing before responding. This has taken some time. Finding my place as a Tibetan-American in a society that prefers white Americans is a delicate procedure. Still, I am hopeful that people of colour will advocate for their values and voices more and more, as I am doing in my own way in this essay.

The Buddha taught his disciples to refrain from identifying with the changing factors of life. The stronger we cling, the more pain we feel, he explained. I know this in my head, but I am still learning it in my heart. Those parts of myself that I choose to solidify emerge like tiny pebbles when my comfort zone is trespassed. I defend those pebbles as though they are organs I need to live, and I watch the teachings slip down the river.

Yes, this life is temporary, and therefore the pains of life are only temporarily real. I'm grateful for the Buddha's teachings to help ease the burn of offences, whether intended or not. I hope I am not mistaken in believing that examining injustice may help to decrease it, as I will be better prepared to address it in the future. By examining these events, I see what is there within me that objects, those hard solidifying parts, and I try to remind myself that what I find is not for me to cling to, but to release with greater wisdom.

My Kind of Exile

Tenzin Tsundue

'I am more of an Indian,
except for my Chinky Tibetan face'

Ask me where I'm from and I won't have an answer. I've never really belonged anywhere; never really had a home. I was born in Manali, but my parents live in Karnataka. After finishing my schooling from two different institutions in Himachal Pradesh, my further studies took me to Madras, Ladakh, and Mumbai. My sisters are in Varanasi, but my brothers are in Dharamsala. My Registration Certificate (my stay permit in India) states that I'm a foreigner residing in India and my citizenship is Tibetan. But Tibet as a nation does not feature anywhere on the world political map. I like to speak in Tibetan but prefer to write in English; I like to sing in Hindi but my tune and accent are all wrong. Every once in a while, someone walks up and demands to know where I come from . . . my defiant answer—Tibet—raises more than just their eyebrows . . . I'm bombarded with questions and statements and doubts and sympathy. But none can ever empathize with the plain fact that I have nowhere to call home and in the world at large, all I'll ever be is a 'political refugee'.

When we were children in a Tibetan school in Himachal Pradesh, our teachers would regale us with tales of Tibetans suffering in Tibet. We were often told that we were refugees and that we all bore a big 'R' on our foreheads. It didn't make much sense to us; we only wished the teacher would hurry up and finish his talk and not keep us standing in the hot sun, with our oiled hair. For a very long time, I sincerely believed that we were a special kind of people with an 'R' on our foreheads. We did look different from the local Indian families who lived around our school campus—the butcher family who killed twenty-one sheep and goats every morning (when the goats bleated with half-cut throats from behind the slaughterhouse, we used to throw stones at the tin roof), the five other families who lived nearby; they owned apple orchards and seemed to eat only apples in different forms! At school, we never saw many people other than ourselves and a few *Ingis* (Westerners), who visited from time to time. Perhaps the first thing I learned at school was that we were refugees, and we didn't belong to this country.

I am yet to read Jhumpa Lahiri's *Interpreter of Maladies*. But something she said about her book has stuck with me—she said that her exile grew with her and that seems to be happening with me too. J.P. Dutta's *Refugee* has a scene in the movie that eloquently puts forth our plight—a father brings his family from across the border into a neighbouring country and is living far from comfortably but is a survivor. Events follow one after another and there comes a scene where the authorities hold him captive and question his identity. He breaks down: '*Wahan hamara jeena mushkil ho gaya tha, isiliye hum yahan aye, ab yahan bhi . . . Kya refugee hona gunah hain*? [It had become difficult for us to live there, so we have come here. And now, here too . . . Is it a crime to be a refugee]?' The army officer is dumbfounded.

A few months ago, a group of Tibetans in New York, mostly youngsters, found themselves in a difficult situation. A Tibetan youth had died and nobody in the group knew the cremation rites. All of them stared at each other. Suddenly they found themselves too far away from home.

> and meanwhile through the years
> our unburied dead eat with us
> followed behind through bedroom doors
> followed behind

Tibetan refugees, like other immigrants in the West from Asia, work hard to earn a living in a highly mechanized and competitive environment. An old man was thus very happy when he got a job that would pay him enough so he wouldn't be a burden on his family's scarce resources. He was put in charge of pressing a button whenever there was a beep. He found it amusing doing that trivial thing throughout the day. He sat there all day with a rosary in his hand, softly murmuring his prayers, and pressed the button religiously whenever there was the beep (forgive him, oh lord, for he knew not what he was doing). A few days later, out of curiosity, he asked his co-worker what the button was for. He was told that every time he pressed the button, he cut the neck of a chicken. He immediately left the job.

In October 2000, the world was tuned in to the Sydney Olympics. In the hostel, we were all glued to the TV set, eager for the opening ceremony to begin. Halfway into the event, I realized that I couldn't see clearly, and my face was wet. I was crying. No, it wasn't the fact that I dearly wished I was in Sydney or the splendour of the atmosphere or the spirit of the games; I tried hard to explain to those around me. But they couldn't understand, couldn't even begin to understand . . . how could they? They belong to a nation.

They have never had to conceive of its loss, they have never had to cry for their country. They belonged and had a space of their own—not only on the world map but also in the Olympics. Their countrymen could march proudly, confident of their nationality, in their national dress and with their national flag flying high. I was so happy for them.

'Night comes down, but your stars are missing.' Neruda spoke for me when I was silent, drowned in tears.

I watched the rest of the show in silence—heavy and breathless. They talked that day of borderlessness and building brotherhood through the spirit of games. From the comfort of home, they talked about coming together for one humanity and defying borders. What can I, a refugee, talk about except the wish to go back home?

* * *

Home for me is real. It is there, but I am very far from it. It is the home my grandparents and parents left behind in Tibet. It is the valley in which my Popola and Momola had their farm and lots of yaks, where my parents played when they were children. My parents now live in a refugee camp in Karnataka. They have been given a house and land to till. They grow maize, their annual yield. I visit them once every couple of years for a short vacation. During my stay, I often ask them about our home in Tibet. They tell me of that fateful day, how they were playing in the lush green pastures of Changthang while grazing their yaks and sheep, and how they had to pack up and flee the village. Everyone was leaving and there was hushed talk that the Chinese were killing everybody on their way in. Monasteries were being bombed, robbery was rampant, and everything was in chaos. Smoke could be seen from distant villages and there were screams in the mountains. They had to trek through the Himalayas and then to India, and they were only children. It was exciting but it was scary too.

In India, they worked as road construction labourers in Masumari, Bir, Kullu, and Manali. The world's highest stretch of metalled road, running from Manali to Ladakh, was built by Tibetans. My parents tell me that hundreds of Tibetans who crossed into India died in those first few months. They could not bear the heat of summer, and the monsoon caught them in poor health. But the camp lived on and had many shifts along the road. Somewhere along that journey, at a roadside, I was born in a makeshift tent. 'Who had time to record a child's birth when everyone was tired and hungry?' my mother says when I ask for my birthday. It was only when I was admitted into a school that I was given a date of birth. At three different offices, three different records were made. Now I have three dates of birth. I have never celebrated my birthday.

The monsoon is welcome to our farm, but not to our house. The forty-year-old tiled roof drips, and we must get to work planting vessels and buckets, spoons, and glasses, collecting the bounty of the rain gods, while Pala goes on the roof to fill the gaps and replace the broken tiles. Pala never thinks about revamping the whole roof using some good asbestos sheets. He says, 'Soon we will go back to Tibet. There we have our own home. Our cowshed has seen some repairs, the thatch is re-laid annually, and old worm-infested wooden poles and frames are replaced.'

When the Tibetans first settled in Karnataka, they decided to grow only papayas and some vegetables. They said that with the blessings of His Holiness the Dalai Lama, it wouldn't take more than ten years to return to Tibet. But now, even the guava trees are old and withered. The mango seeds they dumped in the backyard are bearing fruits. Coconut trees are brushing shoulders with our exile house. Old folks bask in the sun, drinking *chang*, or barley tea, chatting about the good old days in Tibet with their prayer wheels in their hand, while the youngsters are scattered all over the world, studying, and working. This waiting seems to be redefining eternity.

money plants crept in through the window,
our house seems to have grown roots,
the fences have grown into a jungle,
now how can I tell my children
where we came from

* * *

I recently met a friend of mine, Dawa, in Dharamshala. He had escaped to India a couple of years ago, after being freed from a Chinese prison. He spoke to me about his prison experiences. His brother, a monk, was arrested for putting up 'Free Tibet' posters and when tortured in prison, it was he who spilled the beans on his brother. Dawa was imprisoned without trial for 422 days. He was then only twenty-six. Dawa had been working under Chinese bureaucracy for quite some time. He was taken to Beijing from Tibet for formal education early in life and he laughs at China's feeble efforts to indoctrinate their ideas and beliefs of Communism and way of life on the Tibetans. Thankfully, in his case, the Chinese efforts didn't bear fruit.

Two years ago, a close school friend received a letter that put him in the most difficult situation of his life. The letter, from his uncle, said that his parents, who were in Tibet, had got permission for a pilgrimage to Nepal for two months. Tashi, after collecting his brother from Dharamsala, went to Nepal to meet their parents. They had not seen them since their escape to India twenty years ago. Before leaving, Tashi wrote to me, 'Tsundue, I don't know whether I should rejoice that I am finally going to meet my parents or cry because I can't remember how my parents looked . . . I was only a child when I was sent to India with my uncle, and it's twenty years now.' Recently, he received another letter from his uncle in Nepal. It said that his mother had passed away in Tibet a month ago.

I saw the Germans shed tears of joy when broken families from the East and the West finally met and hugged each other over the broken Berlin Wall. I fear the broken families of Tibet will never re-join. My grandparents' brothers and sisters were left behind in Tibet. My Popo-la passed away a few years ago; will my Momo-la ever get to see her brothers and sisters again? Will we be together there so that she can show me our home and our farm?

A Child's Losar in Darjeeling

Tenzing Sonam

My excitement mounted as the days counted down to *Losar*, the Tibetan New Year. A sure sign of its impending arrival was when my mother took me to Shamsu & Sons for a suit fitting. Darjeeling's long history as a British hill station, replete with sahibs and boarding school students, had left its mark on its citizens, who were fond of wearing Western-style suits for festive occasions. Mr Shamsu, an old-school Muslim gentleman, distinctive in his trademark astrakhan hat, was known both for his skill as a bespoke tailor and his inability to deliver on time. Any order placed with him inevitably required multiple failed trips and long harangues from my mother. But such was his workmanship and his honey-tongued spiel that all would be forgiven. Visiting his narrow shop and being briskly fitted by him into a suit always made me feel special and I couldn't wait for the day when I would finally get to wear the suit.

As Losar approached, miscellaneous preparatory activities kept our household in a state of feverish hustle and bustle. In those days, in the early 1960s, our home was swamped by an assortment of relatives and acquaintances, most of who had only recently escaped from Tibet. A set of unusual circumstances had forced my parents to settle in Darjeeling a few years before the Dalai Lama escaped from Tibet in March 1959. Because of its proximity to Tibet, Darjeeling and nearby Kalimpong were important towns on the Indo-Tibetan trade route and had always had a substantial Tibetan population. The Tibetans who came after 1959 called them *Bodpa Nyingpa*, old Tibetans.

Three of my mother's relatives from her village of Sangta, not far from Lhasa, separately made their way to Darjeeling after fleeing Tibet and tracing her whereabouts. They lived with us for a while. My two younger sisters and I cruelly nicknamed them: Shashang Sweater-Nagpo (Uncle Black Sweater) for the garment that he always wore, Shashang Pemo Renjo (Uncle Torn Knees) for his trousers frayed at the knees, and Shashang Kangpa Kyokyok (Uncle Crooked Feet) for his pronounced limp. There was also Somola (Aunty), my mother's first cousin, who showed up one day with her husband and his younger brother after a difficult and dangerous journey from Lhasa. Whenever someone new arrived at our home from Tibet, their haggard and unwashed appearances were signs to me of the terrible situation they had just fled from. There was no shortage of visual references to the state of affairs in Tibet. Cartoons in the local Tibetan newspapers depicted horrifying scenes: monks and nuns bayoneted alive by Chinese soldiers, Tibetans in chains watched over by gun-toting overseers, and the Potala Palace in flames. I would look at the Kanchenjunga range that towered over our town and try and imagine my homeland which supposedly existed just behind its lofty ramparts, a land as mythical as it was godforsaken, overwhelmed now by barbaric and evil Chinese soldiers. But in the benevolent setting of Darjeeling, in my child's mind a gentle and happy place, these troubling ruminations did not last long.

In contrast to my mother's numerous relatives from Central Tibet who passed through our home, there was only *Jhola* (elder brother) from my father's side who lived with us. He was my older first cousin who had joined my father in India in the late 1950s from our ancestral village of Nagatsang, a few kilometres from the famous monastery of Kumbum. Situated not far from the Silk Road cities of Xining and Lanzhou, Tibetans in these borderlands had long been a minority and coexisted with communities of Han Chinese, Central Asian Muslims, and Mongolians. In Tibetan, Xining is called Siling and Tibetans from this area are referred to as Silingpas. Very few Silingpas made it to India in the early days of exile because of the great distances involved and those that did, formed small but close-knit communities based on their distinctive language—a version of the Siling dialect, which has closer affinities to Chinese than to Tibetan—and their culinary habits, which revolved around a love of noodles. Jhola, then in his early twenties, was a soft-spoken and loving older brother who showered my sisters and me with an abundance of affection. Although he was our only relative from Kumbum, a number of other Silingpas were an integral part of our household.

Chief among them was Damba-la, a stony-faced giant of a man, who dominated our kitchen. His hair was close-cropped and a deep, vicious dent marked his forehead. Rumour had it that this was the result of a knife fight with a rival-in-love in Tibet but I later discovered its true provenance. Damba-la was part of a caravan expedition on the Kumbum to Lhasa trade route when bandits attacked them. He and his companions successfully repelled them, but in the melee, one of the bandits struck him on the forehead with a knife. A falling tent pole then hit him on the same spot and exacerbated his wound, leaving him cruelly marked. Many of the Tibetans who found themselves in Darjeeling and Kalimpong before the fall of Tibet were colourful characters with ambiguous pasts who had fled to India to start new lives. Damba-la was no different, the discovery of an affair (and an illegitimate child) with a married lady of high standing had forced him to run away. In Kalimpong, a long apprenticeship at the famous Shanghai Restaurant revealed his true passion—cooking—and he established himself as a master chef in the exile Tibetan community in Darjeeling.

Damba-la was adept at making both Central Tibetan delicacies, particularly those favoured by the aristocracy, and more uncommon ones from Siling, including hand-pulled noodles, chickpea flour polenta, and round loaves of fenugreek-infused bread. As children, we were in awe of him and afraid of his sharp tongue. But behind his stern demeanour and quick temper nestled a kind and generous soul whose craggy face lit up after a few sips of his favourite drink, *payi*—a fermented mash of millet steeped in hot water, served in a bamboo container, and sipped through a bamboo straw. This sweet and potent brew, not unlike good Japanese sake, was a speciality of south-eastern Tibet and a popular tipple in the area around Darjeeling. In later years, Damba-la developed Parkinson's disease and his hands trembled so violently that desperate rattling accompanied even the simple act of lifting a lid from a pan. But this did not stop him from continuing to cook. By this point, my sisters and I had lived away from Darjeeling for many years and the only child left at home with my parents was my young niece Diki, *Jhola's* daughter. The apple of Damba-la's eye, she mercilessly teased him as his disobedient hand struggled with ladles and pots. 'Uncle Damba-la's drumming again!' she would shriek, giggling helplessly. And our once-fearsome cook would shake his head and smile indulgently, regarding her affectionately through rheumy eyes.

Another Silingpa who was in and out of our home during my childhood was Majen (Cook) Yamphel. He had trained at Kunga Restaurant in Calcutta's Chinatown, the headwaters of a stream of Tibetan cooks who eventually spread out to Tibetan and Chinese restaurants from Kathmandu to New Delhi, and in the process helped to evolve a distinctly Indian-Chinese style of cooking that has now become an accepted feature of the Indian culinary landscape. Much to the consternation of my parents, Yamphel loved to drink and gambled away his earnings playing mahjong, sometimes disappearing for days on end. Although not as accomplished a cook as Damba-la, he was nonetheless very much a part of our household and took over the cooking chores whenever Damba-la was otherwise engaged (he was in much demand around town and often hired to cook at parties and other social events). I have fond memories of my father, Damba-la and Yamphel sitting together after dinner, sipping payi and speaking in the incomprehensible Siling dialect.

I caught up with Yamphel many years later, in 1995, when my partner Ritu and I visited Tibet for the first time. He had moved back to his home a few years before and now lived among his many relatives as a respected elder. Meeting him in the unfamiliar environs of Kumbum brought back many happy memories of my childhood in Darjeeling, which, in the context of where I now found myself, seemed impossibly distant. I finally understood just how far my father and his companions had travelled to end up as exiles in Darjeeling. Visiting Nagatsang and meeting various cousins, nephews, and nieces for the first time was a confusing and disquieting experience, tinged more with sadness and alienation than with the joy I had hoped for. My relatives only spoke in the Siling dialect and had it not been for my cousin Yonten Nyima, Jhola's younger brother, who had come to India some years before and learnt to speak Tibetan, I would not have been able to communicate with them. I regretted not having paid more attention to the Siling dialect when I was growing up but my father never encouraged my sisters or me. Perhaps, in the climate of heightened anti-Chinese sentiment that prevailed in the exile community at the time, where Tibetan was the dominant spoken language, he was uncomfortable with this linguistic distinction that separated the Tibetans of his native region.

The mix of Lhasawas and Silingpas in our home made for an interesting fusion of customs and traditions. Damba-la presided over one of the key preparatory rituals of Losar, the making of *khapsey*, deep-fried snacks made of dough that come in an assortment of shapes and sizes. For two days, Damba-la, assisted by my mother and other members of the family, slaved over giant cauldrons filled with bubbling oil, frying khapsey. We, children, couldn't contain our eagerness to sample the freshly sizzling goodies and were shooed away if we got too close to the splattering oil. The crowning moment of the khapsey-frying session was the making of *senz*, a specialty of my father's home region. The preparation of these intricately coiled strings of dough, subtly flavoured with ground Szechuan pepper and deep fried in bundles, requires a special technique and Damba-la was famed for his senz-making skills. We loved to dunk strands of senz into salted, buttered Tibetan tea and then use another piece of khapsey, broken to resemble a spoon, to fish them out. The trick was to eat as many of the senz bits before the 'spoon' itself collapsed into the tea, at which point, we continued with a new 'spoon'. Huge quantities of khapsey of all sizes and shapes were neatly packed into large, newspaper-lined cartons. These would last us through the Losar period and for many weeks afterwards.

The twenty-ninth of the twelfth Tibetan month was when Losar began in earnest. That evening, we gathered for the ritual *guthuk*—literally, 'noodle soup of the twenty-ninth'—bowls of handmade, shell-shaped pasta in a meaty broth. This was more of a Central Tibetan tradition and my mother and her relatives were in charge of its preparation. Each bowl of guthuk contained a dumpling with a secret ingredient hidden in it. This could be a fluff of cotton wool, small chilli, a piece of charcoal, a wild root delicacy called *doma*, or any of a number of other prescribed items. Each item symbolized a trait that ostensibly described the person who ended up with it. Much hilarity and ribbing accompanied the opening of the dumplings; but for us kids, this was a serious and tense affair: we just could not end up with one of the more unpleasant objects, like chilli (sharp-tongued and hot-tempered) or charcoal (scheming and malicious). But miraculously—with some help from the kitchen, I now suspect—we rarely got anything too negative.

For Silingpas, the next day, the eve of Losar, held special significance. The centrepiece of dinner on this occasion was a glistening pig's head, cooked in dark soy sauce and star anise along with a dish of pig's trotters. This was a Siling tradition peculiar to our household as pork is not commonly eaten by other Tibetans, who prefer yak meat, mutton, or beef. On this special evening, Silingpas also considered it important to eat *gyathuk*, egg noodle soup; the fine strands of noodles auguring long life. These traditions probably had roots in Chinese customs that the Tibetans in the Kumbum region had adopted over generations of close coexistence. The more typically Tibetan dish of boiled chunks of beef and mutton with potatoes and radish was also part of the spread, along with smaller plates of stir-fried vegetables. The first time Ritu visited my parents in Darjeeling coincided with Losar eve dinner. The grinning pig's head on its platter, slices of which my father enthusiastically plied her with, compounded by a surfeit of payi, proved too much for her constitution and she had to be gently escorted to bed, much to the amusement of my family.

That night, my sisters and I would go to bed, restless with excitement, our new clothes laid out next to us in readiness. We tossed and turned and whispered in the dark until finally, lulled by the comforting murmur of the adults chatting and drinking in the background, we fell asleep. It seemed like we had barely nodded off before we were shaken awake. The time was 3 a.m. and it was pitch dark outside. Loud bursts of exploding fireworks rent the early morning air. My father, already up and dressed, was ushering in the new year with crackers to dispel bad spirits and negative forces. We hurriedly put on our *chuba*—the traditional gown worn by men and women. One of the first things we did was to prostrate before our family altar and offer *khatag* to it. These long white scarves symbolizing pure intention and compassion are used as an offering by Tibetans for every imaginable occasion, from births and weddings to deaths and farewells. Our altar, which contained statues of various Buddhas and photographs of the Dalai Lama and other high lamas, soon piled up with the khatag.

My parents then sat down and it was their turn to receive khatag from all the younger members of the family. But first, we took turns to prostrate in front of them. Paying homage to one's elders in this manner was yet another Siling tradition and I only realized much later that it was not practised by other Tibetans. In return, our parents gave us gifts of money, which my father neatly packed in red envelopes. Money was freely given to children by their elders during Losar and was an important part of why we so eagerly anticipated it. We were then served *changkoe*, a hot, mildly alcoholic broth made of home-brewed *chang* (barley beer) mixed with *tsampa* (roasted barley flour), dried cheese and sugar. Changkoe was a true Losar treat, not least, in retrospect, for the unfamiliar but pleasant flush of warmth and light-headedness it stimulated in us children. Later, after the morning ceremonies concluded, I finally changed into my new suit and from then on, wore it for most of the Losar period.

It was still dark when the first of our guests arrived. A shout would go up—'The Toongsoong students are coming!'— and a flurry of activity electrified the household as last-minute preparations were made to welcome them. We could hear distant but advancing bursts of fireworks accompanied by loud shouts of *'Tashi Delek Phunsum Tsog!'* the traditional Losar greeting that translates roughly as 'May you have good fortune and good health!' The 'students' were a group of young men in their late teens and early twenties who lived together, first in the suburb of Toongsoong (from which they got their moniker) and later, in a large, dilapidated British bungalow not far from our home. For a number of years in the early 1960s, they could be counted on to be our first Losar visitors. Years later, I found out that they were part of a select group being readied for underground resistance activities. The rambling house they lived in was a safe house from where they were transferred to the next phase of their covert missions. Some would go on to be trained by the Central Intelligence Agency (CIA), which supported the resistance for more than a decade from the late 1950s. They would travel covertly from Darjeeling to Camp Hale, a top-secret facility in the Colorado Rockies created especially for the CIA's Tibetan operation. They would then return to serve as instructors in the Mustang Resistance Force, a clandestine guerrilla army based in northern Nepal on the border with Tibet, or go on undercover missions as radio operators along the Tibetan border, or be assigned to the joint Indo-American-Tibetan intelligence office in Delhi.

Unbeknownst to me, my father was a key figure in these operations. During my childhood, he often disappeared for extended periods. We were told that he worked for the Tibetan government-in-exile and had to travel frequently as part of his job. Even when he was home, my father was always locked away in his office, which was in one corner of our home, and other than at mealtimes, we rarely saw him. Endless lines of Tibetans came to visit him. There was a sense of purposefulness in their serious expressions as they awaited their turn outside his office. My sisters and I were under strict orders not to disturb these meetings. In

1974, I was in boarding school when I came across a news item in the daily newspaper that was pinned to our notice board. The article described the arrest of Tibetan resistance leaders in Nepal, following a standoff between a rebel force in Mustang that they were commanding and the Nepalese army. The news caught me by surprise; until then, I had no inkling of the existence of a Tibetan guerrilla army, far less of my father's involvement in it as one of its leaders. I reread the article several times but there was no mistaking my father's name—Lhamo Tsering—an unusual Tibetan name for a man. A few days later, my mother came to visit me and confirmed the story. And that is how I found out that my father had an entirely different side to his life.

My father was the personal assistant and confidante of Gyalo Thondup, the Dalai Lama's elder brother. They had met when my father was a student at the Institute for Frontier Minorities in Nanking in the 1940s and Gyalo Thondup had arrived in the city to continue his studies under the auspices of the Kuomintang government. They quickly bonded; they were both from the Kumbum region and had the Siling dialect in common. The two fled the Communist takeover of China in 1949 and arrived in India, travelling by sea. The People's Liberation Army invaded Tibet soon after. Following a brief visit to Lhasa in 1952, Gyalo Thondup and my father returned to India, determined to publicize the situation in their homeland and muster international support. They were part of an émigré group of political exiles based in Kalimpong in the 1950s who were actively working to oppose the Chinese invasion.

When Chushi Gangdruk, the Tibetan guerrilla army fighting the Chinese in Tibet, sent messengers to Gyalo Thondup seeking support, he put them in touch with the CIA, which had already reached out to him. As his trusted associate, Gyalo Thondup assigned my father to liaise between the Tibetans and the CIA, and that was the beginning of his long involvement in the resistance. My mother told me many years later that when she was pregnant with me, my father had disappeared without warning. She had no idea where he had gone and there was no way of communicating with him. Gyalo Thondup reassured her from time to time and told her not to worry. Jhola was the only family member with her when I was born in early 1959. My father reappeared a few months after my birth, as unexpectedly as he had left. He had been away in the US being trained by the CIA. Until his arrest in 1974, he served as Chief of Operations of the Mustang Resistance Force. All the times he had disappeared during my childhood, he had been on secret missions to Calcutta to meet with CIA officers, or on extended field trips to Mustang.

I later learnt that even Jhola had actively worked with my father. He was sent to Tibet in 1958 after a quick training in the basics of photography at Das Studio, a well-known photography studio in Darjeeling, armed with CIA-provided camera equipment. He is responsible for some of the only extant photographs of the Chushi Gangdruk at its headquarters in Lhokha in Southern Tibet. One photograph shows Jhola, barely out of his teens, standing proudly with Chushi Gangdruk leaders, one hand gripping a machine gun, his camera hanging from his neck. When the Mustang Resistance Force was established in 1960, he accompanied its first commander, Baba Yeshe, as part of the advance party to scout out the desolate Mustang region and spent a difficult winter when nearly 2000 men unexpectedly showed up to enlist before proper arrangements had been made. The men were reduced to boiling the leather from their shoes for sustenance before the CIA sent supplies.

But we knew nothing of any of this as we waited with excitement for the 'students' to arrive. Preceded by salvos of fireworks and accompanied by loud cries, they made their entrance, a good-looking bunch in their chubas and knee-high boots, with slicked-back hairstyles in what was then called the 'Bengali' fashion. Most men in Tibet kept their hair long and braided; cutting it short was the first step that marked their transition as exiles. The 'students' were ushered into our living room where they offered khatag to my father who they looked up to as their guide and mentor. Tea was served along with stronger libations, khapsey and other snacks. The house soon filled with a stream of visitors who arrived to pay their respects. At some point in the morning, Jhola or Shashang Sweater-Nagpo, or perhaps both, headed out as our representatives to make the rounds of close family friends. They would stagger back a few hours later, completely inebriated, barely able to stand. Losar etiquette dictated that guests had to be liberally plied with drinks and the drunker they got, the more auspicious it was considered. By lunchtime, our flow of guests slowed down and our extended family settled into a slow afternoon of food, drinks and games of cards. We, kids, were allowed to play, for small stakes, a popular card game called *hrithempen*, the Chinese version of Blackjack.

On the third day of Losar, we set out to perform *sangsol*, a propitiatory incense-burning ritual to our tutelary deities and an important Losar tradition to usher in the new year. Dressed in our Losar finery, we proudly walked through town past Chowrastha square and up a steep slope to Observatory Hill, one of the highest points in Darjeeling. A temple to the protector deity, Mahakala, worshipped by both Buddhists and Hindus, stood at its apex and was the focal point of many of the town's religious events. We joined hundreds of festively attired Tibetan families who gathered from all over town. Friends and acquaintances bumped into each other and exchanged loud Losar greetings. We thronged the narrow inner sanctum of the temple to make our offerings. Bells of all sizes hung over the entrance and ringing them was especially entertaining for the children. We jostled to add our share of juniper sprigs, powdered herbal incense, tsampa and splashes of alcohol into roaring oven-shaped incense burners. Smoke from their chimneys wafted thickly over the pine trees that surrounded the temple and released the comforting fragrance of burning incense. Young men from each family clambered up the branches to hang fresh strings of multi-coloured prayer flags, adding to the thick accretion of older prayer flags that knotted the trees. The best part came at the end: a large group of us, young and old, stood in a circle clutching fistfuls of tsampa in our right hands. Slowly chanting '*So*' in unison, drawing the syllable out as long as we could, we raised our fists once, then twice, and then, crying at the top of our lungs—'*Kyi kyi so so, lha gyal lo!* [Victory to the gods!]'—flung the tsampa to the skies in a powdery explosion of white flour.

The days that followed were a whirlwind of parties at our home and the homes of various family friends. For us children, it was a chance to meet our friends and play boisterous and largely unsupervised games of hide-and-seek or cowboys-and-Indians. Hollywood Westerns were a popular staple of Darjeeling in those days and had thoroughly colonized our imaginations. We loved nothing better than to emulate our screen heroes, of whom John Wayne, without question, was our favourite! The adults were either busily rushing in and out of kitchens or eating and drinking and playing cards. Sometimes, there were separate areas where the serious gamblers played mahjong. If we happened to be near one of them when they won a round, they would, much to our delight, give us some money for more luck. At some point, after dinner was served and plenty of alcohol had been imbibed, one of the guests would be prevailed upon to sing. This might be my mother's friend Andrugtsang Kusho, who had a good singing voice. Her speciality was *namthar*, arias from Tibetan opera that were hugely popular but technically difficult to sing. Or it might be Jigme-la, who would sing a *lu*, a style of nomadic yodelling from his home region of Amdo, which to my ears sounded foreign and strangely melancholic. Soon, more guests joined in and before long, the singing gave way to dancing.

More often than not, it was my mother and her friends who took the lead. High-spirited and a little flushed, they cleared some space in the middle of the living room and initiated the dancing. In my childhood, the women always seemed to be the driving force behind these social events, whether behind the scenes overseeing preparations, or being right in the forefront of the festivities. Their dances, usually folk dances from Central and Western Tibet, started at an easy pace. Singing together, the women shuffled their feet in time, their arms gracefully swaying. Midway, the song picked up speed and the dancers shifted gear, their feet stamping ever faster to more frenetic syncopated rhythms. Some of the men joined them and the dancing continued, full-throatedly and uninhibitedly late into the night. By then, we children would long have fallen asleep and if the party was in someone else's place, we would be woken up at an unearthly hour and dragged home, stumbling half-asleep through silent, nocturnal streets.

My mother's close friends included an unusual and distinctive group of women who had only met each other after coming into exile and settling in Darjeeling. They were from different parts of Tibet and came from varying backgrounds, and it is unlikely that they would have crossed paths under normal circumstances. Most of their husbands were involved in the resistance and this was perhaps the catalyst for their friendship. One of my mother's best friends was Jigme-la Nyila, who was from Lhasa. Her name was a composite of Jigme-la, her husband's name, and *nyila*, a common designation for 'lady'. She and her husband ran a popular Tibetan restaurant in town called Café Himalaya and a shop selling

Tibetan curios and tourist trinkets. Running restaurants and shops was a common way for the more entrepreneurial of the recently arrived refugees to make a living. Jigme-la worked closely with my father. One of his responsibilities was to escort small groups of men—including the 'students'—by road from Darjeeling down to the plains near the town of Siliguri. From there, under the cover of darkness, he led them covertly across a fast-flowing river that marked the border with what was then East Pakistan. Once they had safely forded the river, Jigme-la handed the men over to East Pakistani soldiers who were waiting for them at a predetermined spot. He then returned the way he had come, having accomplished the most dangerous part of the mission. The men were taken to a military airstrip near Dhaka where CIA operatives received them. From there, they continued their journey by transport plane, stopping over at US military bases in Okinawa or Saipan before flying on to Colorado.

Andrugtsang Nyila, a gentle and dignified lady also from Lhasa, was the wife of Andrug Gompo Tashi, the renowned leader of Chushi Gangdruk, who passed away in Darjeeling in 1964, succumbing to wounds he had sustained during campaigns against the Chinese. I clearly remember his funeral cortege winding its way along the narrow mountain road from Darjeeling to Ghoom Monastery. The atmosphere was charged with patriotic fervour as a long line of mourners chanted anti-Chinese slogans. I was in the front with Gompo Tashi's sons—Dhondup and Dakpa—all of us around five or six years old. Swept by the emotion of the occasion, we raised our fists and shouted at the top of our voices, 'Tibet is independent!' and 'China out of Tibet!' My father had worked closely with Gompo Tashi before his death, especially in the formation of the Mustang Resistance Force to which many Chushi Gangdruk soldiers were relocated after coming into exile. Many years later, Ritu and I visited Andrugtsang Nyila in a small, downtown Manhattan apartment where she then lived with her surviving family. By then, almost everyone I knew from my childhood had left Darjeeling. Many ended up in the US, driven by the migratory instincts of the exile to find a better life. I hadn't seen Andrugtsang Nyila for many years; I left India when I was twenty and had lost touch with people from my past. She appeared frail and melancholic. The roar of New York traffic, punctuated by its signature wailing sirens, provided a melancholic backdrop against which we relived a few happy memories from our Darjeeling days. Not long after our visit, she passed away.

Then there was Toongsoong Nyila (who, naturally, lived in Toongsoong). A shy and retiring lady, she was from Markham in eastern Tibet and lived alone with her two children. She had a tragic story that I was completely unaware of when I was a child. Her husband, Yeshi Wangyal, an early trainee at Camp Hale, was parachuted into Tibet on two separate occasions. His second mission in 1960 was to his native area of Markham where he and his team were to locate his father, the local chieftain Phurpa Pon, who was leading a guerrilla force. The mission was doomed from the start. Phurpa Pon had already been killed by the Chinese and his greatly diminished group was on the run. Coming under fire from almost the time they landed, Yeshi Wangyal and his men made their last stand in a fierce gun battle where, except for one man who was wounded and captured, they all perished.

The most flamboyant and extravagant of my mother's friends was ABC Nyila, so known because she was the proprietor of ABC Restaurant. She was from Lithang in eastern Tibet. With her flashing gold tooth and her outgoing personality, she had a larger-than-life quality. We, children, were especially fond of her because she was generous with her gifts of money. ABC Nyila was fond of playing mahjong for high stakes, which put her in another league from my mother and most of her friends, who stuck to playing cards for small amounts of money. Her husband, Bugen Gyatotsang, was a relative of Andrug Gompo Tashi and a Chushi Gangdruk veteran. His younger brother, Wangdu Gyatotsang, was a legendary figure, one of the first groups of six Tibetans trained by the CIA in 1957 on the Pacific island of Saipan. He was parachuted by the CIA into his native region of Lithang in 1958 to team up with rebel forces fighting the Chinese. After several battles where his companions were killed, he made an epic escape back to India, journeying on horseback and then on foot for months across the Changthang, the wild and desolate Northern Plains.

My father and Wangdu worked closely together, and I remember him clearly, a tall and strikingly handsome man who, like ABC Nyila, freely handed out large amounts of money to us kids. In the late 1960s, he replaced Baba Yeshe as the commander of the Mustang Resistance Force. My father spent several months with him in Mustang during a tense period of in-fighting that threatened to split the force. In 1974, under pressure from China, Nepalese troops marched on Mustang and demanded the disbanding and surrender of the force. This was when my father was arrested and used as a bargaining chip. Wangdu made plans to rescue him by force. A showdown was narrowly averted when the Dalai Lama intervened with a taped message calling on the guerrillas to lay down their arms. The guerrillas surrendered but Wangdu, along with a small band of men, made a run for the Indian border. He was ambushed by Nepalese soldiers and shot dead. My father and six other guerrilla leaders would spend nearly seven years in a Nepalese prison for their role in the Tibetan resistance.

But I would only piece together these events and understand their significance much later in life. Whatever fears, anxieties, and sorrows our elders carried with them in their hearts at the time, they did their best to ensure that our carefree and happy childhoods were not impacted in any way. Our Losar festivities continued unabated until the fifteenth day and then they officially came to an end. Life slowly returned to normal. My suit, which I had worn throughout, was packed away. I would soon go back to school. Our dwindling stock of khapsey was the only reminder of that special period and one day, this too depleted. Soon, this brief phase of our lives also came to an end and our Losar celebrations were never the same again.

I look back at those days and see them as if from the wrong end of a telescope, dreamlike and distant. I see my mother, her friends and other family members and acquaintances sitting together, laughing, and drinking around tables laden with bottles of beer and large, communal containers of payi with several bamboo straws stuck in them. I see them singing and dancing until late in the night, fuelled by the flush of alcohol and the memory of their recently abandoned homes. There is a youthful and reckless energy to their merrymaking. Despite personal tragedies and news of the worsening situation in Tibet, the future still seems ripe with possibility. They seem determined to keep their spirits up, to reassure themselves that their situation in exile is temporary and that they will soon return to Tibet. But none of them will go home. The years will pass, and they will settle into a liminal state of exile, one foot precariously planted on foreign soil, the other always dangling helplessly towards a homeland receding ever further away. Their children—my generation and younger—will grow up knowing Tibet only through their increasingly blurred and rose-tinted memories. One by one, they will pass away, and our children will not even have that living link to our past. We will leave Darjeeling and start new lives and families in faraway places. Darjeeling itself will change and undergo political turmoil and transformation. It will cease to be the halcyon place of my childhood memories. But I will always remember how, for a short period in the early 1960s, when our connection with Tibet was still fresh, when our elders were optimistic and filled with single-minded determination to reclaim our homeland, we celebrated Losar with total commitment and joyous abandon.

The Awe-Inspiring Culture

Nyen

Translated by Dhondup T. Rekjong

This afternoon, I clipped my fingernails and toenails after a long time. On one hand, I did it intentionally, but on the other hand, I did it not knowing what else to do because of this useless prison life. Like other prisoners, I held a clipper, placed its blades on the smiling line of my nail, and carefully cut each of the nails, one at a time. For me, cutting my nails is a somewhat trivial pleasure. From cutting my nails to filing them afterwards, I get a lot of time to contemplate. However, after finishing the nail cutting, I was not sure if I should consider the scattered clippings on the ground as nail-trash or not.

This place is full of shady prisoners, so a high standard of morality is rare here. In this iron-fenced panel, armies of black shadows can be seen everywhere. Nail clippings are something we are not required to worry about or take responsibility for and they can be left on the ground or thrown away.

Come to think of it, if someone cuts their fingernails at home, they only care to pick up the clippings out of concern for their house's hygiene. If someone cuts their fingernails outside, they may not worry about the clippings and might possibly leave them on the ground. There is a tradition, one that's thousands of years old, in which people pay no heed to nail clippings as they think there's no harm in it. They also think, 'What good would it be to pay attention to this.' That is *their* way of thinking. Perhaps it is also *their* cultural trait.

However, I'm different from *them*.

My nail clippings are also different from theirs. So, what am I going to do with my nail clippings? Am I going to leave them scattered on the concrete without a second thought? Should I leave them there as if no one is watching me? No, that's not how I think. I remember the cultural imprints that my late grandmother passed on to me and the good habits that I learned from my late mother.

I shouldn't leave those rough-edged nail clippings on the ground like that. If I do, the birds might peck at them. The nails might get stuck in their throats or even injure them. So, it's important that I pick up every clipping and bury it in the earth. If I bury them, the birds won't be able to eat them. But where can I find a piece of earth in this prison to bury them?

The whole ground of the prison is covered with this merciless concrete.

Under these circumstances, there's no way for me to bury them in the earth as we Tibetans traditionally do. So, I gathered them all and wrapped them in tissue paper and dropped them into the dustbin.

I think my ancestors are correct about what they say. Today, from the bottom of my heart, I felt the depth of their noble saying, 'One should not forget one's homeland even if it is just a cliff of clay'. Although it is not preserved in the volumes of great manuscripts, this clear and simple saying is as strong as a *vajra* rock.

One's home is definitely not just a bare cliff.

Rather, this overly modest saying about a cliff of clay really refers to the vast grassland. This cliff is also a range of snow mountains. This saying is derived from a long-lived culture and tradition. Culture is not merely found on paper and in ink. Culture is not just grandiose qualities like exposition, debate, and composition. Rather, culture is an irresistible and invisible force, which is equal to an awe-inspiring seasonal wind that effortlessly penetrates the nine-floored iron fence panels of this dark prison.

Because of this cultural courage, no one has been able to strip me naked to date.

Because of having that cultural imprint within me, no one has been able to isolate me. In this dark and remote prison, the thing that consoles me every day and night is the idea of the cliff of clay called home. The notion of the cliff of clay back home serves as a spine for my body; the idea of this cliff of clay back home is like giving my body a new neck.

The reason why I was cautious about my nail clippings is because I am a part of my ancestral culture.

It is clear that my nail clippings won't harm the birds hovering in the sky over the prison. However, every time I see the cluster of barbed wire thorns placed on top of the prison walls, I worry deeply about the foolish birds. I worry they might get caught in the barbed wire.

Thinking about My Teacher on Teacher's Day

Sangdor

Translated by Lowell Cook

They say that tomorrow is Teacher's Day. When I think about it, I've really only had one true teacher. It isn't anyone famous you would've heard of. He was completely ordinary at least from the outside. No one knows what his inner life or lived experience might have been like. Even though it's no longer possible, I still wish I could know more about his inner life. Some people claim that this teacher of mine was a 'hidden yogi'. But I'm not so sure about that. So, let's put that to the side for now. Overall, there's no denying that it was thanks to him that I learned how to both delight and infuriate people by joining word with word, stringing together phrase after phrase, and arranging stories from the past with those yet to come. That's not all I learned from him though. I'll tell you more in time!

His name was Pema Gyaltsen. If we were speaking Lhasa dialect, you'd respectfully refer to him as my *pola*, or grandfather. But since I'm about to make a rather bad-mannered toast to him with some rough language, I'm not going to use any honorifics. I'm going to say he 'died', not 'passed beyond'. And, why not?

Well, even when he was still alive in this world, I never used a single honorific word with him. At that time, I didn't even know how. And now, even though I'm not worried that he might overhear me, I'm going to have to make do with our blunt nomad expressions, that is, straight nomad talk.

In my memory, he's wearing an olive-green Tibetan robe and holding a set of black prayer beads interlaced with a multicoloured guru bead. He said the colours represented the five buddha families. He had yet another set of prayer beads that he called his Tara chanting beads. Those beads were a genuine 'thousand-starred' rosary, specifically for the practice of the Goddess Tara. Whenever he'd perform his recitation of the Tara mantra, a group of us kids would go and collect *tsama tsitok* flowers. He said these were a necessary ingredient in his chanting practice. We crossed through gruff hills, picking flowers up all the way to the red marsh flatlands. On the way, we'd cross through a thicket of willows that made our going hard. Birds of all varieties—woodland birds like *jodangs* and rock land birds like *maris*—would be perched around us. In the end, we would have gathered a great many *tsama tsitok* flowers. They were the most brilliant yellow of yellows. And if you cut off their stems and blew on one, it'd make this funny sound.

It was in this way that I grew up living with my teacher from a young age. I began absorbing his beliefs and mannerisms unconsciously until they eventually became my own. I wouldn't have been able to rid myself of them even if I wanted to.

When I turned nine, my grandfather taught me the Tibetan ABCs or, rather, the *ka-kha-ga-nga*s. Along with this, he also taught me how to connect the letters and later on how to form words. He was a strict man. He taught me in a stern manner and I studied as hard as I could. He'd never let me lay down on my back near our hearth, claiming it'd make me arrogant. In those days, his advice didn't quite reach my ears, but now, when I think back on his words of advice, there might have been something to them. If we, children, were chatting too much, he'd put an end to it saying that it was his wise old counsel. Wasting food will bring about such suffering as the death of children, he'd say. If we did this, our luck would run out. If we did that, our good fortune would dry up. Such were the details he drew from the Buddhist Monastic Code, to tell us about what was allowed or forbidden, what was acceptable or inappropriate.

He had great affection for me. He never complimented me to my face, but to other people, he'd say things like, 'This boy has such an adorable little personality' or 'What an articulate and speedy little reader he is!' He even went so far as to make me memorize our entire collection of daily prayers. Each year he'd also make me recite three major scriptures—the 'King of Samadhi Sutra', 'Perfection of Wisdom in 18,000 Lines', and the 'Fortunate Aeon Sutra'—one time through each. Those three tomes with their ornate cloth bindings and colourful illustrations of deities captured my imagination. On top of these three, he'd also make me recite the 'Sutra of the Ten Bhumis' and the 'Collections of Incantations'.

When my teacher left the house, I'd ruffle through his altar cabinet. This traditional cabinet was painted red and made of high-quality wood. The sides were plainly engraved with images of conch shells in a row. The altar had a top and bottom part that could be detached. The top part held a bronze Buddha statue wrapped in golden cloth. You could only see the protrusion on the Buddha's head peeking out, but boy, would he ever praise that statue's importance and power. On occasion, he'd bow his forehead to rest against the statue and, for a moment, remain in silence. After a little while, he'd take his hands and wipe away the tears. Enshrined on the top section of the altar cabinet were, first and foremost, pictures of the Potala Palace and the Jowo statue followed by the many other holy sites and sacred statues of Lhasa. Arranged here too were photographs of the previous incarnations of Arol Rinpoche and Chubzang Rinpoche. I guess these two masters ranked among his principal teachers. At important moments, he might even pray out loud saying, 'Think of me, ultimate Buddha Arol' or 'Look upon me, primordial Buddha Chubzang!'

In front of these images, he had a set of seven water offering bowls, a bundle of flowers, and his 'all-nighter' butter lamp burning away. The rim of the first water offering bowl was a bit bent. Inside it sat a statue of the deity of wealth, White Dzambala. It was made of natural copper and was about the size of a child's palm. Every morning, he made his water offerings and every afternoon he emptied the bowls. He had separate chants he'd recite while making water offerings and while emptying the water offerings. The lower part of this altar cabinet held lots of texts, many of which had been stitched back together. He had worn-out, old copies of the *Life of Milarepa*, the *Sutra of the Wise and Foolish*, and the *Life Story of Lord Tsongkhapa*. He had a two-volume set of *The Battles of Hor and Ling* from the Gesar Epic, which had their faded covers reattached. Other mended titles included *A Presentation on the Five Traditional Fields of Learning* by venerable Tsultrim Rinchen and the *Life of Thangtong Gyalpo*. Stacked on a slightly higher part inside the cabinet were texts like the three main scriptures I mentioned before, which we referred to as Samadhi, the Perfection, and the Fortunate. These types of books came in long manuscript format or in the traditional loose-leaf style. In the corners of the altar cabinet were incense substances like the six precious medicines, juniper, artemisia, and other cleansing incense powders brought back from Lhasa. So, I guess this is why countless fragrant smells would overwhelm your senses the moment you approached his altar cabinet.

When I recollect all of this, the shape and colour of my teacher's face don't really come to mind today. Even so, I'll never forget some of the things he said to me. He'd tell me, 'As you grow up, you'll need to learn calligraphy. And make sure to study grammar. Then maybe you'll make a man out of yourself.'

In yet another one of his small chests, he had an assortment of common medicinal substances—compounds like 'golden goose egg', 'leaf clad maiden', and 'crystal moon'; substances that went by the name of *palri* white and red herbal pills; triple compounded naropa, dragonbone, sweetwood, and the like. Back in the days when the town was far off and doctors were particularly scarce, he'd be the one to prescribe these common medicines to our family and heal our coughs and colds.

I had a tough time sleeping when I was a little boy. I'd often suddenly wake up in the middle of the night with night terrors and shoot straight up, my forehead drenched in sweat. My grandfather and his wife would come by my side and, in unison, recite the 'Praise to the Goddess Tara' starting from the line, 'With your majestic armour that gives joy to all, you dispel all disputes and bad dreams,' followed by a short Sitatapatra prayer. At the end of this, they'd perform an expulsion ritual. This was quick to put my mind at ease and I'd fall asleep once again. Sometimes my teacher would perform protection rituals for me. He'd not so gently bop me on my head with a text bound in hard wooden covers and chant some recitations. It seemed that, at the time, this also helped.

Grandmother had limitless respect for him. His work primarily consisted of reciting scriptures and staying in retreat. On occasion, he'd ride an ash-coloured horse into town to pick up some food, but those were brief errands. Grandmother took on the responsibility of tending to the yaks and all the other hard and heavy work. The responsibilities particular to nomadic women—the dairy work of milking female yaks, the weaving work of spinning wool, and the collecting and spreading of fresh yak dung—seemed to have been done entirely by her alone.

By and large, this household of ours in which my grandfather was the breadwinner was, at first, rich like the saint Milarepa's. Some say that this was thanks to all the religious rituals and the good fortune of my teacher. But as far as I can tell, it mostly came down to my grandmother's thriftiness and upkeep. Like a 'deer fattened off the land', the roof above our family's head, our pots and pans, food and snacks, and clothes and jewellery grew ever plentiful. They say that an old nomad man once took a jab at my grandfather, saying, 'Hey there now, looks like your family's got what we call "power more renowned by the years and livestock more abundant by the months," doesn't it!'

My teacher grew serious and replied, 'It's not permanent in the least. It's all but a dewdrop.'

They say that around this time our family had over one hundred stocky, thickly coated black yaks that were all healthy and disease-free. We had many stallions and mares too. Nevertheless, we didn't seem to have many sheep. If you were watching while the herd moved out to pasture, it looked like one huge yak, the size of a mountain ridge. There were some twenty animals or so that had been dedicated exclusively to our protector deities that we called divine yak, protector horse, and heavenly ram. They might have just been animals, but it wouldn't be a lie to say their bodies were immaculate. They had pristine wool coats and clear, sharp intelligence. Each year when we would make our petition offerings to the protector deities, there was this infinitely majestic presence. We would have a tall pyre of *sang*, a smoke offering, burning away with scores of little flames while the fragrance of juniper and the aroma of butter wafted in all directions. In the midst of these flames were ritual cakes, in triangular and half-moon shapes, greasily sizzling away. Atop this, the soot and butter sculptures, all smeared together, sat sputtering as they burnt and crackled.

We would smear the horns and tails of these animals with white butter. Meanwhile, protective symbols made of white wool and multi-coloured ribbons would be dangling off their bodies, swaying back and forth in the wind. Ritual water would be used to rinse the yaks from their heads to their mane and then down to their tails. If the yaks would shake the water off as soon as we did this, we would take it as a sign that the protector deities were pleased. My teacher didn't perform many of these types of deity invocations or *naga*-summoning rituals. Yet, whenever he performed rituals to request spiritual protection from the Dharma protectors or to call upon the local deities, it made the audience's hair stand on end. He never made prostrations after doing a smoke offering though, and wouldn't allow others to do so either. He'd say, full of assurance, 'You're not supposed to go for refuge in worldly deities, but merely summon their assistance.' I genuinely felt like he had the ability to control these mundane deities as if they were his servants.

Amid these random collections, a certain bull yak owned by our family, with horns as big as copper ladles, comes to mind. Why now? Well, my teacher, that is, my grandfather purchased that bull yak for me from a place called Arik. This bull yak had a rather large head and ears, and his horns were thick and round. When he grunted, his white, shimmering breath came steaming out. Whenever the day was sunny or when the afternoon clouds parted, he'd plant his horns in the ground and send clods of earth scattering towards the sky. His movements had an air of majestic dignity to them. When this bull yak of ours fought with the other yaks, there was no limit to what he could do. We colloquially call this 'not being able to control his nose'. But what nomads really call these yak fights is 'scufflin'. Us kids would tap his forehead and run away, making him grow wild, mean, and fierce. The tips of his horns shone dark black, and his clumpy tufts of mane ruffled about as his hoofs scraped and clattered on the stones. Even though red blood might be glistening around his mouth and dripping from his nose when he got to scufflin', his bloodshot eyes would keep glancing this way and that with no hesitation. He was so breathtaking in the way he resembled the undomesticated yaks of the wild. Yet, in the end, this bull yak of mine died of a sudden illness. As far as I was concerned, I wouldn't have cared more if, instead of telling me that my bull yak had died, you told me at that moment that World War III had broken out.

Yes, what they say is true, 'The end of growth is decline'. Once, a close cousin of my teacher, that is, my grandfather, seemed to have become possessed by a demon and got into a dispute with our family over land. A fierce yet misplaced feud sprang up and broke my teacher's spirit. With a sense of renunciation for the world, he practised the harsh virtue of 'giving gains to others and taking loss upon oneself' until the bitter end. He resolved to go into exile just like a bird taking flight from a rock. With this, the pasture where my 'navel flower' had been plucked, this pasture that glowed like golden butter was torn away from me. I was too young at that time to have had any authority to get a word in. Otherwise, there is no way I would've let things descend to that level.

During one of those horrible years of exile, the entirety of our family's horses, yaks, and sheep were killed outright, utterly wiped out, with several fierce blizzards taking the blame. The frozen snow took about a month to thaw. Buried beneath it were our dead horses, yaks, and sheep, all frozen stiff. They said that you could see some of the horns and tails of the animals sticking out of the snow.

With one bad thing following another, it was then that my grandmother developed a heart disease or some other similar severe illness and died. As she was passing, I can still vividly recall my teacher propping her up as he sternly asked, 'Do you remember when the two of us went to see the precious Jowo statue in Lhasa? Think of the precious Jowo.'

'I can see him vividly,' grandmother replied. He made a fumigation mixture with bits of the Jowo's robes and burnt it for her. When she was close to death, my teacher placed seven rebirth pills in her mouth, a blessing substance said to bring about liberation when tasted.

After my grandmother passed away, our family had to call her *drinchen-ma*, her graciousness. This is the way we nomads refer to the deceased. Not long after *drinchen-ma* left us, one morning my teacher, that is, grandfather, recited the 'King of Aspiration Prayers' a few times and died. He died without any serious health problems, final wishes or last words. Locals in the village said there had been death omens before he passed away, but whatever the case may be, it's hard when someone dies, and your home is empty. You can ask the corpse about any death omens.

Now, our family had to call him *drinchen-po*, his graciousness. For the time being, beyond his prayer book, there was nothing left in his graciousness' place for our expenses. His prayer book was a narrow volume bound with a grease-stained book wrap. Most of the paper inside was so old and timeworn that it was hard to read. What you could discern concerned the goddess, Tara. It was all recitation manuals, practice texts, and the like. On a few blank pages, there were a bunch of holes punched with the tip of a needle in the shape of little cairns. Attached to this were a few small slips of paper with the notes 'King of Aspirations, ten thousand recitations accumulated' or 'Confession of Bodhisattvas, ten thousand recitations accumulated', and such things written on them in his handwriting.

What I later came to learn was that my teacher, that is *drinchen-po*, had not only entrusted me to the care of someone else, but had also arranged some supplies for me such as a warm and cozy sheepskin coat, a rough and rugged embroidered robe, and a fox fur cap with earflaps on either side. On top of this, he had prepared everything the heart of a young nomad boy could desire—a fancy saddle, some choice stirrups, as well as one of the best cruppers. However, as it took me so long to grow up, others gradually came to take ownership of these items. It's exactly as the saying goes, 'An old man's savings and an old dog's snack!'

Since this teacher of mine was a devotee of the goddess Tara, my biological mother, who was his stepdaughter, was given the name 'Drolma', meaning Tara in Tibetan. My sister too was given the name 'Tare', from the mantra of the goddess. But these are things that it took me a long time to come to understand.

As for us family members, we suffered quite a bit when these two old folks who were like the sun over our heads passed onto the next world. And we suffered more later when my mother became ill when my sister and I were still very young. My mother did get to enjoy herself a bit during her lifetime, thanks to the two lucky old folks in our family—that is my grandfather and grandmother. Yet, in the end, she too did not escape the hands of the Lord of Death.

Today, with the dead and living so firmly decided, I asked someone about how that one guy is doing these days. By that one guy I mean that cousin of my teacher who had forever relegated our family, my teacher's family, my grandfather's family, to yesteryear. They said he had caught a painful terminal disease some time ago and died. Now seriously, I've nothing left to do but reflect on the expression, 'To chuckle at the ways of the world.'

When my teacher, that is, my family's *drinchen-po*, was still among the living, I was never able to ask him anything much as I was too small. I definitely never engaged in any intellectual discussions with him. If only he were still here now. What would he have held in his heart? How much importance would he have placed on spiritual things? Thinking back on it, he was quite different from the majority of spiritual-minded folks in those days in that he was literate. He would often make calligraphy pens out of the wood of superior quality. He'd then mix up some ink and write in all different styles of cursive calligraphy.

When he was still among the living, he took me to watch a *cham*, a ritual dance, at one particular monastery. That monastery followed the Gelukpa lineage, but they nevertheless performed the *cham* dances of Milarepa from the Kagyu lineage. Someone in the *cham* was dressed up like the Venerable Milarepa himself and pretended to sing some of his song-poems like 'Deer Self-Liberated' and others. The character Ara Karnak also seemed real to life. The two of them would act out things like plucking lice from one another's heads. There was a dancer called Thaku Nyi, Double String, who could spin in circles like a wheel for a long time. Hanging down from his waist were thin strings that extended straight out when he started to spin fast. The cords must've been fastened together as they never came apart. He would spin for a long time to the marvel and delight of the children's eyes.

My teacher found great enjoyment in these monastic dances. In fact, he must have been a monk from that monastery during his childhood. He once took me to one of the monastery's monk cells where we ate some porridge delivered by the abbot of the monastery himself. The porridge itself was great, but it was the rich butter inside the porridge that I found most tasty. This was the first time I went somewhere far away together with my teacher.

It may seem like I'm jumping from memory to memory of my teacher's character and appearance, his personality and actions. But to be honest, I don't have that much left in my memory. The tips of his thumbs on both hands were truncated. He said it was from squeezing a battery once in his childhood that exploded and gashed him. Although he was forced to renounce his monastic life on account of the times, he loved that monastery from the depths of his heart and had something close to faith in it. He also held its monks in great esteem. He had instructed us that the monk who should chant at his deathbed had to be from that monastery. When he was close to death, he held up the name of a monk and said, 'The deathbed chanter must absolutely be this monk.' Later, my mother and everyone else called upon that monk and, as far as I can recall, he chanted the 'Sutra of Liberation.'

I've been searching around to see if there was anyone similar to my teacher in traditional biographies or the historical accounts of other Tibetans. I wonder if his style and behaviour aren't just a little bit reminiscent of the famous translator, Marpa Lotsawa. If you had to search for someone with a similar face amongst those alive now, I feel it would be the face of the poet Jangbu. I can't recall my teacher's face so clearly, but I'd go so far as to wager that it was pretty much the same.

In the Embrace of Letting Go

Topden Tsering

Grief holds poorly when one is airborne.

I learnt about my *Ani*'s passing, in Delek Hospital in Dharamsala, hours after I had booked the ticket to fly out to India from California. The past three days since I first heard about her hospitalization had been spent in anguished indecisiveness. I had wanted my father to accompany me so he could say his final goodbye to his nun older sister. But new concerns over his health as well as complications arising from pending Green Card applications for him and my mother prevented me from making an immediate departure. As such when I boarded the Air India flight from San Francisco to Delhi, it was too late.

My seat on the plane was in the middle: between the window and the aisle. On either side was seated an Indian gentleman, each of considerable girth, whose physical generosity was matched by his propensity for yapping. In Hindi, their inquiries, answers, anecdotes, complaints, traded over my head, full of knowing authority, as though America had bestowed on them an entitlement, which they couldn't wait to throw around in their home country. I feigned foreignness; both to the language and the country, but my forgery came with a cost. I was now assaulted by an overload of information and I couldn't even show I was affected by it.

Squeezed between the two—rendered immobile, insular—I felt like an island. Grief was its only inhabitant.

It was like a boulder had been forced on my heart, cold to the touch, enormous in mass, and unforgiving in weight. A deliberate effort, almost an unnatural struggle, was required of me to draw in each breath. When I exhaled, my lungs hurried to vent their fullness, as though guilty about the bounty of life left to them, as though ashamed of the accompanying noisiness. Then followed a brief moment of stillness, when my pain, until now throbbing, threw down roots and put up walls, making way for a suffering that seemed encumbered in eternity.

Mid-flight, some 30,000 feet above the ground, it felt jarring: this feeling of imprisonment in the realm of weightlessness, levity. Jammed between the two talkative, overweight passengers, I feared the crushing heaviness of my heart would rip a hole through the plane, sending us all tumbling down. In either direction there was little space for me to move, which I had hoped I could, so the pain would be more bearable, spread more evenly across my chest.

In my mind's eye, I attempted to bring my *Ani* alive. I looked for a happy image to settle on. I found one. It was in her room in the Ganden Choeling Nunnery where she stood, her face leaning towards mine, reaching for a forehead touch, a Tibetan greeting. Her head was freshly shaven and her eyes shone underneath eyelids that hung low in fleshy folds. A crisscross of wrinkles spread outward from her brows, her cheekbones, her mouth. 'Don't worry about *Ani*,' her pale lips moved. '*Ani* will be just fine.'

The recollection didn't last long. Elbowed out of the frame, another image took hold. This one of a picture my cousin in Dharamsala sent me via Facebook, taken on her first night in the hospital. She was a small bundle on a wheeled bed, at the head of which a younger nun sat, cross-legged so she could keep my *Ani* upright. An oxygen mask covered *Ani*'s nose and mouth, and outside it there was not much left to her face. I couldn't tell if her eyes were open or closed. I had never seen my *Ani* so sick. I had never seen my *Ani* looking so helpless.

I tried to shut out the image: a futile effort. For distraction I looked out the window to an engulfment of blinding light. Reaching up my hand to wipe away my tears, I couldn't escape a sinking feeling.

I had failed my *Ani*.

I had failed my *Ani* by not making it on time, by not being there to bend down over her, to show her my face. The nephew she had doted on, the nephew she had raised like her son when he was a little boy, the almost son she had often told not to worry over her because she would be just fine.

I had failed her by not being there to look into her eyes, to run my hand on her bristly scalp, and offer comfort: 'Don't worry *Ani*. I am here!'

* * *

Upon first hearing about *Ani*'s hospitalization, my younger sister in New Mexico, with whom my parents were staying, and I decided to keep the news from our father.

My *Ani* was Father's older sister, each to the other the only surviving sibling, both belonging to the generation from the other side of history, before occupation, before exile, before India. For the longest time, father had resisted coming to the United States—he didn't want to leave *Ani* alone in India. Mother had visited me several times before and while she liked America, she had to return to be with my father, who in turn wanted to be on hand to look after *Ani*.

For much of his life, between his late thirties and early sixties, Father led a troubled life. Like many Tibetan men from his background, he had an unhealthy appetite for alcohol, which addiction turned what was once a whip-smart and thoughtful man into an abusive husband, father, and brother. By the time he turned a corner, following a fatal health scare (severe liver complications), the first penance he made was towards *Ani*.

For the last fifteen or so years—after his picking up again on the thread of a normal life—father, afflicted with shortness of breath from years of physical inactivity, followed a prescribed routine. At dawn, he'd leave for *Kora*, a round of the wider circumambulation around the Dalai Lama's temple. A rosary in hand, he'd walk laboriously, stopping every so often to catch a breath (Baby steps, my sister would tease him, whenever we'd take a walk and Father would lag behind.) In the afternoon, he'd head for the nunnery, navigating the Bhagsu Road, chock-a-block with honking cars, taxis and autos-rickshaws, his slow strides now challenged into sidestepping over ditches, onto storefront steps, inches away from screeching tires. All this while his hand would be carefully wrapped around the content of his bag: a tiffin containing homemade food.

Inversely, his schedule when he was drinking had been no less predictable. In the morning Father would leave the house an erect man, full of purpose. Late in the night, Father would return home an inebriated mess, borne on the shoulders of fellow tavern-goers. He'd be drenched in a boisterous frenzy, equally given to loudly singing folk songs in his *tod* dialect and issuing, in Hindi, choicest curse words, *sala, benchod, bhoseri*, aimed at no one in particular, but inescapably stinging everyone within earshot.

Ani, much to my father's consternation, took poor care of herself. All her energy was spent reciting Mani, reading scriptures, meditating, and following a litany of spiritual observances. Bring her food and she'd at the most eat four spoonfuls before pushing it in front of a couple of dogs and cats always at her door. There were also the birds that descended on the terrace and the monkeys that roamed a few feet away, on the wooded trail leading to Kirti Monastery and the temple beyond, strewn with gnarly water pipes, baring traps for unheeding footsteps.

Bring her new clothes and shoes and you'd hardly see her in them. Even in the dead of Dharamsala winter, she refused to wear the down jackets and fleeces I'd bring her, citing religious codes against garments with full sleeves. 'It's for a reason,' she'd tell me, 'That a *Choepa's* robes are a simple affair.' A nun's shirt is devoid of accessories, consisting simply of holes to pull over one's head and slip her arms through; her frock is layers of folds held together by a cloth belt; her shawl a billowing expanse of unassuming fabric. Consequently, *Ani* refused to wear anything that had zippers or buttons. No wonder then that all the Uniqlo jackets and North Face fleeces I bought her disappeared into her trunk, to be given away to lay people she knew around town, 'who needed them more'.

On account of these strictures, also neglects, *Ani*, starting from when she was in her fifties, had been a sickly, malnourished woman. While the nunnery served healthy, delicious vegetarian meals, her doctor had recommended that she eat meat for strength. Hence Father's daily routine of bringing her a meat dish, then sitting across from her, making sure she took satisfactory bites, all the while gently berating her for sending away students and well-wishers who stopped by to help with cooking, laundry, cleaning, etc.; for letting in stray dogs and exposing herself to unpronounceable diseases; for not skipping group prayers in the main hall, even in the monsoon, down a long flight of slippery steps, lending dubious grip even to her walking stick.

Their affection was an odd interchange. Exasperation from his side, and, from hers a pretence of being agreeable. Not too unlike twenty or thirty years ago. The only difference was that then the sentiments had been reversed, with the two inhabiting opposite roles.

I can still see my child-self beholding one such scene.

Ani would have hurried to our house upon hearing of a fresh drunken outburst by Father. Its victims: my mother, my younger sisters, and myself. She had meant to offer herself as a shield, an arbiter of reason. By the end of a long exchange of reprimand, imploring, cajoling, she'd herself be reduced to tears. Her calm constitution, tempered by decades of spiritual practices, had frayed in front of a man given to blind rage. Defeated, she'd rise to leave; her eyes wet with tears, before clambering down the steps, while inside the house father retained a picture of hurtful indifference and intent.

As a young boy, the utter injustice of the scene had deeply moved me. Now, as an adult, seeing my father carry so much tenderness for *Ani*, I was equally touched.

As back then, now too, I am struck by the capriciousness of the human condition. By how desperately we struggle against the unforgiving ways of time and its many incredulous tricks.

* * *

A year ago, when I persuaded my father to join me in the United States, he finally relented. But in this country, which my sisters and I had made our home, and which was for most exile Tibetans, like for millions of others from poorer countries, a prized destination, Father existed without interest. Every other day, he'd ask to be connected on the phone with *Ani*. Some days the call would go through, and you'd hear on the other end a meek 'hello'. Father would leave her a series of instructions: to eat well, to dress warm, and to allow her disciples to do her laundry, to bring her food. On her end she'd respond with ready *yegh, yegh*, customary 'Yeses' bearing little sincerity.

On other days the phone would ring and ring and ring before going dead. This would make father imagine the worst. He'd call up my cousin and beseech him to immediately rush to the nunnery and check on *Ani*. His alarm would be impossible to miss, rankled with the vividness of a slideshow: *Ani*, unconscious, lying underneath the altar; *Ani*, writhing in pain, fallen by the door; *Ani*, rushed to the hospital, where she now lay in a bed, a forest of pipes sticking into her nose and mouth.

The missed connections would be from a familiar pattern. Ani would have unsuccessfully fumbled with her cell phone to locate the 'receive' button. It didn't help that my cousin had, as a marker, glued a piece of bright red tape on the incoming key. Or she'd have been groping in the pile of blankets to retrieve the ringing phone without luck, while my father listened on the other end with bated breath.

On the days the calls didn't go through, Father, predictably, would be agitated. Although he wouldn't say it, I could sense him holding me responsible for this unwelcome suspense. I could sense him blaming me for bringing him over and inserting the divide of a whole half world—spanning countries he didn't have names for and an ocean he had not heard of between him and his beloved sister.

Three months ago, Father, who is medically uninsured, had sent us into another health scare.

A complaint about some shortness of breath led to a doctor friend, Cynthia, graciously giving him an examination in her house in the upscale Berkeley Hills. He had found her meticulous check-up hugely satisfying. The prodding into his mouth and ears, the placing of stethoscope on his chest and back—he found these intimacies reassuring. He was amused and doubly gratified, when the doctor, listening to his heart, instructed him to pronounce, 'eeeee'. He had been mildly proud to demonstrate his mastery of the English alphabet. Leaving the house, he expressed surprise that Cynthia was a doctor. So unassuming, he said, and dressed so simply.

A full set of blood tests at a lab followed, which in turn led to trips to various clinics for X-ray, liver tests, and electrocardiogram (ECG). After seeing clouds of white spots on his X-ray, another doctor immediately advised us to go to the emergency room (ER) in a nearby hospital. For the past several days, during our visits to the numerous labs, multiple possible diagnoses had been suggested to me—tumour, bad liver, heart problem. I had kept the reports from both Father and Mother, sharing them on the phone only with my sisters, one in New Mexico, another in New York, yet another in Elmhurst. At the ER, blood was drawn and he was put underneath the hulk of a white machine for a CT scan. Then we were asked to wait for the results.

Waiting—hours slowly ticking away—by a narrow corridor, amid a blur of doctors, nurses, patients, stretchers and other equipment, Father grew restless. Twice, he grabbed men in white coats by their sleeves, calling them '*Dakta Saab*', and asking, in Hindi, why the long wait?

When the results were read to us, Father was relieved. I was overjoyed. Heart problem was ruled out, so was the liver tumour, and lung complications. The diagnoses settled on high blood pressure, diabetes and breathing difficulty. Back to square one. The white mushroom-shaped spots on his X-ray had been abrasions from some thirty years ago after he had survived tuberculosis. The faint bumps on his shoulders, back and legs, as Mother had repeatedly stressed, were reminders of his innumerable falls, in various stages of drunken conditions, all over the town—into ditches, by roadsides, down long flights of stairs. (And to think the brave folks in the 22 Establishment need parachutes, my mother joked, referring to the Indian government's Tibetan Army.)

Cynthia, now taking over, prescribed medicines.

Father, like many Tibetans his age, has a fondness for medicine. In India, when my mother or sister took him to a hospital after he complained of discomfort and the doctor discharged him without a prescription, Father would become upset. 'Not a good doctor,' he would declare. In McLeod Gunj, feeling a hint of headache, stomachache, etc., he'd rush to a Tibetan doctor. If the doctor, after contemplating his pulse with a closed-eye deliberation, decided that Father didn't need to take pills, he'd offer thanks with closed palms before his chest, before heading to another clinic. There, he'd wait for his turn to be seen by another doctor (another contemplation of pulse with a closed-eye deliberation), determined not to leave without small plastic bags full of black and brown pills.

After becoming sober, Father had attached keen attention to his health. At seventy-six, he is amongst the handful of the last of his generation in all of McLeod Gunj. In our neighbourhood above Bhagsu Road, jam-packed with narrow buildings with crooked staircases, from among the nine or ten families in our vicinity, father was the only surviving '*Pala*', the rest having passed, due to various health issues, mostly liver-related.

'The last man standing,' my younger sister, who has spent the most time with our parents looking after them, would quip.

Father gets up early to read Buddhist scriptures and offer prayers, then leaves the house—in Richmond, California, when he is with me; in Albuquerque, New Mexico, with my sister—for a morning walk, before returning for breakfast, after which he plops into a high chair—a tufted leather kind in my house; an upholstered counterpart in my sister's—to watch first all the Tibetan news channels (RFA), (VOT), (VOA), et al on YouTube and on TV, followed by an endless staple of South Indian action films, devouring flying cars and people being kicked around like tin-cans, while twirling his *mani* wheel with one hand.

Intermittently, at Cynthia's advice, he'd pace around the house, even go out for an afternoon walk, admiring spacious stucco buildings with manicured front yards, disapproving structures with wood exteriors, 'like our *Shing-khang* before we put up a building', a reference to the ramshackle of a house full of holes that I was born in. He'd follow a strict diet and, at the prescribed hours, happily pop the pills into his mouth.

A few months after my parents' arrival in the United States, I had submitted Green Card applications for them. Father had been nervous about the time the approval process would take (anything between six months to a year) and the restriction hoisted on him from travelling to India, to see *Ani*.

In the weeks leading to the 2016 US election, Father had watched Donald Trump on TV with amusement. Hearing the then-Republican candidate, to-be-president's anti-immigrant rhetoric, my parents had been alarmed. 'Will our applications be harmed?' mother had asked. 'There is not a chance he'll win,' I had said. I could see father getting worried about the uncertainty that lay ahead. It was no longer just the unimaginable space separating him from *Ani*. Time, too, was increasingly abandoning his side.

Not long before hearing about *Ani*'s illness, I received letters with requests for additional evidence from the US Citizenship and Immigration Services (USCIS). Before the submission of their applications, I had been careful about ensuring the completeness of the forms as well as supporting documents; I had gone over them again and again; I had consulted lawyers and other experts. I was momentarily discouraged, and then I diligently went about gathering the requested documents.

It is unlikely Trump had anything to do with this setback. Still, I couldn't help but wonder about the question Mother had asked when we watched him on TV, looking angry, pointing fingers, while issuing vitriol. It was an uncomfortable idea to entertain. This accidental intersection between perhaps the vilest president in the history of the United States of America bent on overturning the country's legacy of providing safe haven for the disenfranchised, and my parents, first-hand victims of China's illegal occupation, who—now doubly exiled, first from Tibet, then from India where they lived undocumented—presently in the twilight of their years, faced new uncertainties in this country their children called home.

I had just mailed in the requested papers when my cousin called me on Valentine's Day about *Ani*'s medical emergency. Knowing that Father would insist on travelling to India immediately, that he would worry himself sick, my sister and I decided to keep the news from him.

Ani had previously been hospitalized and had recovered. My mother, sisters, and I hoped for the same outcome, while closely monitoring developments through my cousin. Over the next day, she showed signs of improvement. Then she took a turn for the worse. Fast. She couldn't talk; it was hard to tell if she recognized people; at some point, she lost control over one side of her body. The head doctor had advised my cousin against taking *Ani* to Chandigarh or Delhi, six to twelve hours away. She wouldn't survive the bumpiness of the ride, the doctor had said.

Abandoning any thought of bringing Father along, I booked the tickets to Delhi, then onward to Dharamsala.

I was to fly the next day.

Later that evening, driving to a restaurant in Berkeley, I had thought about *Ani*'s loss of movement in the right side of her body.

One of my favourite things to do, when visiting *Ani* in her room in the nunnery, had been to put my head in her lap as she sat cross-legged, twirling with her left hand a rosary half-buried in a red cloth pouch. This was her precious rosary from Tibet from when she was a young nun. A gift from her teacher, it had been blessed by many lamas, including the Dalai Lama, and having thumbed over the beads perhaps millions, trillions, of times, she strictly followed a belief of not exposing the *Mala* made sacred by a long and complex series of *Ngag*, or tantric spells.

Snuggling up to her, I'd put her free hand in mine and gently rub my fingers over her knuckles, her palm. Looking amused, reciting *Mani* under her breath, *Ani* would give me a curious smile. Then, she'd untangle her hand and, raising it closer to her eyes, inspect it closely, as though she were seeing it for the first time. Perhaps looking for the cause of my infatuation with it.

My cousin had described to me how *Ani* had responded, upon waking, to not being able to move her right hand, the same hand I had cupped in my hands to lovingly caress and kiss. In the Delek Hospital in Dharamsala, *Ani* had struggled to raise her head from the pillows, her left hand twirling another rosary to look closely at her unmoving limb. What had gone through her head? Shock, panic, or reconciliation—I wouldn't know.

Out here in the traffic on Solano Avenue, my eyes trained on the cars ahead, my one hand on the wheel, I had felt *Ani*'s fingers slowly slipping away from my other free hand.

I was walking towards a restaurant when my cousin called again. It was dark and in the glow of the streetlights, my shadow gave chase to my heels. '*Ani* is having difficulty breathing,' he said, his voice breaking. I stopped in my tracks, bracing myself. 'She is not breathing,' he said. I had a sense he was hiding something, but I was terrified to pry. Finally, he gave in.

'*Ani* passed a few minutes ago. The nuns are praying, huddled around her bed.'

I had not been prepared for it. I had been praying for *Ani* to wait for me. Holding the lump in my throat, I rushed to find some privacy between parked cars and cried. What had so far been stuck in my throat, trapped in that mysterious place where pain breeds, now came out in loud sobs—an unwieldy ululation, a raspy reverberation of ungainly sound. It was like too much pressure had been put on my heart. I felt air emptying from the cavity as though about to collapse. Yet, all that emptiness, the openness, was not enough to hold the information that I was now withstanding, fighting from its becoming a reality.

Moments later, my phone rang again. It was my sister.

Having come to the end of her hold on secrecy, she had relayed the news to our Father who now came on the phone. He was surprisingly calm. It struck me that despite his alcohol-blurred years during his prime, despite the later affection he carried for his sister, he was a man surrendered to faith. In a matter of minutes, that brief continuum vacillating between here and gone, he had yielded unquestionably to the arrival of death.

He was no longer the one who needed protecting. It was I who needed it with my slippery hold on the belief system of my father, with my need for *Ani* to be forever around.

Father could hear that I was crying. 'Don't cry, son,' he said. 'There is nothing to be gained from shedding tears. It was *Ani*'s time. I am so glad you are flying out to India tomorrow. Be sure to carefully attend to the rites that await her passing when you are in Dharamsala.'

'Be sure to be the nephew to her who she doted upon like her own son.'

* * *

The morning of my flight I learnt *Ani*'s final rites had been scheduled for the day after I arrived in Dharamsala, three days away. Determined through Tibetan Buddhist astrology, it is typical for a body not to be laid longer than a day or two before cremation—a wait longer than that is uncommon. By some stroke of luck, I had been granted the opportunity to see her body—to bid farewell in person—before it was consigned to fire.

Standing before the long flight of steps leading to *Ani*'s room in the nunnery, with my cousin leading I begged for a moment to breathe. The weight I had carried on the plane from San Francisco, then in another to the Dharamsala airport, further in a rickety taxi that took me home in Mcleod Gunj, now threatened to keel me over. I needed to bend down to grab my knees.

Looming before me was the same retention wall I remembered from decades ago. Green moss dotted the partitions between the stone slabs in twirling, fuzzy outgrowths; occasionally, from its midst, sprang a small flower. My eyes rested on one such four-petaled plant, dew-kissed, and near symmetrical. Briefly, I was transported to my childhood when during monsoon I had stood transfixed before tiny rivulets issuing through the cracks, the water gushing off the surface, and where it met the assorted foliage, bouncing off the petals, their membranes wet and quivering. The sight had been one of the highlights during the rainy seasons; the wall had been a canvas and the interplay between the water and the vegetation a picture of constant marvel: abundant entertainment for a little boy, in the community of Buddhist nuns, with no friends his age.

I knew *Ani*'s body lay not in her room but in one of the smaller prayer halls, with dozens of nuns reciting scriptures in rotation and round the clock. In her room, I knew there were two monks, one of them *Ngagpa*, a tantric master, performing the rites to help *Ani* leave behind her earthly attachments. Out in the courtyard, there'd be *Ani*'s students, also their students, as well other nuns and relatives from Father's and Mother's sides.

Reaching the landing, a flurry of activities awaited me: meal-making and serving, tea-making and serving, unfurling, and rolling of *Khatas* (Tibetan greeting scarves offered now for condolence) and burning of juniper. All eyes turned towards me: the apple of *Ani*'s eyes, late by two full days. One of *Ani*'s older students, who

I remembered from when she was a young nun, walked up to me and squeezed my arm. She was fighting back her tears.

'*Ghenla* passed peacefully, without pain. She had decided it was time and had not wanted to be a burden on anyone—very much like how *Ghenla* was when alive, always turning away offers of help, always insisting on being self-sufficient,' *Ani* Choezin said.

Near us hovered four ruddy-cheeked nuns, the oldest perhaps twenty: *Ani* Choezin's disciples. *Ani*'s student and her pupils had been by her side throughout the hospitalization, also other students and, in turn, their pupils. There had been a constant stream of other nun visitors: friends and other members from the *Sangha* (religious community). Also present had been my cousin-brother and four or five other lay relatives. These relatives now asked me to sit down and have tea. 'You must be tired from the journey,' they said.

All the arrangements for the cremation had been made. The younger nuns from the nunnery had picked the wood and stacked them up in a truck before ferrying them to the cremation site, their bare arms bristling against splintered logs. In setting up the pyre bed, they had been helped by three or four elderly men experienced in the final passage of life, from the same local association to which father belonged, '*Toepa Kyidug*'.

Ani waited for you, *Ani* Choezin said. Her disciples nodded their heads, looking at me with sympathy.

In her room, I took in the same interiors I remembered from three years ago when I had last seen *Ani*, before leaving for Delhi to board a plane back to San Francisco. She had gotten up from the bed, unrolled a *Khata*, then putting it on my neck, leaning close and looking into my eyes, said, 'Don't worry about *Ani*. *Ani* will be just fine.'

Looking around the room, I ticked off articles that I remembered from the last time I had been here. It was as if not one item had been moved from its place. I saw the gas stove, the blackened pots, the two or three cups, and the spoon that always seemed to be without company, dangling at an odd angle over the makeshift kitchen counter as though it had just recently been licked off, meant for washing but forgotten. There were the toothbrush, the toothpaste, and the half-used red Lifebuoy soap on the shelves, also the red open-beaked jug *Ani* took out with her toiletries every morning, to bend over the common wash sink, from which to splash water on her face and her shaven head.

On the altar, atop a hand-me-down cupboard from Father, were the familiar statues of deities (Buddha, Tara, Guru Rinpoche), the framed photos of the Dalai Lama, Karmapa and several other lamas, and arrayed before them were offering bowls filled to the brim with water.

Had it been my *Ani* who last poured water into those bowls?

The cupboard held another memory. I would not have been more than twelve or thirteen when my second younger sister, perhaps six, during one of her childish plays had crashed into it, breaking the glass in one panel. A deep cut had been left on her hand, blood flowing everywhere. Panicked, Mother had cried; Father might have been in the house but of that, I have no memory. Mother had ordered me to rush to a nurse who lived a few blocks down, to ask for help. I had run down the steps, taking a sharp right corner on the Bhagsu Road, as fast as my legs could carry me. Finding myself below Nurse Chodon La's house, I had shouted at the top of my lungs, my eyes peeled on the faintly-lit windows, hoping for a shadow to pass: 'Nurse Chodon la, Nurse Chodon la, please come. My sister has cut her hand.'

At some point, the glass had been replaced. And at some point, my resourceful child-self had plastered on the same panel a sticker that read, in sparkly letters: 'I Love City Boy'. Over time, another sticker had been glued on the other panel: a picture of

Guru Rinpoche, a handiwork perhaps of Father, whose root guru was the Indian-origin Buddhist Master. And so, for the longest time, a glitzy advertisement for cosmopolitan attraction shared the same space as the image of an ancient master credited for subduing demons bedevilling the Dharma in Tibet.

The cupboard had been a magical artefact during my childhood years of living with *Ani*, as during my adolescence and adulthood when I visited her, bearing gifts and money. She'd reach her hand into it before producing an apple, a packet of biscuits, or an orange juice. She'd also retrieve from it packets of Mani pills, blessed chords, and amulets 'to keep me safe'. From it, she'd also conjure the same bundles of Indian rupees I gave her, now offered to me in her extended hand, 'for the road, to drink tea'.

Only the solitary table before her bed—on which now sat the two monks, loudly reading from scriptures, banging on drums, and crashing cymbals—seemed visibly disturbed, its original contents cleared away to make way for their scriptures and religious instruments; there were also cups filled with tea and plates heaped with snacks. I wondered about the rosaries, her inkpot, and prayer books that I had seen clutter the table. Mostly I wondered about my hand-me-down school notebooks, in which she practised writing in English, changing between her name and mine.

* * *

The Ngagpa, his head a mop of matted hair, when examining *Ani*'s various religious instruments, expressed admiration. He was especially impressed by my *Ani*'s *Daru*, a full-sized drum with a tiny brass globe attached to it via a string, which one flapped with one hand, causing the ball to bang against the taut surface. The instrument dated from her Nyingma lineage days in Tibet when she practised '*Chod*', a particular ritual of Tibetan Buddhism that focused on the severing of attachments.

Even the cloth cover was from Tibet, faded through half a century, its hand-stitched seams coming loose at various places, the fabric carrying a salty whiff from the land in which she had once been a young novice excited at the life of devotion that lay ahead. Before she had been forced into exile in India, some sixty years ago, by the fear of Chinese soldiers of whose kind she had not seen one but who she had heard were bent on destroying monasteries and nunneries, killing monks and nuns, to wipe out the faith. Her faith.

'She had been a real *Chod-pa*,' the tantric master exclaimed.

'There is no doubt your *Ani* picked the time of her passing,' he said. When *Ani* had been hospitalized, the nunnery was on winter break, meaning in their tending to her the nuns had faced no disruption to their practice: their group prayers, their dialectic debate training, also their school curricula including Tibetan and English classes. There had been no disturbance caused to their schedules when the nuns had stood by *Ani*'s side, offering medication, helping her to nature's calls, praying for her recovery.

With the Ngagpa, I consulted about the Buddhist astrological divination around her passing. The traditional almanac identifies the persons and objects of the deceased's attachments, Buddhist scripture texts (sometimes tomes of them) to be read by a community of monks or nuns, the statues of deities to be commissioned, all to help the deceased in her or his onward journey over the next seven weekly cycles, at the end of which, on the forty-ninth day, she or he enters a vessel for her or his reincarnation.

Given my *Ani*'s fondness for my father and me, I had been sure her soul had remained trapped by our sides. After an entire life spent in the practice of Dharma, her gaze unflinching from death and the realities hereafter, and during which time she had afforded little attention to her own wellbeing, which negligence caused much consternation to Father and me, I had long ago seen this irony becoming real: after death, *Ani*'s refusal to let go of us, which hesitation obstructing her passage into the afterlife, a journey for which she had invested a lifetime of preparation— meditation, scripture-reading, contemplation, strict adherence to conscious living, and constant watchfulness of the mind so that at the end, when the time had come, she could slip into the other side with no mind for who and what she left behind.

Surprisingly, that was not the case. The divination named three entities to which *Ani*'s soul had been tethered. The first was identified abstractly as an 'older' person. The second was some creatures or animals. And the third was leftover food.

It was not hard to make sense of the second and third pronouncements. When alive, *Ani* had had to listen to constant admonishments from Father and me, my mother and sisters for letting stray dogs and cats into her room and allowing them to make their home in the choice corners of her quarter, sometimes on her narrow bed. Occasionally, after we had exhausted our lungs from enumerating the likelihood of contracting dangerous diseases from such unsanitary associations, she'd act genuinely frightened and offer her resolve to not open her doors to the animals again. However, the next day we'd be sure to find her sitting cross-legged, eyes half-closed, one hand twirling a rosary and the other petting a cat in her lap while a dog snoozed at the foot of her bed.

The third object was the food she saved from the meals provided by the nunnery and the dishes brought to her by Father so she could feed the cats and the dogs and the birds on the terrace and the monkeys, which loitered not too far from her doorstep, outside the gate to the trail leading to the temple of the Dalai Lama.

'Your *Ani* is worried about who will feed the animals now that she's gone,' the Ngagpa said, pointing towards the threshold outside which lay two cats and a dog. Then the Ngagpa bent down to lift the cloth covering the kitchen counter and retrieved a plate of cooked meat. There were also whole loaves of bread wrapped up in newspaper, tucked away in a corner.

But who was the 'older' person?

Then, it struck me. During one of our phone conversations, my cousin had mentioned how *Ani* had reacted when *Ani* Sherab had visited her in the hospital.

Ani Sherab and *Ani* had known each other from Tibet when they were teenagers. Years later, they had found themselves in the same nunnery in Dharamsala where their friendship further deepened. The two had been inseparable: walking together to the Dalai Lama's temple for mass prayers on religious anniversaries, enjoying occasional meals in a restaurant in the marketplace, trudging around the circuitous path circling the His Holiness' residence, sitting next to one another during prayers in the nunnery's assembly hall, helping one another with meal-bringing and clothes-washing when either was sick, on Sundays, shaving each other's head and sitting out in the sun, chatting with other nuns. As a young boy, I had also been the beneficiary of love and affection from *Ani* Sherab. As an adult when I visited *Ani* with food and money, my rounds wouldn't be complete without calling upon *Ani* Sherab, whose room, in the same building, was one floor below. By the time *Ani* had been hospitalized, *Ani* Sherab was herself sickly and mostly confined to the bed.

At the hospital, when *Ani* Sherab had visited, my *Ani* had acted strange. By now declared by doctors as incapable of recognizing faces, and despite her almost lifeless condition, *Ani* had struggled to prop herself up and lifting her one hand to remove the mask, she had stuck out her tongue in a traditional show of respect. This had alarmed her caregivers who immediately shepherded *Ani* Sherab out of the room lest *Ani* continued to exert herself.

'Yes, yes,' the Ngagpa said when I mentioned *Ani* Sherab. 'Your *Ani* is worried about her friend's health, given that she has been ill for a long time.'

* * *

Finally, I found myself outside the room where *Ani*'s body lay. A swell and ebb of high-pitched female voices, nuns reading scriptures, greeted me; there was also the crashing of cymbals and banging of drums. Ever since I had heard about her passing, outside a restaurant in Albany in California, I had wanted nothing more than to see her, so that I could fix my eyes on her for as long as possible so that her image—even with her eyes shut and her body stilled—would be permanently seared in my mind, to be forever available for evocation for the rest of my life, until I grew old and my memories faded and I too faced the end of my own life. Nursing this desire on the plane to Delhi, then on another to Gaggal, during the bumpy taxi ride to Dharamsala, then after having dropped off my luggage at home, walking towards the nunnery past the shops, motorcycles, taxis, and the blur of faces, I had been running over, again and again, the moment when I would behold my deceased *Ani*'s face. I had decided that I wouldn't cry; I had decided that I'd kiss her: on her eyelids, on her cheeks.

I had been prepared for the cold touch on my lips.

With the cacophony of chanting from inside, I knocked on the door—more out of habit from having lived in the United States for the last eighteen years than anything—before gently pushing it open. To my right, some thirty or thirty-five faces looked up from the scriptures and towards me before turning their eyes back on the text, reading intently, swaying their bodies. Right in front of me was a screen made of two hanging bed sheets slung over a string running across the room. This could have served as a partition for privacy in a typical room-sharing arrangement. Here, the covering was meant to provide respectability for the deceased, and an illusion of distance to the living, those who inhabited the same space for hours on end offering prayers. From the time *Ani*'s body had been brought here, dozens of nuns changed shifts every four or five hours so that there was not an interval of more than ten minutes when high-pitched prayers had not filled the room, both during the day as well as through the night.

Prying open the curtains, I was not prepared for what I saw. *Ani*'s body was tightly wrapped in a white cloth from head to toe and it lay unceremoniously on the ground on a thin sheet. A poster with ritualistic iconography—a circle, clamped between the teeth of a wrathful deity, showing people and animals in numerous stages of living and dying lay propped against the wall just above her head. Next to it was a picture of the Dalai Lama. A mountain of white scarves was heaped on one side. A small stone, a few flowers and some coloured sands were placed right at the centre along the length of her body.

'Why not at least a mattress?' was the first thought that came to mind as I raised my closed palms over my chest, readying to say a prayer. 'If not a proper bed,' the noise continued.

No matter how hard I tried, the prayers were hard to come. I found disturbing the incongruity of the situation. The *Ani* I had come to see, travelling from California to India, was a white bundle almost cast to a corner much like a bag of dirty laundry. It didn't help that the knot tied over her head, which closed the loop for the shroud, tightly wound around her, reminded me of a toffee wrapping.

The anonymity given to her by the ghoulish disguise was difficult to face. I was unsure if it was the validation of her identity that I was after or a familiar vision on which to hang the words of my supplications. Still I prayed: wishing her to find a speedy reincarnation, as a human being in a household and an environment that gave her, in her new life, the facilities to pursue Dharma, the Buddhist faith; wishing for the removal of all obstacles in her way for the remainder of the forty-nine days, during which, as we believed, her consciousness would roam, across spaces; wishing that our paths would cross again, in this life, or in one of the lives after.

Briefly, I wondered if I had noticed, from the corner of my eyes, the body move, under the white sheet.

* * *

Later that night, back in my house, as I lay in bed, in the pitch darkness caused by the frequent power outages, I ran over again and again my audience with *Ani*'s body and the strange mix of emotions that had overcome me.

As the layers of initial impressions—sensory, aesthetic—with its impulse for contextualizing—why and how—peeled off from my recollection, I was hit by the cold, simple realization.

My *Ani* was gone.

Try as I might, no amount of good or bad things waiting to happen to me, from here on, would prompt her to materialize at our door, as had so predictably happened before. As a little boy, if I had a little cold, there'd be *Ani*, reliably armed with Tibetan pills. If the family returned from our sweater-selling trips in Bareilly in the northern plains, which I'd join during my winter vacation, there'd be *Ani* with hot meals and groceries. If Father slipped into his drunken rage, there'd be *Ani* to cover us children from his violence, and to protect Mother. If I topped my class in the annual examinations, there'd be *Ani* with her *khata*, and her recommendation that we visit the many lamas around the town to offer them thanks. If I'd been caught by a vendor trying to steal a soccer ball at one of the shops in lower Dharamsala, there'd be *Ani* to fall at the man's feet and implore, '*Babuji, maaf karo!* [Babuji forgive me!]'

Try as I might, no whim or urgency to see her would make her available, either in the nunnery—praying in the assembly hall, deep in meditation in her room—or in the marketplace where she'd have gone to shop for fruits for her altar or at the Dalai Lama's temple where she'd be seated amongst the nuns, reading from her scriptures, holding shy conversations with those who'd stopped by to say hello. No longer could I simply walk to the nunnery and barge into her room and see her smiling face. No longer could I creep up on her in the marketplace and get a confused look-over. No longer could I pull at her arm at the temple and steal mischievous pleasure from her all-too-serious pronouncements of having no time for small banters.

In that moment, struggling to train my eyes in the dark on something, anything, I was overcome by the irrevocability and the inescapability of the loss.

Ani was gone forever. Gone forever. Forever.

A Stranger in My Native Land: Kumbum

Tenzing Sonam

Kumbum Monastery grew up around the spot where Tsongkhapa, one of Tibet's greatest scholar-saints, was born in 1357 to a nomad family. Tsongkhapa reformed Tibetan Buddhism and his teachings gave rise to the Gelugpa Order, which became the dominant religious and political force in Tibet. The monastery was consecrated in 1582 by Sonam Gyatso, the Third Dalai Lama, and in time, became renowned as one of Tibet's six great Gelugpa monasteries.

In my father's time, nearly 4000 monks lived here, their collective energy engendering several of Tibet's great religious thinkers and scholars. They came from all over Amdo and from as far away as Mongolia and the Russian Buddhist enclaves of Buryatia and Kalmykia. The monastery was closed soon after communist Chinese forces took control of the region in 1949, and a large section was levelled during the Cultural Revolution. In the late seventies, Kumbum slowly came to life again, but the activities of the monastery were tightly regulated and today, only a maximum of 400 monks can be enrolled. With restoration, Kumbum suffered another fate; its proximity and accessibility to China made it a potential tourist attraction, and in an effort to realize this, the authorities have turned the monastery into a museum-like heritage centre.

* * *

We are staying within the monastery complex, at the residence of Zorgey Rinpoche, one of Kumbum Monastery's high lamas, who is closely connected to my family; the previous incarnation and the founder of the lineage was my great uncle. The present Zorgey Rinpoche is now in his seventies and has lived in exile for the past four decades, the last thirty years in America. Following a family tradition, Nyima is the Rinpoche's steward, and despite his master's absence, represents his interests at the monastery.

All tourists pay an entrance fee to visit the monastery, but pilgrims are exempt. Thanks to our guide, an old monk who works with Nyima, we fall into the latter category. We go from shrine to shrine, making our offerings, joining the pilgrims who are mostly nomads, traditionally dressed and speaking the Amdo dialect. Photographs of the Dalai Lama and the late Panchen Lama are prominently displayed in all the chapels, a reminder of the extent of the Dalai Lama's influence inside Tibet. Pressed up against the pilgrims in the dark interiors of the temples, the hushed sounds of their devotions mingling with the familiar smell of butter lamps and watched over by the serene faces of the giant Buddha statues, I can imagine what Kumbum must once have been like. But the spell is broken by a group of Chinese tourists who barge into our midst, unconcerned by the display of reverence and piety around them, their bullhorn-toting leader loudly explicating in a brutally insistent and shrill voice.

We visit a building that houses displays of the butter sculptures that Kumbum is renowned for—intricate tableaux of scenes from

Buddhist mythology populated by gods and goddesses and lesser beings, all meticulously shaped out of vividly coloured butter. But the skills of Kumbum's butter sculptors are obviously adaptable; one display case encloses a large tableau of the Palace of Heaven at Tiananmen Square, complete with tiny representations of Mao, Zhou, Deng and company, frozen in the archetypal Communist gestures of applause. I marvel at this improbable juxtaposition of the sacred and the stridently profane.

I find it disturbing that most of the monks we encounter speak only Xining Chinese. Has the monastery become a mere showpiece for tourists, its monks placed there simply to provide the requisite colour? It is only after we have been here for a few days that I discover that Kumbum's monastic legacy is very much alive. In one of the old courtyards of the monastery, we come upon a group of about fifty monks engaged in a vigorous debating session—the formalized system of dialectical inquiry that is at the heart of the Gelugpa tradition. The staccato explosions of their ritual handclaps punctuate their excited arguments. To my surprise, they are debating in Tibetan. The majority seem to be in their twenties and would have been born long after the Communist Chinese takeover of Tibet. They would have grown up in a world bereft of religion; Kumbum would have lain empty and in ruins, a decaying symbol of a forgotten past. And yet, here they are, their faith undimmed, once again engaged in the spiritual traditions that are at the core of their identity as Tibetans.

* * *

My father was born in the village of Nagatsang, five kilometres from Kumbum Monastery. Our ancestors were nomads who settled there shortly after the establishment of the monastery in the sixteenth century. From the seventeenth century, large groups of Chinese and Muslim migrants moved into the region and soon outnumbered the sparse Tibetan population. When my father was a child, the three original Tibetan families of Nagatsang were surrounded by over fifty Chinese households and this is the case even today, except the families have multiplied and the village has expanded.

As the youngest son, my father was destined to become a monk at Kumbum Monastery—two of his older brothers were already monks. But my grandfather was unusually far-sighted and realized that unless Tibetans became proficient in the Chinese language, they would increasingly become marginalized in a society that was completely dominated by Chinese and Muslims. So, instead of Kumbum, my father was sent to the local Chinese school and from there, in 1945, to the Institute for Frontier Minorities in Nanking. Soon after he arrived in Nanking, he met and befriended Gyalo Thondup, the older brother of the fourteenth Dalai Lama, who had come to study at the nearby University of Political Science.

My father briefly returned to Nagatsang in 1946. This was his last visit home. In early 1949, the Communists were on the verge of a national victory and their troops were poised to enter Nanking. Gyalo Thondup and my father fled to Shanghai and from there to India. By the time they arrived in India and based themselves in the border town of Kalimpong—then the most important Indian trade post with Tibet—Communist troops were already on their way to the Tibetan capital, Lhasa. The two went to Lhasa in 1952 but their visit was short-lived; the Chinese occupation forces had set up base there and were suspicious of Gyalo Thondup's motives for coming back. After their return to Kalimpong, Gyalo Thondup initiated a number of operations to support the growing resistance movement inside Tibet, the most significant of which was to solicit support from the CIA. My father was delegated to coordinate and oversee the CIA's undercover aid program. Before long, he found himself embroiled in the murky world of espionage and guerrilla warfare, an involvement that dictated his life for the next twenty years.

After the fall of Lhasa in 1959, the resistance forces, supported by the CIA, regrouped in a remote corner of northern Nepal; my father was the key liaison between the two. The CIA pulled out abruptly in 1969, a precursor of the soon-to-come détente between America and China. The guerrillas continued their campaign until 1974 when they were finally disbanded after a tense showdown with Nepalese troops. My father was involved in this confrontation and, along with six other guerrilla leaders, spent seven years in a Nepalese prison as a result. After his release, he worked for the Dalai Lama's Government-in-exile in Dharamsala in northern India and eventually attained the rank of a minister. Fifty years have passed since my father left Nagatsang.

* * *

A few days after our arrival in Kumbum Monastery, my wife Ritu and I visit Nagatsang. The low, rolling hills on either side of the dirt road from Rusar are dotted with neat stacks of freshly harvested wheat, row after row of aesthetically pleasing inverted V's that somehow look quintessentially Chinese. We enter the village; high mud walls surround each dwelling and intricately carved wooden entrances—their frames papered with auspicious Chinese characters—lead into their compounds.

We stop outside the house of one of my relatives. Dhondup, the eldest of my first cousins, comes out to greet us. Inside, a lot of people are gathered—various cousins, their wives, and children— all smiling and laughing and speaking Xining Chinese, while I, also beaming, reply in Tibetan, our greetings spontaneous, warm, and mutually unintelligible. We are ushered into the main room.

There are sofas on either side of a low table and a wood-burning stove in the middle. The walls are decorated with glossy posters of sylvan, Alpine scenes and postcard chalets beside tranquil lakes. Picture frames crammed with snapshot collages hang prominently. I notice photographs of my family, even a few wedding pictures of Ritu and me, and I am suddenly moved by the thought that my relatives, whom I am now meeting for the first time, have spent years of their lives with our pictures on their walls.

Dhondup has flourished since the economic reforms; he is now a building contractor and a rich man by village standards. We are offered small cups of strong alcohol that we are made to knock back in a gulp. Bottles of beer are opened and, simultaneously, cups of a local speciality—green tea, dried fruits and rock sugar steeped in hot water—are placed in front of us. The women serve us; a pork dish, the meat succulent with fat, chicken stewed in soya sauce, stir-fried green peppers with mutton and fried aubergines, all accompanied by steamed and baked bread.

Three of my first cousins sit with us, steadily downing alcohol. Nyima interprets for us; none of the others speaks a word of Tibetan. Dhondup is the most garrulous. He is also the only one who remembers my father: 'Your father used to come home from school and play the flute. We were only children then, but we loved him so much. Oh, I have so much to talk to you about, if only I could speak Tibetan!'

'Is she Tibetan?' asks one of my cousins, pointing at Ritu.

'No,' I say. 'She is Indian.'

'Is she a Tibetan born in India?'

'No, she's a native Indian.' I ask Nyima, 'Have they seen Indians before?'

'Only on television,' he replies.

'He is Tibetan but he looks like an Indian,' says another of my cousins, pointing at me.

'I guess I've lived so long in India that I've become an Indian myself!' I reply to their merriment. But the irony is that in exile, I have had the freedom to develop and express my identity as a Tibetan more completely than my relatives here and unlike them, I was brought up with strong nationalistic aspirations. Here, Tibetans have been a minority for so long that for them even the notion of a separate and independent Tibet is unimaginable.

The morning advances. My father becomes the focus of our conversation. To my cousins, he is the last surviving member of their parents' generation and, as such, the patriarch in absentia. They tell me to convince him to return; they want him to live out his final years in his family home among his many relatives. I promise to convey their message but deep down, I know that my father will never return. He has spent most of his life actively working for the cause of Tibet's independence. For him to return would be an admission of failure, a negation of his entire life's work.

The talk, the alcohol and the rush of memories make Dhondup melancholic, and he unexpectedly breaks down and sobs like a child, hugging me, speaking to me in Xining Chinese, shaking his head and groaning as if racked by some deep, searing pain. I cradle him and try to comfort him, confused, the alcohol gone to my head as well—these unfamiliar surroundings, this stranger in my arms with whom I have nothing in common, and yet who is bound to me by ties that are more deep-rooted than shared memories or experiences.

After a while, we visit the very spot where my father was born; the original house has long since been dismantled and literally divided among three of my cousins.

'These are the beams from the old house,' Dhondup says. 'And that tree was there when your father was a child—take a picture of that, he'll remember it—and that's the spot where he used to sit and read his books or play the flute.' My cousin has recovered from his momentary breakdown, and he is now even more drunk, staggering, grinning broadly, doing an impromptu jig, and saying to me, 'This is one of the happiest days of my life because you have come back to your native land, and we have finally met.'

We are now to pay our respects at the graves of our ancestors. We walk through the village in conspicuous procession, Ritu and me in our Western, mountaineering-style clothes, various cousins and nephews carrying bits and pieces of our gear—my camera bag, the video backpack, a tripod—and my drunk cousin, supported on either side by two boys, singing and lurching wildly. We pass a group of old men sitting beside the road. One of them remembers my father; they had gone to school together as children. He peers at me as if to find some identifying feature that will connect my face to the one he dimly remembers from more than sixty years ago, but he shakes his head, either giving up on the effort or simply not believing that I am who I claim to be.

Just outside the village, in a small clearing beside the path, lie a few unmarked mounds of earth. These are the graves of my grandparents. I am taken by surprise since Tibetans usually cremate their dead or feed their remains to vultures. But here in the Kumbum area, Tibetans have assimilated the Chinese custom of ancestor worship. A cousin burns coloured paper—symbolic money—as an offering while the rest of us make prostrations in front of the graves. Seeing me participate in their family ritual, Dhondup is again overcome by emotion. Wailing loudly, he collapses on top of one of the mounds: 'Grandma! Two of your grandchildren have come all this way to see you, and you are not here to receive them . . .'

We troop across the fields to a site above the village where more mounds are scattered—various granduncles and aunts. From here, the golden roofs of Kumbum are visible at the far end of the narrow valley.

Dhondup is once more in high spirits. 'This spot,' he says, his arms flailing, 'is your father's, and this . . .' he stumbles towards me, 'is your spot and this . . .' he gestures at Ritu, 'is for you!'

The sun is setting. The surrounding hillsides have taken on a warm, golden, almost liquid sheen, and their rows of haystacks stand out, stark and surreal, like a de Chirico painting.

My relatives, like most Tibetans in the Kumbum region, are literally clinging to the last shreds of their cultural identity. They still have Tibetan names and are officially registered as ethnic Tibetans, a minority status that allows them certain privileges, and most importantly, they still maintain their faith in Tibetan Buddhism—the proximity of Kumbum Monastery continues to exert a strong influence on their lives. But in every other respect, they have become indistinguishable from their Chinese neighbours. Until the onset of the Cultural Revolution, their womenfolk could always be recognized by their Tibetan dress without which they never ventured outside, but the madness of the intervening years wiped out that one surviving display of ethnic separateness.

The loss of language and traditions is the first step in the dissolution of cultural identity. Here among my relatives, in this far corner of Tibet, that process seems almost complete.

Nowhere to Call Home

Tenzin Tsundue

Boarding a crowded Delhi Metro train, I was crammed up with four college boys who seemed quite amused by my Tibetan face. As if the grins exchanged among them weren't enough, one boy let out a catcall—'Ching chong ping pong'. I face this every day and usually don't have the time or energy to react to such racist verbal attacks. Since I had a couple of stations to go, I inched closer to the teenager and shook hands with him. While still holding his hand I said, *'Yenna da, yenna wennu?'* (Hey man, what do you want?). They knew it was a South Indian language but couldn't even guess which. Then I taunted him in Hindi: *'Aap ko Tamil nahin ati hai kya?* [So, you don't speak Tamil?].' By then, the entire crowd on the train was staring at us, listening to every bit of the exchange.

To this new-found audience, projecting my voice, I gave an impassioned lecture on Indian nationalism, quoting the Right-wing Indian Prime Minister about the beauty of India's unity and diversity among its 1.4 billion population. By then, the entire coach must have vowed silently never to take on a 'chinky' in public.

Until the mobile revolution, when wires connected the world, we encased ourselves in STD/ISD booths to make phone calls. International trunk calls were expensive, but a certain call package made phone calls to Tibet affordable. Since half of Dharamshala

Tibetans came from Tibet in recent years, they all called Tibet regularly. This was the only direct link between exile and home.

Once, on Losar, the Tibetan New Year, I watched a long line of young men and women outside a phone booth in McLeod Ganj. One by one, the refugees entered the cubicle, spoke to their loved ones in Tibet, cried, and came out emotionally wrecked, then paid and left. I called the booth the Cry Box. I realized that the maximum number of Tibetans in Dharamshala cry during Losar.

That evening, as I walked down the hillside, taking the shortcut through the pine woods and oaks, I reflected that they were fortunate to have someone to cry to, a house to call home. Being exile-born myself and having been deposited in a boarding school as a semi-orphan from early childhood, I find it painful even to write here that I grew up distanced from my family. That night I wrote:

> *'Losar is when we the juveniles and bastards*
> *call home across the Himalayas*
> *and cry into the wire.'*
> (*from the poem* 'How I Lost My Losar')

Through the profound loneliness of being far away from my parents and our imagined homeland, I have often thought that we are children of our circumstances and that history is our father and the culture that nourishes us is our mother.

As refugees, we have been physically uprooted from our homeland, but as transplants, we are unable to settle down in the foreign land. Over and above that, even the future looks bleak today. As born-refugees we have nowhere to call home. My parents' generation looks to the past with nostalgia for the memories of the homeland they left behind, but as exile-borns, for us, more than the borrowed memory—our history—the dream of liberating our country fires our imagination. We look to the future with hope. Freedom is my first inspiration in life.

My parents were teenagers when they followed His Holiness the Dalai Lama into exile, escaping the persecution by Mao's army in 1959. Initially, most Tibetan refugees worked as road construction labourers in the early rehabilitation period. My mother tells me I was born in a tent in a roadside coolie camp in Lahaul valley in the early 1970s.

I must have been a restless toddler. Mother says she used to tie a rope around my waist and peg it on the roadside while they broke stones and laid the road. After my father's death in our camp in Manali, North India, we moved to Kollegal in the South Indian state of Karnataka and pioneered the Tibetan settlement most distant from the Himalayas. I was two-and-a-half years old.

I first heard about Tibet from my grandmother. She was a storehouse of stories. Her tales about Tibet built up an image of a country we had never seen. Our refugee camp was set up on the outskirts of Sathyamangalam jungle, the thickest jungle in all of South India, where the notorious outlaw Veerappan used to hunt elephants and log sandalwood trees—we had truly been rehabilitated in the middle of nowhere. There, in the hot, dense jungles of Karnataka, my grandmother told us stories of snow mountains and yaks; of apples, peaches, and apricots. *Momola* had songs for everything: songs for games, skipping, farm work in our maize fields and the long walks to the local vegetable market. She told us stories of the folklore figure Aku Tompa's wit and wisdom. And this is how we became Tibetan, even after being born in India and never seeing the real Tibet.

Every once in a while, the afternoon somnolence in our village was broken by the shrill call of the Indian woman who came into our camp to sell the popular South Indian rice-cake snack, idli. Bored with our bland and overcooked Tibetan food, we kids would rush towards her. We loved the soft idlis, which were served on a banana leaf and dipped in spicy masala soup called sambar, with a dash of coconut chutney. Sometimes, the ice cream vendor came by on his bicycle, a bullhorn blaring its *pom pom* greeting. On other occasions, it was the bucket exchange man shouting in Tibetan in a long wavering tone: '*Ha . . . yang . . . dung . . . pey . . .*'

Having never left our refugee colony, I had often wondered, and even asked my mother, where these Indians came from, not realizing we were the ones who came from outside, all the way from the high Himalayas. It was not until in school that I first understood that we did not belong to the country we were born into and that we had lost the independence of our country and were now living outside Tibet at India's sympathy. This shattered my little boy's pride. This initial hurt transformed into anxiety as I imagined our people being blindfolded, made to kneel with hands tied behind them, and then shot in the back of their heads. This, their children were made to watch. As the body slumped into the pit, the kids cried.

There came the guilt of living in freedom, while our brethren suffered tyranny, which was replaced by the great resolve to struggle for the freedom and dignity of our people even though it required a herculean effort. This resolve inspired me to take a lifelong pledge. I was eleven years old. Today, I honour this pledge with a red bandana that I wear on my forehead. I have promised never to take it off until Tibet is free and to work for Tibetan freedom every single day.

After schooling, my first foray outside the Tibetan community was to Madras, the capital of the Tamilian world in South India. I was shocked, not only by the people, place, and language but also by the palate. My tummy, raised on Tibetan gastronomy, was being tested by fiery masala foods. My childhood snack, idlis, resurfaced, but this time as the staple main course. In the first week, the tangy masala meals were fun. However, by the third week, my Tibetan digestive system started to give up. The light rice meals not only made us hungry again soon, but the masala burned our guts.

Often, in the middle of the night, I sat up on my bed, pressing a wet pillow to my belly while trying to study. My guts burned and I regurgitated bile. Combined with tackling Shakespeare, Tagore and Subramanium Bharathi, the anxiety kept me up late in my bed in the half-lit room, and I cried deep into the night.

Now, South Indian cuisine is one of my favourites and even after twenty-five years, I can still show off a smattering of Tamil. Where adaptation meets a dead end, creativity takes the lead forward; perhaps exile is the most fertile ground for growth.

Two years ago, I went on a speaking tour of the United Kingdom. Tibetans living in the towns and cities that I visited hosted us. After much speaking, travelling and interviews, when we gathered for dinner with long-lost friends, the food was inevitably rice, dal, and curry, typically Indian. Tibetans may have gone to the West, but they have never left India.

Today, almost 70,000 Tibetans have immigrated to the West, and they have not only become citizens of the world but preserved their identity. However, the third-generation youth is a concern; like most immigrant children, they have inherited the blood and the stories, but, in large part, not the language.

When my classmate and buddy Choegyal dropped out of regular college, friends thought he was straying because of his craze—music. He listened to Hindustani music when none of us had developed a taste for it. He would go '*aaaa aaaa*', drawing clouds in the air with his hands, as he tried to sing intricate ragas. Many years later, I saw him leading singing tours in Australia, packed in an old sputtering brown minivan. He travelled for months singing and telling stories of Tibet in different villages and towns. He sings long arias in the traditional Tibetan pastoral tunes, which are immediately arresting and soulful. A deep sense of longing and loneliness pervades his melodies. Recently, he has been nominated for a Grammy, his first global recognition.

During a phone conversation a few years ago, a Tibetan who lived in Tibet told my friend in Sweden with a great sense of pride that Chinese in Tibet still do not dare to walk alone in Tibetan neighbourhoods, as they fear being knifed or mugged. My friend asked him how that was possible, as the Chinese were now the majority in Tibet. The native observed that the Chinese had not yet overcome their archetypal fear of Tibetans and Mongolians as barbarian and that Chinese exoticization of Tibetan culture has further reinforced this civilizational stereotype.

As a poet and former political prisoner, my friend Phuntsok Wangchuk had always been the first to speak up against Chinese propaganda in Tibet, for which he had been tortured and jailed for six years. But the anti-Japanese propaganda films he had enjoyed in Tibet seemed to have worked on him. As a result, when he first arrived in Dharamshala, he couldn't believe his eyes watching the almost exaggerated politeness and the courtesy regime of the Japanese youngsters who bowed thrice before serving the Tibetan political prisoners with food and clothing.

Tsewang Dhondup arrived in Dharamshala with his wounded arm slung around his neck. He said, 'I hid in the mountains for months and escaped Tibet to bear witness to the atrocities I have seen with my own eyes and suffered myself.' Tsewang was shot twice in the uprising protest that spread across the Tibetan Plateau in the months leading up to Beijing Olympic Games in 2008.

This Uprising gave birth to two movements: the Lhakar movement celebrates and instils cultural resistance, while a series of unabated self-immolations demanded 'freedom for Tibet and the return of His Holiness the Dalai Lama to Tibet'. So far, there have been 155 known cases of Tibetans burning themselves inside Tibet alone, making their ultimate sacrifice of life for freedom.

A while back, a friend's stay with her family in Tibet was cut short and she was told never to return. She told me that the entire country of Tibet has been under lockdown; even the few passports issued have been revoked. Every individual has been registered as a number and pinned down to each small unit of dwelling and their movement is kept under surveillance. Tibet is now a police state.

China's mining in Tibet for lithium, gold, and rare earth is pushing Tibetan nomads and farmers out of their ancestral land, coercing them to rehabilitate in artificial villages, much like how White Americans caged Native Americans into fenced plots called Reservations.

Once on a long train journey through Central India, I sat down on the entrance footboard with a stranger. Like me, my co-passenger, Ramchand, didn't have a reserved seat. Over a cup of chai, he looked at my face and enquired if I was Chinese. Hiding my immediate irritation, I put my best foot forward and declared: '*Hum Dalai Lama admi hain*' (I am a Dalai Lama follower). That didn't ring a bell with him. Now, I found myself in a crisis as his assumption still hadn't changed. Banking on my ultimate resort I said: 'I belong to the Mount Kailash country'. He blinked. For his ignorance, I wanted to take revenge. So, I asked Ram.

Me: Lord Shiva lives on Mount Kailash?
Ram: Yes.
Me: Mount Kailash is in Tibet?
Ram: Yes. Yes.
Me: Mount Kailash has been Shiva's abode for thousands of years?
Ram: Yes. Yes. Yes.
Me: That makes lord Shiva a Tibetan?
Ram: hmmm

I later related this story to a much-entertained audience at Awadh Conclave, the literary festival in Lucknow. And since in the story, Ram has lost Shiva to Tibet, I wanted to compensate the audience. So, I said since His Holiness the Dalai Lama has been living in India for sixty years as a refugee and because he has globally championed India's ancient wisdom and calls himself a son of India, I declared that the Dalai Lama is Indian.

Inspired by Indian freedom fighters like Bhagat Singh and Subhas Chandra Bose, many years ago, I went to Tibet to fight China. Alone. After graduating from Loyola College, Madras, I went to Ladakh, the nearest approach to track a path to sneak into Tibet. I taught English in a Tibetan refugee school near Leh and later made my route across the Tibet border on foot. I was twenty-two.

My plans worked only in crossing the Indian border, but once inside, I got lost in the cold desert for days, nearly died, and later was arrested by Chinese military police. They interrogated me, beat me up, denied me food and sleep, and threw me in jail.

During those long interrogation sessions, they threatened me with execution by a bullet in the back of the head. The legendary story of Chinese public executions the elder generation of Tibetans told us kept flashing through my head. I marked my days on the prison wall with a nail until I lost count. This was the best training I have received in my life.

Today, when I get arrested for protesting the visiting Chinese President, and when Indian police try to intimidate me, I tell them to calm down and say that I am trained by Chinese interrogation and that we could skip the time pass and focus on working together.

We call ourselves refugees to keep alive our dream to return to our homeland and India calls us foreigners—perhaps a leverage against China—though the constitution of India recognizes us as citizens.

In seventy years, Mao Zedong's China has become an economic superpower but, in the process, killed its own Buddha. Tibet has lost one-sixth of its population and almost all the monasteries, but they couldn't change us in seventy years. Today, Tibet's Buddhism may be quietly changing China.

The struggle for Tibet's independence is not just a national movement for me but also a very personal struggle. I have created for myself a personal record; my protest actions have sent me to jail sixteen times, while speaking tours have taken me to twenty foreign countries. I have always felt rejuvenated and spiritually liberated after each jail episode. I have found freedom in jail; I have learned to live with strangers charged with murder, rape, and robbery by sharing food, a room, and a toilet. I have learned to live with a hanky as a towel, a finger for a toothbrush, shoes as a pillow and a shirt to cover myself when I sleep on the floor.

I live an old lifestyle, that of a wandering minstrel. I travel for months touring towns and cities, telling stories and reading poetry. I sell my books, and that pays for my food and travel. Although my income is small, my expenses are even smaller. I live a simple and minimal, need-based life. I live in two pairs of clothes. My friends think I have only one, but I have two; I wear them in turns.

Home is not a house but the purpose that takes us places, and sometimes away from our own home. Reasons to live can make strangers family, and no country foreign. When we come out of our comfort zone, we learn to make ourselves feel at home, anywhere. Stuck at home with old habits and malice, a house can turn into a prison, sometimes. Once, a prince from the Ganges left his family and kingdom in search of higher truth and never returned. He found a key to happiness which, even to this day, is practised as the path to freedom, and for many, this is home.

The Lottery

Tenzin Dickie

We called it the lottery, the lottery to go to America. It was a list of a thousand names. How did the Tibetan government officials decide who got on this list? Did they fold thousands of names into thousands of tiny rolls of paper, mix them up for good measure, and pick out a thousand lucky winners?

Before the lottery, the only lotteries we knew about were school raffles, which my brother Tendor had a knack for winning. His luck held through several years of raffle drawings before it vanished abruptly, and he stopped winning. One of the last things he won was a pair of beautiful black ankle-high leather boots that all the female teachers had their eyes on. Later, they came to our apartment to try them on. They were elegant, comfortable, enduring; the leather was soft and flexible, and the zip smooth and seamless. The shoes must have been Italian. Back then, even if you had the money for such luxurious items, which of course none of the teachers had, you couldn't have found shoes like that anywhere in India, even in the bazaars in Delhi. One by one, each woman tried to slip a bare foot into a shoe and one by one, each gave up in resignation—the toes were too narrow, the arch too high, the ankle too tight. The shoes would not fit anyone. 'Cinderella's shoes,' my mother said.

I knew all about Cinderella and her shoes from the Ladybird books that my mother brought me from the school library. I knew about Snow White too and Sleeping Beauty and the Little Mermaid—beauties with skin as white as snow and hair as black as ebony or yellow as silk or red as sunset. None of these princesses looked anything like any of the women I knew. My mother put the shoes away. We'll keep them for you when you grow up, she promised. I arched my feet and smiled with secret delight. I was eight. I had years to grow into my Cinderella shoes, but I knew that when I did, they would fit. They fitted no one else but they would fit me. I know now that in the original French fairy-tale, Cinderella's shoes weren't glass at all but fur. The translator mistook the word '*vair*' for '*verre*' and transformed fur to glass—the translator must have been a man because a woman would know that glass shoes are for looking at and not for wearing. Still, this blunder rectified a detail, transforming the shoes from ordinary fur to transcendent glass. Fur after all can be stretched, while glass shoes must be made just for you. Different objects have different symbolic values. Imagine Eve or Snow White biting into a mango. It just doesn't work.

So, those were the lotteries we knew; school raffles in which the most you won was a teddy bear or a pair of shoes that fit no one. Lotteries such as my friend Sonam buys now, the PowerBall with tens of millions of dollars for the winner, and the scratch tickets that my mother likes to buy and scratch out, the meagre winnings always slightly less than the initial outlay, these were unknown then in India. Shows such as *Kaun Banega Crorepati*, the Indian version of *Who Wants to Be a Millionaire*, were unthinkable. India was still recovering from the economic slumber of its Socialist Nehru years, its markets opening slowly to the world. Coca-Cola, which you could find all over Kathmandu, had yet to come to India. On the rare occasions that we could afford soft drinks, we drank the local imitation Thumbs Up and wondered how it measured against the original. India was poor and Tibetans poorer still. The idea of a lottery that made you rich, a lottery that gave you a new life, was not just ridiculous but subversive.

And then it came. The lottery to America, the lottery that split our future. We knew our future—we would have our parents' refugee lives, our parents' exile futures. We would grow up, graduate from our Tibetan boarding schools, go off to Indian colleges in the great cities of the heartland, make friends with Indians, but not too well because it wasn't for us to make love or war with them, and then return to our Tibetan settlements in the north or south to work in our own schools and communities, in our own government. With America came the possibility of living outside these settlements, the possibility of unsettling. With America, the future split infinitely.

* * *

America. *Chigyal.* Outside country. Abroad. *Nubchok.* The West. The west was a composite, the land of the yellow-haired, blue-eyed *Injis.* We were inordinately curious about them, that mysterious charmed species that stepped through India so lightly, smiling at complete strangers and taking their photos. We couldn't help but be infected by some of the obsequious reverence the Indians had for these Injis, so recently their overlords. The confidence with which they acted like people for whom things went right all the time was awe-inspiring for us, a people for whom things had gone so wrong. They were a people who had a place not just in their own world but every other world they chose to enter, whereas we had no place anywhere, not even in our own world. Whether the Injis came from England,

America, Germany, or France made no difference to us. They were Injis with their yellow hair and colourless eyebrows, skin pale pink like that of baby mice. They had a smell too, not rancid like the Indian smell but rather delicate and distinctive, something faintly sweet, like decaying rose tissue. It was not an unpleasant smell.

There were very specific things I knew about Injis. I knew they were a proud people who could accept kindness only when they did not need it. We had had two Inji guests at a special school dinner once. Before the dinner, our principal made an announcement to the entire school: one of the two Injis was blind but not one of the teachers or the students was to help him because he would be insulted and offended. What a proud and narrow-minded people, we thought, who would take kindness for contempt. But we knew they could be kind. Machen Phuntsok, the cook, and the only person at Patlikuhl who had travelled abroad insisted on their kindness. In fact, he hadn't travelled so much as he was shipped abroad, with a cardboard notice hanging around his neck, his destination written in a foreign hand, while helpful yellow-haired strangers bore him along through different airports to the correct arrivals gate in Switzerland, where he was joyfully retrieved by his relatives.

Another time, a group of Inji tourists stopped by the school on their way to Manali. They had these strange cameras slung around their necks. They took a few photos on the playground and handed out these photos right then and there to the overjoyed subjects. Of course, they got mobbed. They spent the rest of the afternoon taking portrait pictures of us one by one. I jostled my way into the line. I had been in family pictures before, but never in a photo just by myself. For many of my schoolmates, it was their first photo of themselves. After I had my picture taken, I held the square grey-white sheet of paper by its tip, watching the grey-white fog colour into an image of myself. I looked startled, as if I had been there all along but was only now noticing it.

* * *

For all that the lottery changed my life, I don't remember how I heard about it. Did I hear of it from my parents? The other staff children? One week the conversations in the staff room were about the new Hindi movie in the cinema and the love affair between Miss A and Gen B and the next, they were all about America. Who wanted to go, who did not want to go but was going to sign up anyway because regret always came too late, who would survive, who would have to learn English, who thought they would be unhappy but what was there in Patlikuhl for them anyway, with a pay that was just enough to last from month to month with nothing saved towards your future, your children's future.

Years later I would learn the specifics. It was Representative Barney Frank, a Democrat from Massachusetts, who introduced the Tibetan provisions to the 1990 Immigration Act to allow one thousand Tibetans entry into the country. For fear of Chinese displeasure, the American government would not give either refugee or immigrant status to Tibetans, but Congress had finally settled on a compromise: Tibetans would be recognized as 'displaced' rather than 'refugees' and given a thousand immigrant visas. Then all we knew was that the American government had said to our government: we'll take a thousand of your people.

It wasn't just visas that were available that year. The Tibetan government was also given a certain number of scholarships to send their civil servants to American universities for further study. My father signed up for a scholarship and my mother for a visa. In the months after they signed up and before they were selected, I don't remember them acting any differently. They acted like nothing would change. So, for me and my brother, life in Patlikuhl went on much as before. We went to classes, returned to the apartment for lunch and dinner, played with the other staff children and went to the bazaar on walks with our parents. We had no idea that everything was to change so drastically.

Looking back, I don't think they thought at all that they would be chosen. Having spent their formative years in hardscrabble refugee camps on the Nepalese highlands and then harsh Tibetan boarding schools in the Indian northeast, they had never been sunshine children. As grownups, they scorned happy-go-lucky adults whose façade of cheerful heartiness seemed constructed to dispel intimacy. Both had an instinctive sense of the world as an antagonist or an opponent to be outwitted and outmanoeuvred. They did not win raffles or lotteries. My father, the rationalist, did not believe in counting his blessings until they were hatched in the palm of his hand. My mother, the realist, took anxious care not to want anything too openly or eagerly because she knew the universe would only create an obstacle to spite her.

Gen D la, my physical training teacher, had no such compunction. He was triumphant after he signed up, long before the selected list came back. He knew with full and joyous certainty that he was going to America, and he was going to thrive there. He was the right person to go and thrive, certainly. His English was very good and he made sure everyone knew it. He liked to carry about a thick English novel with a finger in the book to keep his page. He had a defensive aggression that earned him no friends in a small place like Patlikuhl but might serve him well in a crowded city in a very individualistic society. He was good-looking but very dark, and some of the female teachers said dismissively, 'like an Indian'.

We were afraid of him. We knew his kind—insecure men who were ill at ease with their place in the world, men who could be kind and entertaining one second and cruel and dangerous the next. His was a cavalier, light-handed cruelty that cost him nothing. During our physical training (PT) class, sometimes he let us loose on the basketball ground with a few balls but other times he made us stretch out on the ground and hold painful positions for far too long. There was this one position that we hated—we had to lay on the floor perfectly straight and then hold our legs up off the ground at a 45-degree angle, straight and unmoving, for what felt like an eternity of pain. The position wasn't so bad for the first half minute but after that, pain descended, growing into an unendurable fire thrumming through every inch of your body, the only thing sustaining you the sure knowledge that if you didn't contain and confine this pain, if you let it break, worse followed. Someone would cry, still holding that pose. Then he released us, and we lay there gasping and quivering like drowning children rescued from a wet grave.

During this period (I believe it was during this period but could it have been later?), Gen D la took an extra interest in the English language and sometimes kept us in the classroom during the PT period to talk about the finer points of English. 'What's the difference between "listen" and "hear"?' he asked, sweeping his eyes over the class while we stared stupidly at him. Weren't they the exact same words? 'What's the difference between "look" and "see"?' When he translated the words into Tibetan, we understood the distinction he was trying to make. Of course we knew. But the fact that I had wrongly collapsed the distinction between these English words now magnified the distinction I felt anew between the Tibetan words, the awful difference between looking and seeing. I felt the vast philosophical and empirical drop that separated one shore from the other and felt the full force of that narrow strait where intention met grace and looking turned into seeing. It was my first conscious understanding of words, of their intellectual as well as tactile properties, as a vehicle for ideas. For that, I am grateful to Gen D la.

He told my brother's class that he was going to America. He didn't tell us. Perhaps he thought we were too young to appreciate the glamour of such a move. He said to them he was meant to be in America. It was just the right place for someone like him. He could see himself on the streets of New York, playing basketball with his black friends, hanging out with them just like one of them. He had such a specific vision of himself in America. The others who entered the lottery, my parents included, had no such vision—they had signed up for a new life with no idea of what it meant.

* * *

When the results of the lottery came to Patlikuhl, Gen D la wasn't among the chosen few after all. My parents were. My mother would be among the first thousand Tibetans to be resettled in the United States. My father was selected for a fellowship. (It was around the time of my father's return two years later that I first heard the words Fulbright and Harvard and many more years before I understood what those words really meant.) The others who got the lottery were Miss A and Miss E, my mother's friends, as well as Miss F, her nemesis, and our neighbour from across the hall. Some of the other staff, the school secretary, a couple of cooks, a tailor and a dorm mother, were also on the list.

That period passed in a blur. My memories of what followed are fragmented—I know my mother cried and cried and cried although I don't remember it. She thought I was too young to be left behind in boarding school but of course, there were kids as young as five at Patlikuhl. At eight, I felt quite the adult. However, I had never bathed by myself—my mother boiled large pans of hot water and bathed me once a week in the kitchen sink—and I still wet the bed at night. Now she watched me bathe with a scrub in her hand that she visibly restrained herself from using, only directing me to scrub harder here and rinse cleaner there.

Bathing was easy, I just had to remember to wash the back of my neck and the hollows at my heels. But I agonized over my midnight sickness. I knew I would only go a night or two before exposing myself and wetting my bed and then, shame and ignominy. I would be called *'Chingshara-Pisspot'*—a name that would follow me for the rest of my life. They would taunt me in the morning when they saw the stain on my bed—did it look like a map of Tibet, of India? How would I look my classmates in the eye? My face burned at the humiliation. I walked to and from classes with a grim look on my face. Some of the teachers patted me kindly on the head and others said, 'Now you must take care of yourself, become more responsible.' Yet others said, 'Kids much younger than you live in the dorms. You'll be fine. You are a big girl now.' They assumed I was miserable about my parents' leaving for abroad. I was only thinking, how do I stop peeing in bed? How do I fix this thing that was so wrong with me?

I wonder now if I would have felt my parents' leaving more keenly if I hadn't been obsessively panicked about the entire school learning my secret shame. I know my brother felt the coming separation much more keenly than I, but he was always the sensitive and soft-hearted one—from my youngest days at Patlikuhl, I had a hard edge at my core, a natural boldness that would sustain me through to my early twenties when it finally vanished without my noticing. This boldness wasn't courage, it had nothing to do with honour—rather it was a useful unawareness, an un-selfed consciousness that insulated me from everything outside me.

The other teachers came to our apartment to congratulate and console my parents. My mother gave them tea and sobbed like a child, her face in her arms, great heaving sobs as the sleeve of her blouse got wetter and wetter. Gen Ngawang Dorjee from the Head Office in Dharamsala, who must have been on a tour of the Tibetan Children's Village (TCV) schools, said to her, 'It's really alright, you know. You don't have to go if you can't bear to. You can give your place to someone else. Anyone else will be happy to take your place.' My mother sniffed and said, 'No, I mean, I will go in my own place.' Everyone laughed and my mother laughed too. Gen Ngawang Dorjee said, 'Well, what a strange woman you are. Why are you crying your heart out then?'

My parents made their preparations for departure. My mother arranged to put Tendor and me in dorm no. 4. She chose that dorm because Mama Yangchen was known to be a kind dorm mother who never beat her kids and because my mother had done her a favour once and felt Mama Yangchen to be in her debt. We all went to look at the dorm, my parents, Tendor, and I. The rest of the school was in class, so the dorm room was completely silent and empty as Mama Yangchen led us down the aisle. We walked between the two long columns of empty bunk beds spotlessly made up with striped-blue cover sheets tucked in and smoothed out with uniform precision. The boys were on one side and the girls were on the other, but my mother insisted that my bed should be next to Tendor's in the boys' line, on two upper bunks next to each other. She didn't want either of us sleeping underneath another child because that would demean our fortune and diminish our intelligence.

Gen D la made preparations in his own way. Soon afterwards, to everyone's surprise, Gen D la and the school secretary announced that they were getting married. They had a ceremony right before the bride left for America.

* * *

I can still picture this next scene. We waited for the bus from Kullu. We waited by the side of the road, clustering in front of the samosa shack. Other teachers had come to say goodbye to my parents and other staff who were leaving. My mother's eyes were red-rimmed and her smiles meant to thank her colleagues for their wishes kept collapsing before they began. Behind our group, the proprietor of the snack shop, a fat lalaji in a soiled kurta, sat before a vat of oil, making jalebis. He squeezed out the batter from a cloth bag in his hand, thick white lines that quickly turned golden in the darkish oil. Beside the pyramid of samosas, there was a sack full of tiny blackish-red berries heaped in a small mound. When you bought them, you got them salted with masala in a paper cone. They were pitted inside so you chewed as best you could on the tart-sweet flesh and then spit out the pits.

Finally, the bus came, pulling up with a belch. No one got off the bus except the conductor. The teachers offered and exchanged *khatas*, wishes, hopes, and prayers. Some of the male teachers loaded the luggage on top of the bus. The conductor blew his whistle a few times and shouted out *jaldi, jaldi* [quickly, quickly]'. My mother squeezed Tendor and me tightly and repeated the list of things we must do: we were to eat our meals properly even if we didn't like the food, stay clean and keep our clothes neat, study hard and be responsible, and stand up for ourselves. She kept breaking off. My mother could never control her emotions—they always escaped her, especially her anger, her grief, her despair. My father hugged us and then pulled her into the bus, into the sea of curious Indians who craned their necks to watch the scene. A man gave up his seat. The Indians were always respectful of weeping women. Then the bus drove away. As the conductor's last shrill whistle lingered in the air, the other notes of the bazaar—the bark of dogs, the song of birds, the symphony of men spitting, the chorus of customers haggling—revealed themselves in a swell of sound.

My brother wiped his eyes and put his arm around me. I didn't cry. It felt too much like being on stage, like play-acting. I still wanted those tart berries, and I had money that day, but I was too embarrassed to buy them, not because of how it would look to the teachers who assumed I was heartbroken but because it seemed like such an adult thing to do. I was embarrassed by the glamour of that commercial transaction. We walked back to the school with the other teachers.

Although this is how I remember my parents leaving, both of them leaving at once on that bus, in actuality, my father was only escorting my mother. He came back and left again a short while later. But try as I might to tease out that time, I only remember that day of departure, the day my brother and I became dorm children.

All our clothes were packed up into different trunks, and Tendor's and mine were brought to our dorm. Other things, some furniture, some decoration pieces, were distributed to our parents' friends. Others were left for my aunt, my father's younger sister, a new teacher at Patlikuhl who would move into our apartment. The Cinderella shoes that my brother won in that lottery, which were to be kept safe for me, disappeared in the chaos and we never found them again. I didn't miss them, and in fact, forgot all about them until now.

When Tendor and I got back to school, the last period of the day was still in session. We could hear our schoolmates in the classroom buildings—a burst of applause here, a roar of recitation there. Our dorm was quiet and empty when we walked in, our footsteps disturbing the dim silence. I walked along the aisle with my brother, passing row after row of identical, blue-sheeted beds, and suddenly realized that I had no idea which bed was mine.

The Journey

Pema Tsewang Shastri

Like many Tibetan refugees, I along with hundreds of Tibetan children came to India in 1965. Although my so-called date of birth is 7 July 1956, I was actually born in the year of the Wood Horse, 1954, in a place called Phudrak, situated in the district of Saka in the U-Tsang province of Tibet. I have some recollections of my birthplace, with its enchanting landscape of mountains, valleys, and pastures. I have seen herds of wild yaks, wild horses, antelopes, and gazelles grazing peacefully on the pastures.

Phudrak was a small hamlet with a mostly semi-nomadic community whose economic life depended largely on its livestock (yaks, sheep, goats, and horses) and spiritual life depended on its monastery (Phudrak Monastery). My grandparents and my father were originally from Lithang, Kham. Though our family was not rich, we weren't poor either. My parents were living a content and happy life with their eighty-plus yaks and *dris* (female yaks), about 300 sheep and goats, and fifteen horses. In Tibet, and especially among the nomads, those who possessed *kartri-naktong* (10,000 sheep and 1000 yaks) were considered rich. Phudrak monastery had around sixty to seventy resident monks and its abbot was appointed by the Sera monastery, one of the largest monasteries in Tibet. The simple life of the community revolved around this monastery. It was not only our place of worship, but also our school, hospital, court, and entertainment centre.

Since ours was a semi-nomadic family, my grandfather and father, along with other men from our community went to Lake Tsatso to the north to collect salt during the winter. Tsatso in Tibetan means lake of salt. Their trip to Tsatso, to and fro, generally took them more than two months. In the summer, they went to Nubri (a small border town currently under Nepal) to the south to barter the salt and wool for rice, fabric, molasses, utensils, and farming tools. I always looked forward to their return from Nubri as they brought various kinds of candies and cotton clothes.

In summer, we moved constantly from one pasture to another with our herds, often camping in beautiful valleys with sparkling blue waters and lush green meadows dotted with colourful wildflowers. I played with the neighbours' children and, sometimes, during the summer, we ran around naked on the banks of a river or the shores of a lake. We watched people dancing around a huge bonfire at night. I especially liked watching my father and others scaring away packs of wolves with their muskets. I also remember sleeping outside with my grandfather, looking at the moon and the thousands of twinkling stars in the sky. Our food generally consisted of *tsampa* (roasted barley flour), meat, and dairy products. Elders drank lots of butter tea and we children drank milk and whey.

Whenever there was a lunar eclipse, the adults said prayers and beat drums and other available utensils to frighten away Za Ogral, the demon with the broken throat, who was believed to be swallowing the moon. The elders said Za Ogral tried to swallow the moon but the moon always came out of its cut throat. Legend has it that once Za Ogral swallowed the mythical hero Ling Gesar along with his horse. But Gesar cut the throat of Za Ogral with his sword and came out. Since then, whatever Za Ogral swallows, whether it is the moon or sun, comes out from the opening of its throat. At that time, I believed in this story.

Later, when I studied science in school in India, I realized that lunar and solar eclipses are caused by the rotation of the moon around the earth, and the earth around the sun. When I told my father about my scientific discovery that the sun is stationary and the earth and other planets revolve around the sun, my father did not believe it. I showed him how it worked with the help of a torch and balls. But he still did not believe it, arguing that if that were the case, then we would all fall from the earth, when it moved in space. All the waters of the oceans would spill over into space. I told him that such things do not happen because of the earth's gravitational power. But there was no way I could prove gravity to him.

The story of how I ended up in India is a little different from that of other Tibetans. In the winter of 1960, our family—me, my father, mother, sister, and my father's parents—embarked on a pilgrimage to Mount Kailash and Nepal. Even though the so-called Chinese People's Liberation Army (PLA) had already arrived in our town, there were no travel restrictions at that time. Some Chinese military personnel, my parents told me, even helped us on our way to Mount Kailash by offering their voluntary protective service from what they called brigands and reactionary guerrilla forces. My parents thought that, unlike some armed groups of Tibetan robbers, masquerading as Khampa guerrilla forces, the Chinese military men were well-disciplined and helpful to the ordinary people. A few months before our pilgrimage, a group of well-armed twelve Tibetans had come to our place, and forcibly taken away two of our best horses, ten yaks, and twenty sheep. It seemed that some groups of greedy Tibetans, in an attempt to enrich themselves, took advantage of the political situation of the time and began robbing other fellow Tibetans. Like the Wild West, Tibet had its share of robbers and cowboys. The name of

Garnak Yeshe Sangpo, an extremely dreaded and ruthless chief of brigands, still rings in my ears.

One of the horses they took away from us was called Mogro—a greyish-white horse—which was meant for me. I very much loved riding horses when I was young. So my father always told me that Mogro was meant for me when I grew big enough to ride by myself. I always dreamt of riding Mogro on the wide steppe with a musket slung across my back. But the brigands and later the Chinese dashed my hopes and instead I ended up riding bicycles in India.

I remember seeing some Chinese when we were living in Wachen Trango. A small group of Chinese, in blue uniforms, lived in a small building and a larger group, in khaki uniforms, lived in a larger building. The latter also had a clinic manned by a beautiful lady who spoke Tibetan. I, along with some other children, used to visit some of the blue-uniformed Chinese, who at times gave us candies and other eatables and other times taught us Chinese songs. There were a couple of Tibetan-speaking Chinese in their group who were called *Thongsi* ('interpreter' in Chinese). Whenever we saw them, they taught us a Chinese song which went, '*Tongfa ho thayang she/ Tongfa toe la yashi Mao Tsetung . . .*'

Most of the Chinese cadres smoked a lot and they ate rice with chopsticks with a dexterity that amazed me. One bright sunny day when I, along with three of my friends, was playing near the larger building, I found a half-pack of cigarettes beside a pile of trash. Out of curiosity, we lit one cigarette each and smoked. After a couple of puffs, I began coughing profusely and the cigarette slipped from my hand into the folds of my *chuba* and badly burned my stomach. When my mother saw the burn injury, she took me to the clinic. A beautiful young Chinese nurse attended to my burn. She first cleaned the wound with a cotton ball, applied a blue liquid on the wound, and then bandaged it. She asked me to come to the clinic the next day as well. My injury was cured after three or four visits to the clinic, but the scar still remains and reminds me of the incident.

From Wachen Trango, we went to Gang Rinpoche (Mount Kailash), did a number of circumambulations around it and then headed towards Nepal. Of course, I did the journey and circumambulations on horseback. We had brought five horses and ten yaks with us till Nubri. Leaving behind the animals, tent, muskets, and other belongings with our friends in Nubri, we walked towards Kathmandu.

It was around March or April of 1961 when we were done with our pilgrimage tour of Kathmandu and were returning to Tibet via Nubri. Nubri was a small farming town in Nepal but populated by Tibetans. Almost all the local people were Buddhist and they spoke Tibetan with a slightly different accent. Some of the Nubrians (*Nubriwas* in Tibetan) were traders and they had been doing business with Tibet for centuries. My family had a business partner in Nubri by the name of Bu Drukha; I still remember his two-storied house near a small stream that ran through a network of terraced fields.

I clearly remember that on our journey back home we met many Tibetans fleeing Tibet. It was such a strange situation for us. Finally, we were returning to Tibet and our Tibetan brothers and sisters were fleeing Tibet. Many of them—old, young, male, female, and children—were in rags and looked emaciated and exhausted. Most of them were begging for food from the Nepalese villagers on their journey. We also met a few groups of young Tibetans with rifles on their shoulders. They told us that they were *Tensung Makmi*, the Dharma-protecting army, who fought many battles with the Chinese army until all their ammunition and provisions were exhausted. Later on, I realized that they were some of the Chushi Gangdruk—Four Rivers Six

Ranges—warriors. These Tibetan escapees not only told us many horrendous stories of imprisonment, rape, plunder, massacre, and sacrilege by the Chinese in Tibet but advised my parents not to return to Tibet. But my parents, particularly my grandparents, were determined to return home. They were reluctant to forsake all their property back home—the house, the farmland, eighty-five yaks and dris, three hundred sheep and goats, and fifteen horses. They thought it was too much to leave behind everything they owned back in Tibet and live in a strange land without any income or source of sustenance.

As the streams of Tibetan escapees continued to pour from Tibet, heading for Kathmandu and India, we stayed in Nubri for nearly three years, waiting and hoping that the situation inside Tibet would change for the better. Then, one day my father said that the abbot of Phudrak monastery, along with twenty-five monks, had arrived in Nubri. The abbot advised my father not to even think of returning to Tibet. The abbot also told my father that returning to Tibet would be tantamount to knowingly jumping into an inferno to retrieve one's belongings. But my parents were still not willing to forsake their property in Tibet and backtrack their journey to Kathmandu. Then came one of the members of a family from our own village who told us that all our property, the animals, the house and the farm in Tibet had been confiscated and that my father and grandfather were branded as reactionaries and enemies of the State, in absentia, by the Chinese. This bad news, along with the other information that many of the Tibetan children were forcibly being sent to China for education, and that many Tibetans were sent to prison and labour camps on the pretext of flimsy and cooked-up charges, changed the minds of my parents. But my grandparents still insisted on returning saying that they don't want to die in an alien country. They did not like the hot and humid climate of Nepal.

In the meanwhile, one of our shepherds in Tibet had sent a verbal message through someone saying that he was ever ready to return his share of our family's sheep and goats whenever the family returned. This message further encouraged my grandparents. Despite my parents' protests and pleas, my grandparents left for Tibet with a couple of traders from Nubri. That was the last time I saw and heard of my grandparents. We never even knew whether they made it safely to Tibet or not.

Four months after my grandparents left for Tibet, my mother gave birth to my youngest sister in 1963 in Nubri. During our stay in Nubri, my parents, in order to feed our family, had to sell or barter all their valuable possessions like the yaks, horses, and jewellery. One by one, everything went except for a three-eyed *Dzi* and a *Gau* (charm box). While in Nubri, my father, persuaded by some of the Tensung Makmi (the Dharma-protecting Warriors) joined Chushi Gangdruk (Four Rivers Six Ranges) and served in it until the time we left Nubri for Kathmandu. During his short stint in Chushi Gangdruk he, in groups of six and ten, sneaked into Tibet twice for what they called reconnaissance/raid missions and ambushed a Chinese convoy of three trucks during his second mission. They were able to bring back five Chinese rifles, two pistols, and some ammunition. The leader of the Chushi Gangdruk group in Nubri at that time was Gen Rakrak. My father told me that there were sixty people in Gen Rakrak's group and all of them served voluntarily without any remuneration. My father, later on realizing the hardship of our family, resigned from the service before we left Nubri for Kathmandu. With the sole purpose of receiving a blessing from His Holiness the Dalai Lama and sending us to school, my parents decided to follow the other refugees and came back to Kathmandu. Another reason for leaving Nubri must have been that there was no source of income for our family. During that time in Nubri, all I remember of it was that

Nubrians ate only *sengong* (boiled dough either made from corn or millet flour) and boiled potatoes almost all the time.

As soon as we arrived in Kathmandu my father sold his Dzi to a Manangi guy and the money procured from the sale sustained us for some time. After a few weeks in Kathmandu, we were dispatched to a Tibetan refugee transit camp in Trisuli, which is about two or three hours by bus from Kathmandu. The majority of Tibetans in Trisuli were from Kyirong. Hundreds of makeshift bamboo shacks were built everywhere to accommodate people. There were many tents as well. Our family was given one of the empty spaces in one of those long bamboo shacks which were partitioned into several rooms. From afar the camp looked like a military cantonment. But the atmosphere within the camp was indescribably disgusting in terms of sanitation and over-crowdedness. The condition of most of the people was abjectly poor and the children were malnourished. Not a day passed without someone dying either from disease, malnutrition or from the heat. I still wonder how we survived those horrible days in Trisuli. Although all the children who attended a day school were given half a mug of milk and a morsel of boiled bulgur (wheat) in the morning before class, almost all of them still looked hungry. Attendance at school wasn't compulsory. Many children, therefore, avoided their classes and ran into the nearby forest to look for berries and other fruits. Some children even worked, along with their parents, at a dam construction site to earn a little pocket money. I also remember working there for a few weeks. Imagine little boys hauling mud and stones with a huge bamboo basket on their backs instead of going to school. But when hunger rules, education doesn't seem to have any value.

One day an old acquaintance of my parents from our native village came to visit us. His name was Karma and he had a petty business of selling trinkets to the villagers. My parents were very happy to have someone from our native area. He stayed with us for some time, and one day he asked my mother if she wanted to sell her Gau. Her Gau was an elaborately designed silver amulet—studded with rubies and turquoises and strung together with a necklace of rubies and pearls—weighing approximately three pounds. Karma also told her that the Gau would fetch a better price if sold to an antique dealer he knew in Kathmandu. He also insisted that he would take me with him to Kathmandu. So, my parents sent me to Kathmandu with him. Karma suggested that on our way to Kathmandu we would visit some of the Nepalese villages so that he could trade some of his trinkets. I went with him on foot for a whole day and just before sunset, we arrived at a small hamlet which consisted of about ten or fifteen houses. We stopped at the village Dara—the water fountains, the source of the village's drinking water. Like most of the Daras in Nepal, it also had a rain shelter. Karma told me that we would be spending the night under that rain shelter. We both collected some dried wood from around the Dara and he started making a fire to prepare tea and food. While making the fire he asked me to take a couple of small earrings and bangles from his bag and exchange them for a cup or two of rice from one of those village houses. The nearest house was about 200 meters from the Dara.

As per Karma's instruction, I took some earrings and bangles and visited some houses to see if someone was willing to exchange those for some rice. A middle-aged lady with a small girl came out from the first house. I asked her whether she would like to exchange some rice with the trinkets in my hand. She took one pair of earrings and gave me a bowl of rice. I was encouraged by my first attempt to conduct business and went to the next house. The old woman in that house did not buy anything but gave me some amount of rice anyway. I was happy to receive that much rice from the two houses and returned to Karma. When I got to the Dara, Karma was nowhere to be found. Even the fire he was making had gone cold. There were two ladies at the Dara who were filling up their pitchers with water. I asked them whether they had seen Karma. They told me that there was nobody when they arrived at the Dara. It was getting dark and there was no trace of Karma. I was so overcome by fear that I started calling his name loudly many times and began crying at the same time. After a while I realized that he had planned it all so that he could have my mother's Gau. For some time, I did not know what to do next. I felt like a deserted duckling in an ocean. I was only about eight or nine years at that time. But, fortunately, I knew a little Nepalese which helped me a great deal in communicating my helplessness to the villagers.

With a heavy heart, I went back to the lady with whom I had exchanged a pair of earrings for some rice and told her that Karma has deserted me and that I don't know what to do. The lady was stunned after hearing what had happened; she very kindly invited me inside her house and told me that I could spend the night there. She gave me some cornbread with hot milk and let me sleep in her courtyard. The next morning the lady asked me whether I knew the road back to my parents. I told her that I knew the road, but I intended to go to Kathmandu instead to look for Karma. 'Are you crazy?' she asked. 'You will get lost in Kathmandu and there is no way that you can find this person in such a big city.' She continued, 'Even if you find him, he might kill you for that ornament. So don't ever think of going after him.' She also gave me five rupees and some oranges for the road back.

I was very touched by the unexpected kindness and sympathy that the lady had shown me. As a gesture of my gratitude, I gave all the remaining earrings and bangles to her and thanked her. After having some tea, rice, and dal, I retraced the road back home. I got home around 4 or 5 p.m. and narrated the whole incident to my parents. They were shocked and at the same time very happy to find me alive and safe. They said, 'You are even more valuable than the Gau.' My mother cried a lot on that day and told us that the Gau would have fetched at least Rs 1000. One thousand Nepalese rupees in those days was a fortune.

This incident taught me two different lessons. First: when a man is blinded by greed then his heart becomes as cold as ice. Second: kindness and compassion transcend the borders of nationality and race. And then who knows but Karma might have accumulated enough merit to deserve that Gau from us, and it might have been our family's karma to lose it.

There is a saying in Hindi, *'Jis dane par jiska nam likha hein, wo dana wohi khaye ga.* [Whosoever's name is written on a grain of rice, that grain will be eaten by that very person.]'

The Man Who Can Never Go Home

Lhashamgyal

Translated by Tenzin Dickie and Pema Tsewang Shastri

Now that it's almost twenty years since I left my homeland, I finally have to properly consider the question of whether I can ever go back home again.

There's a Tibetan saying that an old man's country is like an old bird's nest. Although I am not as old as all that, I have now spent more years away from home as a wanderer than I have spent living in my home. Sometimes, for no reason at all, I feel that I am drifting farther and farther away from my homeland and my hometown. It's a feeling that pierces the heart as if I have been separated from a beloved. I am someone who has a great attachment to his homeland. Some thirty years ago, the great writer Dhondup Gyal wrote in one of his essays, 'Although I live in a city that is like a heaven, I can't stop this longing for my beloved homeland.' In the same way, living my life in Beijing, I can't stop missing and longing for my homeland. Every year, I look for opportunities—or rather excuses—to make several trips back home. These few days of return act like a temporary pain reliever, and for a little while, I am good again, the longing in my heart alleviated. However, as time goes on and my life continues far away from my homeland, the pain of this non-return has become like a tumour in my heart.

I am now finally facing the real issue at hand—when will I be able to go home forever? A permanent return?

A few days ago, I reread my favourite writer Milan Kundera's 2004 novel, *Ignorance*. The first time I read it, I was a graduate student and I had only been in Beijing for a few years. Fourteen years later, reading this book again, I realized that I hadn't understood it at all the first time. Kundera writes about leaving one's country and then returning, and he creates a very vivid impression in the reader's mind of people who are never able to return to their country. Kundera gave the name 'émigré' to those who, due to geography or time, drifted further and further away from their homes. Of course, I see now why I didn't understand this novel when I read it years ago. At that time, I had not become an émigré yet, so how could I understand an émigré's story? How could I understand a novel that had been written by an exile? Now many more years have gone by. Now I have come to understand more and more clearly that I am myself an émigré and exile, I can see that this novel is like a mirror, reflecting the real joys and sorrows that come from a wandering life. I think I can say that I understand this novel on a deeper level now. The émigré is someone who cannot return, someone who cannot go back home but must live out the rest of his life elsewhere. And it's not just this body made of flesh and blood that can't go back home, but it's the mind—the laughing, crying, and grasping mind—that can no longer go home.

I wonder if there is anyone in the twenty-first century who still dreams the 'emigration dream'. Perhaps compared to before, there are even more such dreamers. Ever since human beings began, in every stage of development, searching or travelling or innovating, they are yet always unsatisfied. Whether it's the mind or the body, it's separated from something, it's pursuing something; this pursuit is in our veins, our bloodstreams. History shows countless people have been separated from their homelands and have become émigrés and exiles. I think it's something in people's nature that leads them to become émigrés and exiles. However, in the old days, our culture, politics, and economy were all different, particularly, transportation. Transportation was not at all convenient, so that there was not then, as there are now, masses of people far from their hometowns. This mass of wanderers, they are a new phenomenon. In just one generation, there are vastly more people who started leaving their hometowns and seeking their lives and livelihood elsewhere—this is a strange new thing about people. It is in this context that I understood that I had also become someone who senselessly and unfeelingly left home to seek a living elsewhere, and I console myself by reminding myself of this general background.

Wanderers preserve a dream in their hearts—the dream of their return, someday, to their home. But this home, this home that they so dream of recedes to such a distance that return becomes impossible, and this is the great tragedy of the exile which must be lived out. Having lived this long in Beijing, both my body and mind have grown accustomed to the people and environment and life in this big city, to the streets and avenues, the parks, the crowds, the nightlife, the air, and not only these but also the food and other material objects, along with the rules and regulations, the busyness of life here and the exhaustion that comes with city living. After many years of resisting and rejecting the uniform customs and conventions of life in Beijing, now I not only accept them, but they have become a habit with me. Man is a strange animal, containing such contradictions! The home where I lived my earlier life was a farming village blooming with spring greenery and houses surrounded by hills, with the joy of cuckoo songs in summer and the sweet smell of fresh air rising from the waving green wheat fields, with a blue autumn sky, the neighing of horses and the grunting of yaks, the bleating of sheep, the barking of dogs, the crowing of cocks, and, in winter, a white world covered with snow. Then there were the leisurely ways of the villagers, lingering on the roads, their greetings when they ran into each other, their smiles of humility amid the fragrance of *sang* offerings—I left all these behind me and yet they keep crowding into my familiar life in Beijing. I usually try to dismiss the nuisances and disappointments of my familiar life here, returning instead to the nostalgic memories of home, consoling myself with a sigh of relief. This quality of one person having two faces is common to all exiles. I have become a two-faced person, with one face completely adapted to the life of Beijing and the other face still an exile who is passionately attached to my beloved country. I must confront and accept the city where I live for my livelihood; the faraway country of my birthplace has become a resting place, which I keep in the depths of my heart. Beijing has become my present and future while my country has become the past and distant from me. In this paradoxical situation, like most exiles, I too have become a third category that does not belong to either side. It is difficult to find the concept of a home within or without. In the end, like a cloud, I am completely seized by an unsettled thought.

Nevertheless, in reality, can I return home by sacrificing my present life? Do I even want to return? If I take my love for my parents and family, my love for my homeland, my love for my people—is the weight of this collective love strong enough to summon my wavering soul back home? Until now, it seems I haven't seriously considered this thought. In my nearly twenty years of this itinerant life, I have been trying to avoid this question as far as possible. I don't want to face these questions. Like pebbles inside my shoes, they give me pain as I walk on the road. I spent years and months, one piling on top of another, amidst these contradictions. After these fragmented years piled up higher and higher, finally I became comfortable or at least I looked fairly comfortable from the outside. Now I realize the meaninglessness of the question of whether I desire to return or not, and I have to think about whether I am actually able to return or not. This is likely the most significant issue confronting wanderers like me after many years.

Irena, the most important character in Milan Kundera's meticulously created *Ignorance* returns to the Czech Republic after twenty years. The Czech Republic has experienced a lot of disasters in recent history. It was ruled by Germany under the treaty of 1938. After regaining independence in 1945 with the help of the Soviet Union, within three years, a communist government was established, and the previous capitalist system was abolished. Then in 1989, after more than thirty years, it regained freedom from the Soviets and restored the capitalist system. Irena's character went into exile in France as soon as the communist system was implemented in her motherland. She returned to her country within the first one or two years after the Czech Republic regained freedom from Soviet rule. When the author writes about the protagonist returning to her country after more than twenty years, he sets up the following reunion scene between Irena and some of her childhood friends, 'In the beginning, they did not say anything about her life abroad and in that manner, more than twenty years of her life was cut short. At this time, through a question, they tried to combine her past and present life, which she had left a long time ago, together. That was akin to trying to cut the wrist and then paste it directly to the shoulder or attempting to cut the ankle and then paste it directly to the knee.' With this example, the author shows the difficulty faced by Irena the protagonist, of not being able to return to her motherland. In fact, though there are differences in individual circumstances, this is the shared difficulty faced by all exiles who were separated from their motherland long ago.

In 1999, when I left Tibet and went to Beijing, the people in my hometown were a relaxed and cheerful bunch, despite having hardly any modern amenities and facilities available. Their lives were still untouched by the profit motive, business, and capitalism. The women wore Tibetan *chubas* and wore their hair in braids; they washed their hair with the liquefied bark of elm trees. The men walked with yellow hats on their heads. Only those in mourning went around without hats.

In my more than twenty years of absence, a huge transformation has taken place in this remote area. Recently when I visited my country, I witnessed big and small vehicles constantly blowing their horns and continuously running on the tarred highway. On the street, I saw many young ladies with their hair dyed and hanging loose, I met many fashionable young people, similar to the ones that I might meet on the streets of Beijing. They walked with an Apple iPhone in their hand, earphones dangling from their ears. Sometimes, when I looked around me, even when I was back in my hometown, I felt as if I were still in Beijing. If Beijing were a person, then that person has now arrived at my birthplace. In fact, it seems he has been here for some time. During this twenty-year period of my absence from my place of birth, my mountain village home has transformed like a snake shedding its skin.

What transformations took place here? Did it change naturally or was it changed? What are the pros and cons of such a transformation? I really don't know. My ignorance in this subject is akin to the ignorance of the human race about some of the unanswered questions that still remain. But what I clearly realized was that my hometown now was not the same hometown that I couldn't stop thinking about in Beijing. The country in my mind was the country that I left when I first began my journey, it was the country that existed twenty years ago. I have no familiarity with the transformation wrought about in this remote area during this twenty-plus year period. From this most important historical transformation of my country, I have been completely detached, an actor unable to get on the stage of cultural transformation. After a span of twenty years, it is very difficult now to match my countrymen in keeping the same tune as they sing and performing the same steps as they dance.

I think that every exile wishes that the image of one's beloved birthplace, fixed in one's heart, may remain the same as when he first left on his journey. Nonetheless, in this world where everything is impermanent, it is impossible to find anything that stays the same forever. Moreover, after these things are carried away by the river of time, what permanent and unchanging thing awaits you? This transformation of my country makes me feel that I have lost touch with it. I no longer find that sense of restful peace in my hometown memories. It no longer feels possible to find the genuine smiles of old on the faces of locals. My behaviour and outlook, my perceptions and my lifestyle, my values and my aesthetics—acquired during my more than twenty years away— seem to have become barriers to my return. In brief, the longer I become habituated, adapted, and addicted to my life in exile, the more difficult it is for me to come back home and find loving handshakes, tight hugs, and deep conversations that never needed any explanations.

Even though that's the frustrating reality, during the entirety of my long stay in Beijing, my wish to go back home has never changed. My wish to return and my inability to actually return have become the primary contradiction of my life. Within this contradiction, the limited time remaining in my life is slowly diminishing, passing in this way. In the end, this may be my karma. This may be the unavoidable karma that always confronts all exiles like me. The relationship between an exile and his country is like the relationship between a kite and the kite flyer. However high a kite flies in the sky, it still remains attached to a string. The kite flying higher and higher into the sky is like a man going further and further away from his country. The country is like the kite flyer who, even as he flies the kite higher and higher in the air, wants the kite to remain forever attached to the string. How wonderful is that string-like link between exile and homeland! Can we call this link 'nationalism' or love for one's country?

As for me, even though I have realized now my return may be impossible, yet I always find myself still trying to go back to my homeland. Although this life in Beijing is the path in front of me and my future, I have always been a person who walks looking backwards and towards the past. The reason I left may have been to pursue a far-away place or future career, but now I think that my life cannot be freed from the vision of my country. It seems the string in the hands of my country has already decided the length of my life's journey.

Kundera writes at the end of *Ignorance*: 'At the university, she used to be seduced by the dreams of voyages to distant stars. What pleasure to escape far away into the universe, someplace where life expresses itself differently from here and needs no bodies! But despite all his amazing progress, man will never progress very far in the universe. The brevity of his life makes the sky a dark lid against which he will forever crack his head, to fall back onto earth, where everything alive eats and can be eaten.' And so he has summarized the karma of all exiles. However far we may go, we are unable to go very far in the end. If this is true, then I can accept that my life is also a life that cannot travel too far from my motherland and yet at the same time is unable to go back home.

At any event, if there is a next life, I pray that I may be reborn again in my homeland, the land of snows!

Three Years in Lhasa

Tsewang Yishey Pemba

The British Mission was situated at Dekyi Lingkha (Park of Happiness), half a mile away from the city of Lhasa and close to the hill of Chakphori. We were not very far away from Norbu Lingkha (Jewel Park), the pleasant park with several summer palaces of the Dalai Lama. From Dekyi Lingkha, we could see the top of the Potala Palace and in the distance, the monastery of Drepung, the largest in the world, nestling at the base of a rocky mountain. A stream ran near the Mission and a little further away was the Kyichu River. There were groves of weeping willows and poplar trees. The main buildings, where the British resident lived and where there was a radio station (code ACAYN), had at one time been the summer residence of the incarnate lama of Kundeling monastery, a former Regent of Tibet like the Radreng Rinpoche. The British diplomat and Tibetologist Sir Charles Bell notes that 'the regent had never lived in this house during the winter, and it was feared that we might find it cold then, but it was chosen because it was clean.'

My father's house, the place where l was to spend three-and-a-half years of my life, was within walking distance of the main buildings. Inside was a stone-flagged courtyard with two peach trees, a long verandah curtained to serve as a kitchen and servants' quarters, a shuttered office and a large room which was used as a living area. It contained a British mountaineering tent erected to be used as a bedroom; the pockets inside the tent served as drawers. In this tent, my father, mother, and us four children slept. There was no plumbing in the house, and for that matter, Tibet had none in any houses then. Water for the kitchen and for washing was drawn from the nearby stream and then stored in large bronze cauldrons. There was no toilet, and for such purposes we used the back of the house. When I think of it, the whole accommodation for a family with four children was ludicrous in the extreme and most primitive, especially that tent inside a room, but for me, it was home.

When I first arrived in Lhasa, the Norbu Lingkha, the summer palace of the Dalai Lama, was empty because the Fourteenth Dalai Lama had not yet been discovered and the regent, Radreng Rinpoche, stayed at his monastery at Shide. Norbu Lingkha was built by the Seventh Dalai Lama in 1783, about a mile from the Potala, where he had his winter palace. It was surrounded by a mile-long square wall on each side. We used to go there sometimes to watch the Tibetan soldiers' drill. In those days, Tibet had a standing army of about 10,000 men. The Dalai Lama's *Kusung* (bodyguard) wore western uniforms and Wolseley helmets and marched smartly to a fife. A drums-and-bagpipes band with tall drummers wearing leopard skin ponchos played tunes such as, 'God save the king', 'Cock the north', 'Highland laddie', 'Marching through Georgia', and 'Auld lang syne'. The top-brass Tibetan troops were stationed at Drapchi, a little distance away from Lhasa, where there was an arsenal and a mint; these troops wore khaki Tibetan uniforms, Tibetan knee-length boots and kept their hair in pigtails and wore earrings. They were said to be dour fighters who had kept the Chinese at bay in Kham in the 1920s. The Kusung soldiers blew bugles, signalled with hand flags in semaphore and gave British

Aldershot commands in quaint Tibetan accents and intonations: '*Ber thar rite, queek mach!*', '*Eeslope amms!*', '*Thundey ees!*' What a British Guards' regimental sergeant-major or a United States Marine Corps trainer at boot camp would have made of all this is a matter of conjecture. The heaviest arms the Tibetan army possessed were mountain howitzers and Lewis guns. Many years before, when Tibetans had been fighting the Chinese in Lhasa in 1911-12, innovative countrymen had produced homemade cannons, but these killed more Tibetan gunners than Chinese and had been dubbed *megyo kukpa* or fool cannons by the populace, which made Lhasa folks comment, '*Megyo kukpa che chay, gyabngey kukpa nyey chay; trön pe nang gyi beba, kepa chaney ehadu!* [Firstly a fool cannon, and then secondly a fool gunner; a shot has broken the back of a frog in a well!].' Tibetans love making fun of themselves.

* * *

In Lhasa, there were only Tibetan native schools and a school for monk officials in the Potala. Of course, children learnt to read and write in the innumerable monasteries and nunneries but their education was perforce religious. The Tibetan Muslims educated their children in Urdu and taught them to read and write Arabic so that they could recite the Quran. At first, there was no school teaching modern subjects at Dekyi Lingkha. My father was my private tutor, and he was a strict disciplinarian who taught me English, Hindi, and arithmetic. However, in 1938, Radreng Rinpoche requested the British to start a school for some boys specially selected by the regent's officials and this became my second school after my first one in Yatung. Almost no books on Tibet mention this school, possibly because there were only about a dozen boys and no classrooms; studies being held in the open air, in the courtyard in front of my father's office. Our teacher was

Tseten Nangdi, a Tibetan from Yatung who had been educated at the Scottish Universities Mission School in Kalimpong. He was thirty-one years old, a smiling, rosy-cheeked, athletic man, a footballer, with—surprisingly and exceptional for a Tibetan—curly close-cropped hair and a small Hitler moustache (The Fuhrer was then at his zenith and about to launch World War II within a year). In fact, I thought he had a striking resemblance to Himmler if he had stuck to his chicken-farming and not become the chief of the Schultz Staffel. This resemblance was enhanced by Mr Tseten's steel-rimmed spectacles. However, he was the least Nazi of men. He played the harmonica with stirring verve and his favourite tune was 'Marching through Georgia'. He stayed with Mr Dongjesur, the Nepalese dentist friend of my father who lived in the city and had become very rich fixing dentures and gold teeth, much in fashion in Lhasa society then among both sexes. I think Dongjesur was the only dentist in the whole of Lhasa at that time. Actually 'Dongjesur' was the name of the area of Lhasa where the Nepalese lived but he was known to everybody as 'Dongjesur Babu'. Mr Tseten rode to work on his bicycle, perhaps the only man in the whole of Lhasa to do so, and it took him ten minutes to reach Dekyi Lingkha. One of our students was also the son of the Nepalese representative in Lhasa, and he used to come riding on a pony escorted by a Nepalese soldier.

Mr Tseten taught us English, Hindi, and arithmetic and sometimes we drilled outside near the willow trees and played games. 'This is the queen', 'This is the king', 'The cat sat on the mat' (and for the more intellectual, a complicated version: 'A big, fat cat sat on the mat.') were the standard English sentences that we tried to master. There was also, 'This is a fig', an exotic fruit I never saw in Tibet and did not encounter until I came across it in Delhi in 1981. No Tibetan language was taught, sadly, as in the milieu of those days, any knowledge of Tibetan was considered a waste of time.

One day, Migmar, the biggest boy in our lot, was summoned to read from his English textbook by Sir Basil Gould. He was told to read, 'A cat sat on the mat,' but when Migmar pronounced 'a' like 'a' in the English alphabet, Sir Basil had looked displeased and had insisted that it should be pronounced 'er,' which flabbergasted Migmar. He returned crestfallen to our class and described his ordeal, unable to make out why 'a' should be pronounced in two different ways. No doubt Bertrand Russell would have made much of this incident and would have been delighted by this semantic puzzle occurring in the heart of mysterious Tibet in the holy Forbidden City.

Tseten Nangdi advised me that when I went down to India for schooling, I must go to an English-medium school, which, although meant for the children of *sahibs*, would eventually benefit me, immeasurably. He told me not to go to the Kalimpong School where he had been and where the teaching was in an Indian language. He said that I should aim to become a lawyer, as they made the most money. He also told us of a game called 'boxing' and said that 'boxers' could fell an ox with a blow; this was perhaps a reference to Joe Louis, whose pugilistic sun was then rising. I remember, particularly, an evening walking home with him. We were going through some dunes near Sera monastery where we had gone to see a ceremony and the sun was setting, casting a golden glow over the sand when he again reminded me to insist with my father that he send me to an 'English' school.

One of my good friends at our school was Gendun, a few years older than me. He came from the household of the head of the Kundeling monastery, which had about a hundred monks, and was close to Dekyi Lingkha. Mr Tseten told Gendun one day to construct an English sentence with the word 'cock' in it, and Gendun was complimented when he shouted loudly, 'There are many cocks at Bagmari.' The monks at Bagmari keep a large number of cocks, I know not for what reason.

Many years later, in London, Sir Basil Gould showed a film he had taken in Lhasa of the Bagmari temple with its cocks and I heard him make the only joke I ever heard from him: 'You'll notice there are only cocks at Bagmari,' he told the attentive British audience, '. . . no hens . . . it may be bad for the monks . . .'

One day, Gendun produced a thick red book, like the account books that crafty Marwari businessmen in India maintain to flummox officials of the Indian Internal Revenue—no mean feat. Gendun told me that the book held the key to the English language, and that anybody reading it from cover to cover would master that language. This intrigued me considerably because I always wanted to master English. But to this day, I have no idea which book it was, this magic compendium!

Gendun and I often went to that part of the Lingkor (the sacred path for pilgrims), close to Dekyi Lingkha, where with eyes shut, one tried to put one's fingertip in a hole in one rock. Once, just before I left Lhasa, we went there, and I succeeded in performing the feat. Gendun was delighted and assured me that we would certainly meet sometime in the future. He gave me an image of the Buddha Tsepame (Buddha of Infinite life), taught me to say prayers to him and said that this Buddha was my guardian. Some years after I left Lhasa, my mother told me that he had become a minor government official and that his sister Sedon had become a nun. In the turmoil following the entry of the Chinese Communists into Tibet in 1950, Gendun's family was scattered and could not be traced. I have heard rumours that he had emigrated to Canada as a refugee. Perhaps if he should read these pages, he might wish to contact me and make the prophecy of the rock wall of the Lingkor in Lhasa come true.

Acknowledgements

This collection was a long time in the making. I first contacted a core group of Tibetan writers in 2017 about a book of Tibetan essays, and am so thankful that they all agreed to write or scrounge something up. The collection grew in scope over the years, and I added more writers as time went by. Right from the beginning I conceived this book as something that might help clarify, maybe even define the modern Tibetan essay. If the book comes close to achieving that in any way, it is due to the talent and generosity of the contributors between these pages.

As always, my first thanks go to my family. My parents Pema Tsewang Shastri and Chodon Tenzin for their unwavering love and support. My brother Tenzin Dorjee, my first teacher and my first reader, who keeps me true. Sister-in-law Tsering Choden. My dearest friend Tenzin Palkyi.

My gratitude to my aunt Somo Yangzom and her family, including her youngest daughter Tshering Shrestha and especially my cousin brother the late Tharchan Shrestha, and his wife Acha Dema. I would also like to thank Uncle Tashi, Tenor and their families. Tsering Wangmo Dhompa, whose *Nation of Two* first showed me what the modern Tibetan essay could do. Dhondup T. Rekjong and Pema Bhum, Tenzin Tsundue and Bhuchung D. Sonam for always supporting my literary ventures.

I want to thank my friends for all the love and laughs over the years: Tashi Yangdon Tsarong, Tsephel Thangpe, Tenzin Youdon, my forever roommates Theresa Chan, Elena Sorokin, Cathy Cohn, my Bhutanese sister Kuenga Wangmo and my work-wife Katie Tsuji, my writer sisters Muna Gurung and Iona Liddell, Sonam Wangdue, Praveen Chaudhry and Souzeina Mushtaq, Tenzin Tsetan Choklay, Sonam Tsomo, Kunsang Kelden, Tenzin Wangyal, Chungpo Tsering, Tenzing Rigdol, Tenzin Dolker, Dechen Dolma and Jessica Rubin-Wills.

My professor and translation guru Susan Bernofsky for her generous support. And Joe Shay and Laura Zimmerman for their love and kindness from the first day I landed in America.

I want to thank the following people for their support of my writing: Tenzin Choegyal, Shelly Bhoil, Tenzin Nawang Tekan, Tsering Shakya, Thupten Jinpa Langri, Lowell Cook, TN Khortsa, Tsering Yangzom Lama, Paul Beatty, Stacey D'Erasmo, Stanley Harsha and Gray Tuttle.

I want to thank colleagues from whom I have learned so much: Lobsang Nyandak and Tsewang Phuntso from the Office of Tibet, Alexander Gardner and Catherine Tsuji from The Treasury of Lives, and Jann Ronis, Philip Menchaca and Kelsang Lhamo from the Buddhist Digital Resource Center. Dafna Yachin, Arthur Fischman and Patricia Gruber. Andrew Quintman and Kurtis R. Schaeffer.

I completed a significant chunk of this work in 2018–2019 while I was in Kathmandu on a Fulbright fellowship. I am grateful to the Fulbright Commission and the U.S. State Department, and I thank Tom Robertson, my Fulbright director, for his support. I thank Sameen Yusuf, Beth Prosnitz and Atul Bhattarai for comradeship in Nepal.

I am grateful to Swati Chopra and especially Elizabeth Kuruvilla at Penguin India for championing this book.

Contributors

Pema Bhum is a writer and a researcher. He is the author of two memoirs of the Cultural Revolution—*Six Stars with a Crooked Neck* (2001) and *Dran tho rdo ring ma* (2006)—as well as the critical essay *Heartbeat of a New Generation*, now translated into three languages. He has served as the director of Late Library for seventeen years and currently serves as the executive director and co-founder of Latse Project. He holds an M.A. in Tibetan Studies from the Northwest Nationalities Institute in Lanzhou, Gansu Province (PRC), where he also taught Tibetan language and literature. After arriving in India in 1988, he founded the first independent Tibetan language newspaper in exile, *Mangtso*, and the Tibetan literary magazine, *Jangshon*. He teaches at Stanford and Northwestern universities.

Lowell Cook completed his M.A. in translation, textual interpretation and philology from the Rangjung Yeshe Institute in 2017. He is the author of *Tibetan Pure Land Buddhism: Mipham Rinpoche on Self-Power and Other-Power* (2019), the translator of Sangngak Tenzin Rinpoche's *A White Conch Spiraling Toward Happiness: Poems of a Tibetan Master*, and a recipient of the National Endowment for the Arts grant to translate *A Frostbitten*

Flower and Other Stories: The Complete Fiction of Dondrup Jyel. He has contributed translations to *Samye Translations* (formerly Lhasey Lotsawa), *Lotsawa House*, *TibShelf, High Peaks Pure Earth, Yeshe* and the *Journal of Tibetan Literature*. He aspires to help share the richness of Tibetan literature with the world.

Tsering Wangmo Dhompa is the author of the poetry books, *My Rice Tastes Like the Lake, In the Absent Everyday* (2011) and *Rules of the House* (2002), all from Apogee Press, Berkeley, and three chapbooks. Dhompa's first non-fiction book, *Coming Home to Tibet,* was published in the US by Shambhala Publications in 2016 and by Penguin India in 2014. She was born in India and raised in the Tibetan refugee communities in India and Nepal. Dhompa teaches in the English Department at Villanova University.

Tenzin Dickie is a poet, writer and translator. She is the editor of *Old Demons, New Deities: Twenty One Short Stories from Tibet* (2017), the English language anthology of modern Tibetan fiction.

Tenzin Dorjee is a writer, activist and musician based in New York City. He is a doctoral candidate in political science at Columbia University and a senior researcher at Tibet Action Institute. His work has appeared in the *Washington Post, Foreign Policy, Journal of Democracy, National Interest, Tibetan Review, Huffington Post* and *Oxford Encyclopedia of Politics and Religion.*

Chime Lama is a Tibetan American writer, translator and multi-genre artist based in New York. She holds an M.A. in divinity from the University of Chicago and an M.F.A. in creative writing from Brooklyn College. She serves as the poetry editor of *Yeshe: A Journal of Tibetan Literature, Arts and Humanities.* Her work has been featured in the *Brooklyn Rail*, *Exposition Review*, *The Margins*, *Street Cake*, *Volume Poetry* and *Cadernos de Literatura em Tradução*, n. 24 (Notebooks of Literature in Translation), among others. Her poetry collection, *Sphinxlike*, is forthcoming from Finishing Line Press. She teaches creative writing at the Rochester Institute of Technology (RIT).

Lekey Leidecker is a Tibetan writer and poet born and raised in Berea, Kentucky. Her family is from Pemako. She divides her time between New York City and London. Her poems and essays have been published in *Yeshe*, *The Pomelo*, *Diaspora Baby Blues*, *ANMLY*, *Genre: Urban Arts*, *Rigorous*, and elsewhere. Her first poetry collection is forthcoming from Blackneck Books in 2023.

Lhashamgyal has published ten books in Tibetan and Chinese, including works of translations. He is a five-time recipient of the prestigious Drangchar literary award and numerous other such prizes, including the China Nationality Literature Award and the National Steed Award for Minority Literature. His short stories and essays have been translated into English and Chinese. His novel *The Dear One from Tibet* བོད་ཀྱི་གཉེན་སྡུག has been translated into Japanese and is also forthcoming in French.

Jangtse Dhonko (Nyen) is a well-known Tibetan poet and a former political prisoner. He was born in 1978 in Chongchuk county in Amdo, Tibet. He was a government official at the local history research centre until his arrest by the local police on 21 June 2010, who accused him of inciting separatism through his writings. Nyen is his pen name. He has published three poetry books, *Wild Born* in 2016, *Dexterity* in 2007 and *Revenant* in 2002.

Jamyang Norbu is a Tibetan freedom activist, novelist and writer of the blog Shadow Tibet. His novel, *The Mandala of Sherlock Holmes* (1999), is an account of the detective's adventures in India and Tibet. His new book *Echoes from Forgotten Mountains: Tibet in War and Peace*, is coming soon. He presently lives in New York City with his wife and two daughters and heads the High Asia Research Center at Jackson Heights.

Dechen Pemba is founder and editor of High Peaks Pure Earth, an online platform that publishes English translations of Tibetan poems, songs, and other writings by Tibetans inside Tibet. Dechen is based in London, UK, and also serves as a researcher and consultant on Tibet-related issues.

Dr Tsewang Yishey Pemba, a writer and a doctor, was born into a Tibetan family that worked for the British Mission in Tibet. He became a surgeon in London, a fellow of the British Royal College of Surgeons, and helped found a hospital in Bhutan. He wrote the novel *Idols on the Path* (1966) and an autobiography titled *Young Days in Tibet* (1957). His memoir, *Tibet as I Knew it*, has just been published posthumously.

Gedun Rabsal, a researcher and translator, works as a senior lecturer at Indiana University Bloomington, where he teaches Tibetan language and culture within the Department of Central Eurasian Studies. His numerous publications include his autobiographical account, *Let's Go into Exile!* (*Gro skyabs bcol la 'gro*), his research on Tibetan literary history, *A Comprehensive History of Tibetan Literature* (*Bod kyi rtsom rig gi byung ba brjod pa rab gsal me long*) and his Tibetan-language translations of American classics such as Ernest Hemingway's *The Old Man and the Sea* and Jack Kerouac's *On the Road*.

Dhondup T. Rekjong is a Tibetan scholar and doctoral candidate in religious studies at Northwestern University. His writings have appeared in *The Wall Street Journal*, *Chicago Tribune*, *The Journal of Asian Studies*, *Lion's Roar*, and *The Treasury of Lives*. He is an editor of *The Tibet Reader*, forthcoming from Duke University Press.

Mila Samdub is a writer and researcher based in New York and New Delhi. He studied creative writing at Bard College in upstate New York, environmental design at Yale School of Architecture, and was a curator at Khoj International Artists' Association in New Delhi. He works on the aesthetics and infrastructures of digital governance in India.

Ann Tashi Slater's fiction, essays and interviews have been published by *The New Yorker*, *The Paris Review*, the *New York Times*, *The Washington Post*, *Catapult*, *Guernica*, *Tin House*, *AGNI*, *Granta*, *Kyoto Journal* and the *HuffPost*, among others. She is a contributing editor at *Tricycle*. Her writing also appears in *Women in Clothes* (2014) and *American Dragons* (1993); a translation of fiction by Reinaldo Arenas was published in *Old Rosa* (1994). She is working on a book about bardo and the art of living.

Bhuchung D Sonam is a Tibetan poet, writer, translator and publisher. His books include *Songs from Dewachen* and *Yak Horns: Notes on Contemporary Tibetan Writing, Music and Film and Politics* (2012). He has edited *Muses in Exile: An Anthology of Tibetan Poetry* (2004) and has compiled and translated *Burning the Sun's Braids: New Poetry from Tibet* (2017). In 2022, he edited *Under the Blue Skies: A Tibetan Reader*, an anthology of stories and poems. He is a founding member of TibetWrites and its imprint Blackneck Books. His writings are published in the *Journal of Indian Literature*, *HIMAL Southasian*, *Hindustan Times* and *Tibetan Review* among others. He was awarded the 2022 Ostana Prize Youth Award in the category of 'Writings in Mother Tongue' for his literary contributions.

Tenzing Sonam is a filmmaker and writer. His film work includes award-winning documentaries, narrative features and video installations. His writings have been published in *Civil Lines*, the *Hindu*, *Indian Quarterly*, *Asian Film Archive*, *Monde chinois*, and *Himal Southasian*. He wrote the screenplays for the films *Dreaming Lhasa* and *The Sweet Requiem*, which he co-directed with his partner Ritu Sarin. With Sarin, he is the founder-director of the Dharamshala International Film Festival.

Half Tibetan, half English, **Chhimi Tenduf-La** works at an international school in Colombo, where he provides university counselling. He has written three books: *The Amazing Racist*, *Panther* and *Loyal Stalkers*.

Topden Tsering, formerly editor of Tibetan Bulletin, is a Bay Area-based writer. His essays and articles have been published in various newspapers, journals and magazines, including *San Francisco Chronicle*, *Outlook Magazine*, and *Himal Southasian*. His stories have also appeared in *Under the Blue Skies*, an anthology of fiction and essays by Tibetan writers in the diaspora.

Catherine Tsuji is an editor at The Treasury of Lives, an online biographical encyclopedia of Tibet.

Tenzin Tsundue is a Tibetan writer and activist. His books are *Nowhere to Call Home*, *Tsengol: Stories and Poems of Resistance*, *Semshook: Essays on Tibetan Freedom Struggle*, *Kora:*

Stories and Poems and *Crossing the Border*. He has been anthologized in *Modern English Poetry by Younger Indians*, edited by Sudeep Sen, Sahitya Akademi, 2020, *Old Demons and New Deities: 21 Short Stories from Tibet* edited by Tenzin Dickie, OR Books, USA, 2019 and *Voices in Exile*, edited by Rajiv Mehrotra, Rupa, 2013. He is the winner of the Picador-Outlook Prize in nonfiction.

Sangdor (ཟེང་རྡོར) is a poet from Amdo, eastern Tibet. At a young age, he was recognized as being the reincarnation of a Buddhist master, but later renounced this title and his robes to devote himself entirely to writing. His poetry is associated with the 'new metrics' style (bcad gsar) and is known for breathing new life into classical forms by playfully mixing colloquialisms, modern terminology and proverbs within traditional meters. He is a prolific author with some twenty-plus titles to his name.

Pema Tsewang Shastri is the author of three novels—including *Cold West, Warm East* (2000)—as well as a work of historical fiction, a collection of short stories and a collection of Tibetan sayings, *Like a Yeti Catching Marmots*, published by Wisdom Publications. A former Fulbright Scholar at Harvard University, he has translated works by Dr Gene Sharp and Charles Dickens. He is a foreign rights manager at Wisdom Publications.

Fiona Sze-Lorrain is the author of the novel *Dear Chrysanthemums* (2023), five poetry collections—most recently *Rain in Plural* (2020) and *The Ruined Elegance* (2016)—and fifteen books of translation. She lives in Paris where she works as a zheng harpist and an editor.

Tsering Woeser is a poet, essayist and blogger and one of the most prominent voices of the Tibetan independence movement. Three of her books have been published in English, *Forbidden Memory:*

Tibet During the Cultural Revolution, Tibet on Fire: Self-Immolations against Chinese Rule, and *Voices from Tibet: Selected Essays and Reportage*. Woeser's first major book of literary writings in English translation, *Ocean, as Much as Rain*, translated by Dechen Pemba and Fiona Sze-Lorrain, is forthcoming from Duke University Press. Woeser has received the Prince Claus Award and the U.S. Department of State's International Women of Courage Award. She lives under close surveillance in Beijing.